The
Inclusion
Facilitator's
Guide

The Inclusion Facilitator's Guide

by

Cheryl M. Jorgensen, Ph.D.

Mary C. Schuh, Ph.D.

and

Jan Nisbet, Ph.D.

·P A U L·H·
BROOKES
PUBLISHING C⁰®

Baltimore • London • Sydney

Paul H. Brookes Publishing Co.
Post Office Box 10624
Baltimore, Maryland 21285-0624

www.brookespublishing.com

Typeset by Auburn Associates, Inc., Baltimore, Maryland.
Manufactured in the United States of America by
Versa Press, Inc., East Peoria, Illinois.

Case studies are derived from the authors' actual experiences. In most
cases, pseudonyms have been given and identifying details have been
changed. Real names and identifying details are used by permission.

Readers may access free of charge additional figures and forms that
accompany this book at http://www.brookespublishing.com/
inclusionfacilitator. Use of these materials is granted for educational
purposes only; the duplication and distribution of these materials for a fee
is prohibited. You will see the copyright protection at the bottom of each
photocopiable page.

Library of Congress Cataloging-in-Publication Data
Jorgensen, Cheryl M.
   The inclusion facilitator's guide/by Cheryl M. Jorgensen, Mary C.
Schuh, and Jan Nisbet.
      p.   cm.
Includes bibliographical references and index.
ISBN-13: 978-1-55766-707-6 (pbk.)
ISBN-10: 1-55766-707-1 (pbk.)
   1. Inclusive education—United States.   2. Mainstreaming in
education—United States.   3. People with disabilities—Education—
United States.   I. Schuh, Mary C.   II. Nisbet, Jan.   III. Title.
LC1201.J6695 2006
371.9'046—dc22   2005028573

British Library Cataloguing in Publication data are available from the
British Library.

Contents

About the Authors vii

Acknowledgments xi

Introduction: The Next-Best Thing   *Jan Nisbet* xv

1 From Special Education Teacher to Inclusion
   Facilitator: Role Revelations and Revolutions
   Mary C. Schuh and Cheryl M. Jorgensen 1

2 Ten Promising Practices in Inclusive Education:
   The Inclusion Facilitator's Guide for Action
   Cheryl M. Jorgensen 25

3 Transforming Hearts and Minds: The Inclusion
   Facilitator's Role as a Change Agent
   Cheryl M. Jorgensen 65

4 Participatory Decision Making: The Inclusion
   Facilitator's Role as a Collaborative Team Leader
   Cheryl M. Jorgensen 103

5 Facilitating Student Relationships: Fostering Class
   Membership and Social Connections
   Cheryl M. Jorgensen 125

6 Reconsidering Assessment in Inclusive Education:
   Identifying Capacities and Challenges within
   Students, Teams, and Schools
   Cheryl M. Jorgensen 139

7 Identifying Nontraditional Supports: The
   Inclusion Facilitator's Role as an Information and
   Resource Broker
   Mary C. Schuh 167

8 Restructuring to Support Inclusive Education:
   Organizational Structures that Enable Inclusion
   Facilitators to Succeed
   Cheryl M. Jorgensen 183

9 Preservice Education of Inclusion Facilitators:
   One University's Program
   Cheryl M. Jorgensen 197

Appendices
A Competencies that Form the Foundation of the
   University of New Hampshire's Inclusion
   Facilitator Teacher Education Option 209

B Supports for Students with Significant Disabilities 213

C Agenda Template for a Team Meeting 219

D Guidelines for a "Day in the Life" Observation 221

E Sample Functional Behavior Assessment 225

F Sample Positive Behavior Support/Intervention Plan 233

Index 239

About the Authors

Cheryl M. Jorgensen, Ph.D., Project Director and Research Assistant Professor, Institute on Disability at the University of New Hampshire (UNH), 10 West Edge Drive, Durham, New Hampshire 03824

Dr. Jorgensen directs a 4-year model demonstration project for the U.S. Department of Education, Office of Special Education Programs, titled "Beyond Access: A Model that Promotes Learning of General Education Curriculum Content for Students with Significant Disabilities" and teaches in the UNH graduate program that prepares inclusion facilitators. She is also the co-coordinator of a project that prepares future Ph.D. faculty researchers in the area of autism spectrum disorders.

Since 1985, Dr. Jorgensen has worked with public school teachers, parents, and administrators to increase their commitment to and capacity for including students with disabilities in general education classes. She co-coordinated the INSTEPP in-service training project, New Hampshire's Statewide Systems Change Project, and the Equity and Excellence in Higher Education Project. For the past several years, her work has focused on the restructuring of policies, organizational structures, and teaching practices that naturally facilitate inclusion and learning for all students.

From 1992 to 1996, Dr. Jorgensen directed a federally funded school restructuring and inclusion project titled "Including Students with Disabilities in Systemic Efforts to Reform Schools." Based on that project and the experiences of colleagues across the United States, she authored a book titled *Restructuring High Schools for All Students: Taking Inclusion to the Next Level* (Paul H. Brookes Publishing Co., 1998). Dr. Jorgensen edited the *Equity and Excellence* newsletter, co-authored (with Stephen N. Calculator) *Including Students with Severe Disabilities in Schools: Fostering Communication, Interaction, and Participation* (Singular Publishing Group, 1994), and has authored several chapters in other inclusion texts.

Mary C. Schuh, Ph.D., Associate Director and Research Assistant Professor, Institute on Disability at the University of New Hampshire (UNH), 10 West Edge Drive, Durham, New Hampshire 03824

Dr. Schuh is a Research Assistant Professor in the Department of Education at UNH. She received her master's degree in special education from Syracuse University and her doctoral degree in education from UNH. She has been with the Institute on Disability at UNH since its inception in 1987 and is the Project Investigator on numerous projects related to family and consumer leadership development and educational systems change activities in the areas of preschool, students with emotional and behavioral disabilities, higher education, and students with complex medical issues.

Dr. Schuh has more than 20 years of experience in inclusive schools and communities and project management. She is working on systems change in the areas of personnel preparation, leadership development, assistive technology, and inclusive education. In addition, she teaches a course titled Introduction to Exceptionality at UNH.

Dr. Schuh is the author and co-author of numerous chapters and publications related to inclusive communities and serves on the Boards of Directors of several nonprofit organizations including the Disability Rights Center. Dr. Schuh is a founding board member of the Alliance for Community Supports, an organization devoted to serving the needs of young people with emotional and/or behavioral issues through a process of wrap-around support and self-directed futures planning. She travels extensively nationally and internationally, providing technical assistance and learning from others about promoting social justice and full community participation for individuals with disabilities and their families.

Jan Nisbet, Ph.D., Director and Associate Professor, Institute on Disability at the University of New Hampshire (UNH), 10 West Edge Drive, Durham, New Hampshire 03824

Dr. Nisbet is a tenured associate professor in the Department of Education at UNH. She received her doctorate in education from the University of Wisconsin in 1982 and her bachelor's degree in physical therapy from Simmons College in 1978. She has been conducting research and writing for 24 years on topics related to deinstitutionalization, school restructuring and reform, transition from school to adult life, supported employment, inclusive adult lives, community services and supports, and issues related to aging and disability.

Dr. Nisbet is a former President of the Executive Board of Directors of TASH, an international organization focused on improving the lives of individuals with severe disabilities and their families through research, training, and advocacy. She chairs the Program Committee for the national Association for University Centers on Disability. Dr. Nisbet also is a founding member of the Board of Directors for the Endowment for Health, New Hampshire's Health Care Conversion Foundation, where she serves on the Program and Strategic Planning Committees.

Dr. Nisbet has published extensively in the field of severe disabilities. She also serves on numerous editorial and advisory boards and presents nationally and internationally. She is Principal Investigator on many state- and nationally funded projects related to the community integration of individuals with disabilities and continues to contribute to public policy reform efforts in New Hampshire and throughout the United States to improve the ability of people with disabilities to fully participate in their communities. She strives to integrate social responsibility and advocacy with academic research, teaching, and service.

Acknowledgments

In 1987, Marsha Forest from the Centre for Integrated Education and Community in Toronto visited New Hampshire to lead workshops for families and educators on the topic of inclusive education. That same year, Carol Tashie moved from Oregon to New Hampshire to become the state's first inclusion facilitator. Jocelyn Curtin, who experiences Rett syndrome, was among the first students with significant disabilities in New Hampshire to become a full-time member of a general education class in her neighborhood school. We would like to acknowledge the contribution of these three women to the lessons we have learned about facilitating inclusion, and we dedicate this book to them.

As international consultants on inclusive education, Marsha and her husband, Jack Pearpoint, led a revolution of sorts in the late 1980s regarding how students with significant disabilities were educated. Inclusion, Marsha said, was when a school made a commitment to educate all students in the mainstream of general education classrooms based on a belief that diversity enhances a school's community. Marsha argued that inclusion went beyond ideas of mainstreaming or integration, where students with disabilities were periodically integrated into a general education classroom but were primarily educated in a segregated class setting.

Marsha talked not only about the shift that was necessary in people's beliefs about educating students with disabilities but also about the professional role changes that were integral to making inclusion work. During her visit to New Hampshire, she coined the term *inclusion facilitator* to describe a special education teacher who was responsible for coordinating all aspects of students' inclusive educational programs. Instead of teaching a classroom full of students with significant disabilities, the inclusion facilitator collaborated with classroom teachers, parents, paraprofessionals, and therapists to figure out what supports would be necessary for all students to be a part of the social and academic life of the general education classroom. Marsha felt strongly that as long as a special education teacher had responsibilities in both special and general education classrooms, inclusion would not be successful. Her influence on inclusive education continues even after her untimely passing in 2000.

In 1987, Carol Tashie moved from Oregon to New Hampshire and answered an advertisement for a special education teacher of the "severely and profoundly handicapped." Carol had worked for several years in a school for students with significant disabilities and had begun a pilot program where her students came together for part of the day with students from the general education kindergarten located in the same building. She came to believe that educating all children together had benefits for students with and without disabilities, and unbeknownst to her soon-to-be employers, was eager to help all of the students in the district's self-contained classroom make the transition into general education classes on a full-time basis. Carol was the only applicant for the job, and when she talked about the idea during her interview, the school didn't challenge her. They were just hoping that she would take the position!

Carol's experience bore out Marsha's beliefs about the key role of an inclusion facilitator. During Carol's first year at her new job, she worked with the school's principal, parents, classroom teachers, and other staff to make each of her six students fully participating members of age-appropriate general education classes. Carol no longer spent her evenings designing lesson plans for her six students but rather designing adapted materials based on lessons taught in the general education classroom. During the day, Carol spent time in each student's classroom, assisting the general education teacher with whole-class and small-group instruction. Carol facilitated regular team meetings where students' academic, social, medical, and behavioral issues were discussed, and she empowered all members of the team to solve any problems that arose.

After 2 years in this role, Carol wanted to share what she had learned with other families and schools. For the next 15 years, she worked for the Institute on Disability (IOD) at the University of New Hampshire (UNH), directing several state- and federally funded projects that helped move New Hampshire into a position of national leadership in inclusive education. Today, she spends several days each month consulting throughout the United States about inclusive education, though she focuses most of her energies on peace activism.

In 1987, Jocelyn Curtin was an 8-year-old who was bussed across town to a self-contained classroom for students with significant disabilities. Her mom, Marlyn, had just completed New Hampshire's

Family Leadership Series, where she rekindled her vision for Jocelyn to have a typical school experience alongside her friends and neighbors who didn't have disabilities. When Jocelyn was ready to enter third grade, Marlyn began a 9-year advocacy process that resulted in Jocelyn's membership in general education, her graduation from high school in 1997, and a fulfilling adult life in the community.

Jocelyn's inclusive education was not perfect. There were years when her teachers understood the goals of inclusion and other times when Marlyn struggled all year to make Jocelyn's education meaningful. In some of the schools that Jocelyn attended, a special education teacher served in the role of inclusion facilitator, and Marlyn remembers how much easier those years were. She had an advocate on the inside whose sole responsibility was facilitating belonging and meaningful participation for students with significant disabilities. Since graduating from high school, Jocelyn has become an instructor in the Inclusion Facilitator Teacher Education Option in UNH's Department of Education, and her class presentations are cited by students as some of the most meaningful learning experiences in their graduate education.

The stories of these three women are part of the history of inclusive education. The emergence of the inclusion facilitator role and the lessons we learned from these women are woven throughout this book.

A book like this does not get written without real commitment from a publisher, and Lisa Benson, Rebecca Lazo, Steve Peterson, Janet Betten, and Kathy Thurlow from Paul H. Brookes Publishing Co. were instrumental in guiding this book into print. We appreciate their support and patience.

Last, but certainly not least, we are grateful to Julie Moser for her invaluable editorial assistance as we were drafting the manuscript. She shared not only her advanced technical skills but also her beliefs in social justice and inclusive community.

Introduction
The Next-Best Thing
Jan Nisbet

The Inclusion Facilitator's Guide is based on 20 years of work in New Hampshire, other states, and several European countries. Each of the authors has worked with hundreds of students, families, and schools to build their capacity to include all students, and each brings her own perspective, mental models, and experiences to the book. This introduction represents my reflections on the role of the inclusion facilitator in the school reform process.

I have been privileged to work with many educational reformers in universities across the United States. Common to each of their perspectives is a deep respect for children with disabilities and the right of these children to be fully participating members of inclusive public schools and communities. I have served on boards of numerous professional and advocacy associations and served as an expert witness in several landmark legal cases. For the past 18 years I have directed the New Hampshire Center for Excellence on Disability with the expressed mission "to advance policies and systems changes, promising practices, education and research that strengthen communities and ensure full access, equal opportunities, and participation for all persons." For the last 17 years, I have guided and observed these authors' work at the Institute on Disability at the University of New Hampshire. I hope that this book will generate discussion, deep reflection, and friendly criticism that leads us all to become better facilitators of inclusion for all students.

INCLUSION FACILITATORS COMBINE THE ROLES OF GOOD TEACHERS, MEDIATORS, AND SOCIAL CHANGE AGENTS

The role of an inclusion facilitator is consistent with the gradual move of children with disabilities from segregated environments to general education classrooms and neighborhood schools. The purpose is noble; the reality is difficult. In the absence of overall educational reform that recognizes, values, and supports children with disabilities to learn together with those who are not labeled, inclusion facilitators are the "next-best thing." I say this from an armchair where I watch the trends; cheer any school that embraces full inclusion; and grimace at the lack of fundamental reforms at the policy, funding, and higher education levels.

We ask much from an inclusion facilitator. In some schools, inclusion facilitators are part of a cohesive team that embraces the concept of full inclusion, and they work closely with other teachers to ensure that students are learning, have access to the most up-to-date technologies and instructional strategies, and are members of their classrooms in the truest sense of the word. In other schools, inclusion facilitators are social reformers. They work to develop learning teams out of isolated service providers, cajole administrators into reforming school policies to end exclusion, and advocate for individual children who are labeled and educated on the periphery of general education. Finally, there are those who assume the role of teacher in a self-contained classroom, believing that they can change the school, one child at a time, from a learning environment that segregates to one that embraces diversity.

The most strategic, personable, and skilled will be successful. Inclusion facilitators must understand diverse learning styles and strategies, technology and access, and social relationships and facilitation, but they must also understand power, bureaucracies, people's concerns, decision making, negotiation, and community organizing. This fact makes the inclusion facilitator more than a teacher—it makes him or her an agent of social change. This role requires skills unique to this period in educational history.

SUCCESS IS PROPORTIONAL TO THE IMPLEMENTATION OF EDUCATIONAL REFORMS THAT EMBRACE INCLUSION AND DIVERSE STUDENT LEARNING STYLES

In New Hampshire, the Chair of the State Board of Education proposed a new initiative that is sure to disrupt many existing notions about education and its bureaucratic structures. The initiative, called Real World Learning (RWL), is characterized by extending the process of education beyond traditional school environments and formally adopting rules for measuring and rewarding student achievement in real-world learning environments (New Hampshire State Board of Education, 2004). The goal is to weave into the fabric of education a greater variety of learning experiences that will help prepare students for the real world both during and after completion of traditional classroom education.

This reform proposal requires general education teachers to assume different roles, becoming facilitators, coaches, mentors, and bridge builders between students, the school, and the larger community. This new role for content area teachers nicely parallels the role and responsibilities of the inclusion facilitator, and, if the RWL proposal is adopted and implemented, it will provide an opportunity for general and special educators to work together on improving learning outcomes for all students.

INCLUSION FACILITATORS AND
CRITICAL FRIENDS HAVE A LOT IN COMMON

In the 1990s, the concept of *critical friend* was embedded into the school reform lexicon by the national school reform organization, the Coalition of Essential Schools (Olson, 1994). Cheryl Jorgensen played the role of critical friend and inclusion facilitator at Souhegan High School, a Coalition School in Amherst, New Hampshire. Unlike other schools, Souhegan High School started with principles of the Coalition of Essential Schools and added an emphasis on the inclusion of students with disabilities, which had not been clearly articulated in the Coalition's original mission. In many ways, Jorgensen's roles were interchangeable. The ability to see things as an outsider but to have the curriculum, teaching, and attitudinal tools of a teacher proved invaluable as the school attempted to include all students in general education classrooms. During the school's first 4 years of operation, Souhegan High School staff learned many lessons about school reform, inclusion, and the role of the inclusion facilitator (Jorgensen, 1998).

The inclusion facilitator serves as both a peer and a critical friend. His or her success will be proportional to the school's commitment to an inclusive mission, vision, and values. The inclusion facilitator must be an excellent teacher and mentor and, at the same time, a master of the art of negotiation and change agentry. Being an inclusion facilitator will continue to be a sometimes lonely and frustrating job until university teacher education programs prepare all teachers to believe that all children can learn and should be taught in heterogeneous classrooms.

Although schools like Souhegan High School embrace the concepts of diversity and inclusion, there are still too many students who are left out and educated separately. There must be a constant flow of new teachers who value diversity and inclusive teaching practices as well as educational environments that adopt reflective practice and are committed to whole-school learning. Without this influx and commitment, the inclusion facilitator will only affect some children for small periods of time, and after the child leaves middle school, for example, and goes on to high school, he or she may face 4 years of resource rooms and trailers that send the clear message that some do not belong or are too difficult to teach.

We must be careful not to focus too much on the inclusion facilitator as the point of innovation. It is not enough to have a new kind of teacher or a new member of the school personnel. The new kind of teacher must coexist with changes in the curriculum, teaming, school climate, and community engagement. The title of *inclusion facilitator* should also be a label assigned to administrators, who should share many of the same skills as inclusion facilitator teachers. School administrator preparation programs often coexist with special education administrator programs, but they are treated as separate. Why?

It is true that there are legal, procedural, and fiscal complexities associated with the Individuals with Disabilities Education Act of 1990 (PL 101-476) and its amendments, Section 504 of the Rehabilitation Act of 1973 (PL 93-112), and Medicaid, but in the end, funding streams and roles must be integrated in a way that ensures that all students receive a high-quality education. The Regular Education Initiative included this as a proposal in the early 1990s. Because attitudes had not changed, many people feared that if funding streams and roles were fully integrated, then students with disabilities would not benefit from targeted resources and supports. Thus, there is an ongoing reluctance to fully merge resources, programs, and roles.

INCLUSION FACILITATORS EMERGE FROM IDIOSYNCRATIC PERMUTATIONS OF HIGHER EDUCATION SPECIAL EDUCATION, GENERAL EDUCATION TEACHER TRAINING, AND COMMUNITY ORGANIZING PROGRAMS

Seymour Sarason wrote,

> The preparation of educators should have two related, difficult, and even conflicting goals: to prepare people for the realities of schooling, and to provide them with a conceptual and attitudinal basis for coping with and seeking to alter those realities in ways consistent with what we think we know and believe. (1993, p. 129)

The terms *inclusion facilitator* (Jorgensen, 1998), *change agent* (Fullan, 1993), *linker* (Havelock, 1971), *community organizer*, and *bridge builder* (McKnight, 1995) stand apart from the word *teacher* even though teachers assume many of these roles formally and informally. The term *teacher* conjures up a set of characteristics that are historical and often stereotypical—a person focused almost exclusively on student learning in his or her classroom.

Rarely does one associate the word *teacher* or use it interchangeably with the word *change agent*. This is in part because the roles typically are not interchangeable due to the lack of clarity or consensus in teacher training programs about how to organize certification programs and curriculum. Special educators often complete coursework separately from their general education counterparts. Community organizing or systems change courses are not offered as part of the curriculum. There is some attention given to collaboration, teaming, and working with families in university coursework, but few new teachers graduate with a deep understanding of their emergent and important role as agents of change in their school. Even if they perceive their role as such, they do not have the skills or support to begin the long journey of change that requires understanding power and bureaucracy, organizing teachers and families to work toward change, and engaging in continual self-reflection and constant learning as they move forward (Senge et al., 2000).

Inclusion facilitators are really teachers who emerge within the larger context of teaching for social justice and recognize the relationship between individual learning, environmental influences, social attitudes, and past experiences (Darling-Hammond, French, & Garcia Lopez, 2002). Fullan (1993) reminded readers that teaching is a moral profession that requires the skills of change agentry. In addition, Senge and colleagues identified systems thinking as a learning discipline necessary for effective schools and education that can be "a powerful practice for finding the leverage needed to get the most constructive change" (2000, p. 8).

Sarason has argued for a fundamental restructuring of teacher education. His experience as a practitioner at Southbury Training School in Connecticut, an institution for people with disabilities, is reflected in his ongoing criticism of labeling, separation, and segregation of students with disabilities within schools.

> What I find both discouraging and appalling is how educators at all levels of responsibility assert agreement with the goal of helping each child realize his potential and then say nothing about how the organization and culture of schools undercut that goal, about how teaching children, not subject matter, is made impossible. I am not advocating that teachers become agents of social change. I am advocating that they become agents of school change, that they not see themselves as powerless victims of an uncomprehending public. (1993, pp. 127–128)

Each of these educational leaders has influenced the conceptualization and development of the inclusion facilitator—a role that embodies moral understanding of human rights, social justice, inclusion, and belonging for all students; knowledge of the importance of working across disciplines within a community as a collaborator; the ability to teach and problem-solve to create a universally designed curriculum and teaching strategies that can benefit all students; and recognition of the importance that families and friends play in the educational and social development of children with disabilities. Fullan (1993) and Senge and colleagues (2000) referred to a similar set of core capacities as personal vision building, inquiry, mastery, and collaboration. Although vague language related to these core capacities can be found in the special education teacher standards promulgated by the Council for Exceptional Children and the National Council for the Accreditation of Teacher Education, the means by which these essential core capacities are interpreted in teacher education programs determine whether new teachers acquire them (Council for Exceptional Children, 2003).

In my broad experience in the field since the 1980s, I have encountered only a few teacher education programs that focus on, rather than allude to, the skills necessary to support the requisite organizational and personnel changes necessary to bring about full inclusion of students with and without disabilities. As a rule, institutions of higher education do not prepare their graduates to bring about or manage change. The question is "Why?" Sarason (1993) argued that, with the exception of John Goodlad, few scholars have engaged in critical discussions of teacher education programs and the necessity for change. The development of the inclusion facilitator as an agent of school change falls outside of traditional and most current special education and teacher preparation programs.

In a recent Advanced Seminar in Special Education at the University of New Hampshire, I asked the students, "What is a special educator? What skills do special educators need? What are they supposed to do? How are they different from so-called regular educators?" The answers were all different. Some confusion ensued, and we agreed that they were confused because the design and purpose of their education was confusing.

Some saw themselves as facilitators, some only as classroom teachers. Others saw themselves as consultants. All agreed that they were expected to be many things to many people depending on the status of inclusive education or special education practices in their schools.

Higher education could help straighten out some of these issues if there was more clarity in teacher education curriculum and a clearer vision and articulation of the role of special educator—if one exists. The role of the inclusion facilitator is clear, but it exists as a subtype, a specialization, or a mutation.

INCLUSION FACILITATION IS ABOUT MENTAL MODELS

What we believe about children with disabilities affects how we work and teach. If a teacher believes, for example, that children with autism have enormous capacities for communication and that movement dysfunction plays a strong role in their inability to easily demonstrate what they know, then he or she intervenes in a certain way. If he or she believes that the "least-dangerous assumption" (Donnellan, 1984) is to presume competence within all children, then he or she views each child as capable of learning complex information. If administrators believe in the importance of natural proportion as a context for learning, then they structure classrooms so that about 85% of students do not have disabilities (Brown et al., 1983). If they believe in the positive behavioral approaches, then they organize schools and interact with students in ways that communicate respect and use instructional supports that encourage appropriate behavior without using aversive procedures (Sugai, 1996).

Inclusion facilitators embrace these mental models. They operationalize them depending on their school culture and context: one system at a time, one school at a time, one classroom at a time, or one child at a time.

REFERENCES

Brown, L., Ford, A., Nisbet, J., Sweet, M., Donnellan, A., & Gruenewald, L. (1983). Opportunities available when severely handicapped students attend chronological age appropriate regular schools in accordance with natural proportion. *Journal of The Association for Persons with Severe Handicaps*, 8(1), 16–24.
Council for Exceptional Children. (2003). *What every special educator must know: Ethics, standards, and guidelines for special educators* (5th ed.). Arlington, VA: Council for Exceptional Children.
Darling-Hammond, L., French, L., & Garcia Lopez, S. (Eds.). (2002). *Learning to teach for social justice*. New York: Teachers College Press.
Donnellan, A. (1984). The criterion of the least dangerous assumption. *Behavior Disorders*, 9, 141–150.

Fullan, M. (1993). Why teachers must become change agents. *Educational Leadership, 50*(6), 12–17.

Havelock, R. (1971). *Planning for innovation through dissemination and utilization of knowledge.* Ann Arbor: University of Michigan, Institute for Social Research.

Individuals with Disabilities Education Act of 1990, PL 101-476, 20 U.S.C. §§ 1400 *et seq.*

Jorgensen, C. (1998). *Restructuring high schools for all students: Taking inclusion to the next level.* Baltimore: Paul H. Brookes Publishing Co.

McKnight, J. (1995). *The careless society: Community and its counterfeits.* New York: Basic Books.

New Hampshire State Board of Education. (2004). *Real world learning (RWL): New Hampshire comprehensive educational reform.* Concord: New Hampshire Department of Education.

Olson, L. (1994, May 4). Critical friends. *Education Week,* 20–27.

Rehabilitation Act of 1973, PL 93-112, 29 U.S.C. §§ 701 *et seq.*

Sarason, S. (1993). *The case for change.* San Francisco: Jossey-Bass.

Senge, P., Cambron-McCabe, N., Lucas, T., Smith, B., Dutton, J., & Kleiner, A. (2000). *Schools that learn: A fifth discipline fieldbook for educators, parents, and everyone who cares about education.* New York: Doubleday.

Sugai, G. (1996). Providing effective behavior support to all students: Procedures and processes. *SAIL, 11*(1), 1–4.

From Special Education Teacher to Inclusion Facilitator

Role Revelations and Revolutions

Mary C. Schuh and Cheryl M. Jorgensen

The role of the special education teacher has changed dramatically since the 1980s. The focus of educational law and practice concerning students with disabilities has shifted from gaining student access to education to improving student academic results, as measured in part by their progress within the general education curriculum and their membership in general education classrooms (Hardman & Nagle, 2004; Individuals with Disabilities Education Act Amendments of 1997 [PL 105-17]). As a result of this shift, special education teachers are being required to assume different and more comprehensive responsibilities (Lipsky & Gartner, 1997). Despite this change in the role of the special educator, few teacher education programs have been on the forefront or have even kept up with this trend. Although the ability of educators to teach all students well has become a rhetorical high ground, this goal has yet to be reflected in traditional general or special teacher education programs (Brownell, Rosenberg, Sindelar, & Smith, 2004). Thus, there is a need to define roles, responsibilities, and titles that bridge the gap between changing expectations and the way that special educators are being prepared.

This chapter will describe areas in which the special educator's role has changed most dramatically, including

- The evolution of job titles, position responsibilities, and knowledge and expertise

Preparation of this chapter was supported in part by a grant from the U.S. Department of Education, Office of Special Education Programs, #H324M020067.

- The shift from classroom teacher to facilitator of supports through team collaboration
- The increasing emphasis on advocacy and schoolwide leadership
- The increasing responsibilities as liaison between school, home, and the community

EVOLUTION OF A NEW ROLE

Throughout the years, efforts to include all students into the general education setting have been known by many names. *Mainstreaming* was the term used in the mid-1970s to describe the practice of having students with disabilities receive most of their education in separate classes, although part of their school day was spent in general education classes such as art, music, and physical education. *Integration* was coined in the late 1970s to describe the practice in which students with disabilities were full-time members of general education classes, even if they continued to learn from a different curriculum and had different expectations. Today, *inclusion* is defined as the practice of educating all students in general education classes, including those students with the most significant disabilities, with support being provided to enable both students and teachers to be successful.

Many people who are trained as professional special education teachers experience a contradiction between their academic preparation and what is expected of them in the field. In the past, early definitions of best practices included community-based functional skills programs, individualized education programs (IEPs) that emphasized therapeutic interventions, pseudofriendship programs such as peer buddies, and segregated classrooms. Today, best practices for students with disabilities demand that teachers acquire a different set of skills during their initial and continuing professional education, such as strategies for teaching all students literacy skills, creating socially just school communities, facilitating authentic friendships, embedding service learning into the curriculum for all students, being accountable for every student's achievement, and promoting inclusion in general education (Jorgensen, 2003).

For many special educators, moving from special education to general education is as awkward as visiting another country without knowing the language or the cultural expectations. The authors of this book searched for special educators who have experienced this educational and cultural change firsthand, making the transition from teaching in self-contained classrooms to supporting students with disabilities to become fully participating members of the general education classroom and school.

One indicator of this transition is the introduction of a new job title and role for many special educators: inclusion facilitator. An Internet search of the term *inclusion facilitator*, conducted in August 2004, produced more than 1,000 references. Schools and school districts across the country (including those in San Francisco; Greenwich, Connecticut; Delaware; Lisle and Indian Prairie, Illinois; White Elementary School, Kansas; Maine; Allegheny County, Maryland; Newton and Belchertown, Massachusetts; Ewing, New Jersey; New York; Altoona, Pennsylvania; Pasadena, Texas; Utah; Vermont; and Fairfax County, Virginia) and around the world have developed new job titles to describe those teachers who facilitate the inclusion of students with disabilities into general education settings. These titles consist of inclusion facilitator, inclusion teacher, integration facilitator, inclusion support teacher, inclusion specialist, learning specialist, and inclusion consultant, among others. In addition, many other teachers, such as life skills teachers, resource teachers, educational liaisons, and special education teachers, fulfill the role of facilitating inclusion, even though their job titles do not use the term *inclusion facilitator*.

Dr. Douglas Fisher, a faculty member in the teacher education program at San Diego State University and author of many publications about inclusive education, remarked

> No terms are the same in California as they are in the rest of the country. But, we are good at translating. In San Diego, the position of a teacher who supports inclusion of students with significant disabilities is called "inclusion itinerant," whereas it is called "inclusion support teacher" in Palm Springs, and "advocate teacher" in East County.

Regardless of the job title or position description, this new role requires significant changes, especially for those teachers whose previous duties primarily involved teaching students in "special," self-contained classrooms. What are these teachers' biggest challenges in their new role as inclusion facilitators? What prepared them for this changing role? What information and skills do they wish they had before assuming what has been the career challenge of a lifetime?

To answer these questions, one of the authors, Mary Schuh, interviewed four self-defined inclusion facilitators: Elaine Dodge, Sandy

Hunt, Catherine Lunetta, and Frank Sgambati. All four are educators who have been in the field anywhere from 3 to 27 years and were trained as special education teachers. Interviews were conducted by telephone, in face-to-face conversations, and through follow-up e-mails if clarification was necessary. Dr. Schuh developed questions to learn about the following:

- Their titles and responsibilities
- The knowledge and skills they believe are necessary to be effective as inclusion facilitators
- The shift from classroom teacher to facilitator of supports through team collaboration
- The increasing emphasis on advocacy and schoolwide leadership to support all students
- Their increasing responsibilities to serve as liaisons between school, home, and the community
- Their views on what it takes to create sustainability within their school communities

Evolution of Position Responsibilities, Knowledge Needed, and Job Titles

The evolution of job titles and responsibilities related to the practice of including all students in general education settings is similar across school districts. The interviews revealed that educators who work as inclusion facilitators—no matter what their title—must develop a wide range of knowledge in addition to educational, administrative, and communication skills. Because contemporary position responsibilities have expanded across a number of skill sets and fluctuate daily, inclusion facilitators must also be able to respond to change flexibly, quickly, creatively, and competently.

Biographical Information Inclusion facilitators are known by different titles, and the interviewees shared diverse experiences related to their current role expectations.

Elaine Dodge On leave from her school position and currently working as Distinguished Educator for the New Hampshire Department of Education, Elaine travels around the state providing training and technical assistance to teams who are developing students' alternate assessment portfolios. When she first entered the profession, she taught at a segregated school for students with disabilities. For the last 20 years, however, she has worked in public schools supporting the inclusion of students with significant disabilities.

When Elaine worked as the inclusion facilitator at Moultonborough Academy, New Hampshire, her title was Life Skills Teacher. Working with approximately eight students, all with varying needs, Elaine's job required her to wear many professional hats. Her students varied in age and grade level, disability label, and the priority of their educational goals.

"Most of my students were working on a regular high school diploma, so I had to support them in mainstream classes, supervise their paraprofessionals, and facilitate the input of related service providers," she recalled. Elaine also taught a remedial reading class for middle school students and a high school–level consumer math class. She needed to be skilled in teaching reading and math to a diverse group of students, and as a team leader she had to employ highly developed communication and management skills.

Sandy Hunt Sandy has been a special educator for 27 years, including her current position as an elementary school inclusion coordinator. She taught for many years at Mt. Lebanon School, in Lebanon, New Hampshire, which pioneered inclusion in New Hampshire in the 1980s. Sandy now supports 25 students with significant disabilities in four different schools. Sandy's position responsibilities include providing support to general education teachers, serving as the team leader to plan and implement student supports, serving as home–school liaison, and evaluating and supervising paraprofessionals.

"I am not in any one school for a whole day, so I connect the paraprofessionals to their teachers and principals. I am a support teacher to the process," she described. In this configuration of the inclusion facilitator role, Sandy must effectively use a range of skills including evaluation and supervision, time management, and scheduling to accommodate the four school sites. She also uses her solid background in education in her role as the specialist assigned to students with severe disabilities.

Catherine Lunetta Before getting her master's degree in education, Catherine worked for more than 20 years as a social worker. Her current title is Special Education Liaison, and her responsibilities are wide-ranging. She is the administrator who coordinates the development of students' IEPs and their initial and 3-year evaluations, and she facilitates team meetings for a variety of purposes.

"That is the easy stuff," Catherine laughed. "My more important responsibilities are making sure that students are successful in inclusive classrooms and making sure that the supports are in the classrooms to accommodate their needs and the needs of the overall class and teachers."

Catherine supports 20 students in one elementary school (in grades 3–5) who experience a variety of educational challenges, such as hearing difficulties, attention-deficit/hyperactivity disorder, English as a second language, learning disabilities, behavioral challenges, autism spectrum disorders, and multiple disabilities. Catherine's role changes from consultant to administrator to expert, depending on the situation. Similar to other inclusion facilitators, she must possess a high level of knowledge across a variety of educational fields to succeed in her role.

Frank Sgambati   Frank has had a long and productive career in special education. He began his career as an assistant teacher of children with significant disabilities who attended a program in a church basement before the first federal special education law (i.e., Education for All Handicapped Children Act, PL 94-142) was passed in 1975. From 1978 until 1987, he was a teacher at Laconia State School and Training Center, which was at that time New Hampshire's state institution for people with significant disabilities. Shortly before Laconia became the first public institution in the United States to close in 1992, he left to work for the New Hampshire Department of Education as the first state consultant for students labeled as having "severe and profound" disabilities. These students were being educated in public schools for the first time, and Frank's job was to provide training and technical assistance to local teams. Frank collaborated closely with the Institute on Disability (IOD) at the University of New Hampshire (UNH) during his work with the state department; after working together with this organization to help many schools become more inclusive, Frank decided he needed to experience firsthand what it was like to support students in general education classes.

From 1991 until 1995, Frank worked as an inclusion facilitator in the Kearsarge Regional School District; from 1995 until the present, he has been a technical assistance consultant with the IOD supporting local schools' capacities to educate all children within inclusive general education settings.

Knowledge and Skills When students were first included in general education classrooms, most parents and educators were content if students were invited to birthday parties, received telephone calls from classmates, and were generally accepted into the classroom community (Falvey, 1995; Strully & Strully, 1989). Increasingly, however, all concerned individuals are paying greater attention to students' learning, including the development of literacy skills such as reading, writing, and technology use, and the acquisition of core academic knowledge (Erickson, Koppenhaver, Yoder, & Nance, 1997; McSheehan, Sonnenmeier, & Jorgensen, 2002; Wehmeyer, Sands, Knowlton, & Kozleski, 2002). Thus, inclusion facilitators must have demonstrated competence in general education, special education, and a variety of facilitation skills (e.g., consulting, mediation, coaching) to be successful in their roles. Each inclusion facilitator interviewed expressed frustration about his or her preservice education. They recommended that undergraduate and graduate programs provide future special education teachers with a clearer understanding about their roles and the experience and educational background needed to work in the field.

Sandy explained that her work currently focuses on connecting students with their classmates and supporting meaningful access to the curriculum. She commented, "Back when I was prepared to be a teacher, people didn't think that students with significant disabilities could access the general curriculum, so they didn't teach us to have high expectations." Sandy has worked in her role as inclusion facilitator for 11 years, learning primarily through in-service training workshops, participation in special model demonstration projects, or simply through "trial by fire."

Catherine wished her degree program had taught her more about managing the actual classroom teaching process, such as how to effectively support two students in one class when they are not performing at grade level or have physical or behavioral challenges. She remarked,

> I wish I had learned more in the area of literacy instruction and curriculum adaptation techniques for all students. I don't want to just supplement what is happening; I want to be qualified to have a good basis on how to teach students.

Catherine said that her special education degree program did not provide her with an adequate background in general education. She took one reading class, but it was not enough to prepare her with the skills she would need in her role as inclusion facilitator.

"Reading is so important . . . and there is so much self-esteem and social relationships tied to reading," she noted.

Elaine considered it crucial to improve students' reaching and grasping, to focus their eye gaze, and to teach them other access skills. "Skills need to be drilled, learned, and generalized," she added.

To improve student outcomes and increase access to and participation in general education settings, an inclusion facilitator must connect the knowledge and skills needed to coordinate and implement a variety of student supports. Elaine had to learn about collaboration and teaming skills, technology, and augmentative and alternative communication (AAC) on her own. "Most assistive technology wasn't available when I started, [so I had to] keep an open mind about new approaches and to become as computer literate as possible and stay abreast of new developments."

Because the knowledge needed to work effectively as an inclusion facilitator is broad, the interviewees identified a variety of competencies needed to prepare for their roles, including

- Administration, management, and collaboration skills

- Teaching techniques—especially literacy

- Specialized knowledge in the areas of movement, personal care, communication, assistive technology, and emotional-behavioral and social relationships

These broad knowledge and skill areas have been organized into a set of competencies for inclusion facilitators based on research (Ryndak, Clark, Conroy, & Stuart, 2001) and recommendations from a variety of national professional organizations such as the Council for Exceptional Children, TASH (formerly The Association for Persons with Severe Handicaps), and the American Association on Mental Retardation (AAMR). Appendix A, described more fully in Chapter 9, contains a description of the competencies that form the foundation of the UNH's Inclusion Facilitator Teacher Education Option.

Job Titles   Job titles may seem incidental, but creating and using an accurate title consistently and throughout differing cultures and fields helps others to identify and understand what might be expected from the person holding a particular position. The terms *principal* and *superintendent,* for example, are precise job titles that evoke an understanding of the responsibilities and skills needed for the two positions. Most interviewees expressed this need for clarity in their job titles and felt the term *inclusion facilitator* best represented their roles.

Frank did not even have a job title during the years he served as a de facto inclusion facilitator in a regional school district between 1991 and 1995! Nevertheless, he had firsthand experience with the evolutionary change from special education teacher to inclusion facilitator. He recalled

> *I saw myself as a change agent as well as someone who had to do a lot of training for families [and] general and special educators, as well as supervise paraprofessionals and support teams. I also saw myself as the liaison between families and schools and a link to the school board. The term "inclusion facilitator" was accurate for the day-to-day support that I provided to students and their teams.*

Frank understood the importance of creating clarity around the position and advocated that his job title be *inclusion facilitator* to meet the emergent literature and research in the field, as well as the daily, far-reaching responsibilities of the position.

Although Elaine and Catherine are comfortable with the term *inclusion facilitator,* Sandy expressed some unease about her current title as an inclusion coordinator because she wondered if it inaccurately related to the concept of an inclusion program. She cautioned,

> *[The term inclusion coordinator] is an oxymoron. When you indicate that someone is an inclusion coordinator and attached to a specific program, this is in direct conflict with the effort to include all students in age-appropriate typical grades and classes.*

Sandy believes that the language people use has an impact on the way people view teachers' responsibilities. She pointed out,

> *Long ago when these positions were conceived, we were bringing students back [from out-of-district placements] so it was our job to "include" children who were never in the building. I think we are way beyond that, and it makes sense to revisit the title.*

Frank also warned about viewing the title as a panacea. He noted,

> *I think the inclusion facilitator title is adequate, but you can't put too much into titles. I would love for the day to*

come when we didn't need the title. If we truly realize the goals of best practices in [inclusive] education, we can all become teachers and get rid of specialized titles.

This sentiment reflects an understanding posited throughout this book: An inclusion facilitator role is the "next-best thing" in the educational frontier, but the ultimate goal is for schools to include all students in age-appropriate general education settings naturally.

From Classroom Teacher to Facilitator of Supports Through Team Collaboration

Stainback and Stainback (1996), Vandercook and York (1990), Thousand and Villa (2000), Weiner (2002), and others concurred that a major key to the success of inclusion is the involvement of students, teachers, specialists, administrators, parents, and community members, all working together in collaboration. Villa, Thousand, Paolucci-Whitcomb, and Nevin (1990) proposed that "the very process of engaging in collaborative teamwork can facilitate the invention of a new paradigm of collaboration. The process of collaboration requires continuous adaptation in order to make room for multiple perspectives" (p. 279).

The teaming process exists within schools through a variety of formal structures such as site-based management and decision-making teams, reflective practice groups or study circles, curriculum committees, grade-level teams combining special and general educators, and student-specific teams. Individuals with diverse knowledge, skills, and backgrounds come together to develop common district policies, norms of classroom practice, and student-specific solutions.

For Frank, the change from a classroom teacher to a facilitator of supports and team collaboration was not easy, but he realized that collaboration among families, schools, general education, and special education was essential.

"The concept of teaming and working together is critical to student success," he stated emphatically. He continued, "[When we first started inclusion in our district] nobody had much information that was very helpful in terms of figuring it out in the classroom." Frank also found the change to be difficult around the area of service delivery because many of the related-services providers took students out of the classroom (Giangreco, Reid, Dennis, & Edelman, 2000). Frank also faced issues surrounding technology during his role transition—ranging from getting information about what was available to actually using it to support students with complex needs.

Sandy's educational background in elementary and special education did not include any crossover courses. She recalled,

I didn't have any training in my undergraduate or master's program about working with other adults and the importance of collaboration, and I think that is huge. In my training you addressed the disability—you didn't accommodate to the learning environment, and you certainly didn't learn to work as a member of a team to address the opportunities and challenges of educating students with disabilities in general education.

Elaine's transition has been a gradual one. She added,

You can't go in the first year and make tremendous waves. You have to go in and make changes gradually. The challenge is to accept the reality of where the school is philosophically and set your sight on small successes to build on. It was important to build the team concept by getting to know people, their personalities, their mission, and what was important to them and then pulling them all together.

Advocacy and Schoolwide Leadership

Inclusion facilitators are teachers who emerged within the larger context of teaching for social justice, in which teaching is viewed as a moral profession requiring skills of change agentry and leadership rather than those of a mere technician (Fullan, 1993). Elaine, Sandy, Catherine, and Frank all portray the characteristics of teacher, advocate, organizer, and leader in their roles. Dedication, experience, and self-taught skills have worked for them, but each acknowledged the need for preservice preparation and professional development that provide current and new educators with leadership and advocacy skills.

"I was nervous as hell when I first started because I didn't know if I could do it," Frank confessed, explaining that there were few workshops on inclusive education when he began working as a de facto inclusion facilitator.

What I had in my favor is that I was really open and committed and hard working. I think what made me successful

*in the role is that I was able to move people to support what
I was doing.*

Frank listened and tried not to judge, made sure to tell people that
he did not have all of the answers, and promised to work with them
to help them figure things out. He continued, "Being hands-on in
the classroom made a big difference. When I went to school to learn
to be a teacher, there was nothing to prepare me for the role of inclusion facilitator."

Frank's biggest challenge during his role transition was the per-
vasive attitude that inclusion "can't work for all kids." He felt that
he had to convince and show people that good education means supporting all kids in general education classes and maintaining high
expectations, regardless of a student's unique characteristics. According to Frank, special education perpetuates the myth that some
kids can benefit from being in the mainstream and some kids cannot. He observed,

*In many ways I felt like an advocate for the student and a
teacher for the adults. Every part of the education system
contradicts fully supporting all students and much of the
time it [the decision about who was included and who
wasn't] was pretty arbitrary. This was a constant challenge.*

Frank tackled the problem by developing his own leadership skills
in order to advocate for necessary changes.

"I learned this role by the seat of my pants," Sandy concurred.
She felt she was personally and professionally in the mindset to
work as an inclusion facilitator well before there was an emphasis on
including students with significant disabilities in general education.
When she had worked in a self-contained program for preschoolers,
there had been a child care center nearby for children without disabilities. Even then—27 years ago—she found herself asking why
these children were separated when they could learn from one
another. "What prepared me for this role was growing up in the field
and being drawn to staff development that was geared toward information about inclusion." Sandy took advantage of as many professional development opportunities as possible, and similar to Frank,
she had to forge her knowledge and experience of advocacy and leadership through self-directed professional development.

Although many inclusion facilitators would never describe
themselves as leaders or advocates, Catherine observed, "In fact
that is exactly what I need to be to facilitate positive outcomes for
students with disabilities in general education classes." It is not

unusual for her to be in the position of justifying or advocating for the presence of a student with significant disabilities in ordinary routines. Catherine mused,

> *I used to think this was not my role. But if it is not my role, then it becomes the primary responsibility of the parent. I have seen too many families work too hard to make sure their children with disabilities get a quality general education with supports. It shouldn't all be on the parents. This is my responsibility, too.*

Liaison Between School, Home, and the Community

Strong relationships between schools, families, and the larger community offer opportunities for greater connectedness; an expanded understanding of resources available to support students, families, and schools; and an increased likelihood for successful transitions between school and home and ultimately to adult life. Relationships of mutual support are critical across organizations in community life and, according to Michael Peterson, Co-Founder of the Whole Schooling Consortium, "Our challenge is to create and support community—the common bond holding us together, which, in turn is supported and maintained by our relationships" (1996, p. 292). Because schools and families are essential to the fabric of community life, they must forge a partnership that consists of a shared understanding of what constitutes successful outcomes for all students and shared resources necessary to achieve those outcomes.

This concept implies that inclusion facilitators need to be knowledgeable about the variety of agencies affecting the lives of students and their families. Lourie, Katz-Levy, and Stroul (1996) described an approach called *unconditional care* that results in policies that seek to create an inclusive entrance into services and prevent discharge or exclusion from what is naturally available to students without disabilities. This approach also requires that students with disabilities receive access to specialized supports and services to meet their unique concerns. Although comprehensive systems of care, also known as the *wrap-around approach,* were initiated to respond to the needs of children and youth with emotional and behavioral disabilities, there is widespread agreement that this process benefits all children and their families with complex needs, regardless of their disability label. The wrap-around systems of care approach acknowledges that there are many service providers in the lives of some families, and thus all service providers need to work collaboratively to address the family's needs within their home, neighborhood school, and local community.

Unfortunately, recognition of the importance of wrap-around services together with the skills to bring services to the family has not traditionally been taught in preservice educational or professional development programs. Catherine, for example, wished she had learned more about community resources so that she could better support families beyond the school day. She lamented, "It would have been good to have a better understanding of how to access these resources to solve the challenges that students and families face at home that end up impacting their time at school."

Elaine regretted that she wasn't trained to work with parents to understand what is important to them or how to negotiate win-win solutions between the parents and the school. Some parents, she said, want their children to learn to read and write and support their inclusion in general education core curriculum, but others appear to value social relationships for their children above all else. Still others are concerned with having their children learn basic functional skills and do not see the importance of having their children attend academic classes such as social studies and science. She recalled,

In the beginning, parents looked at me like I had two heads when we stated that there was value to some of the [general] education classes that they might not have considered before. We needed to walk them through and show them how in the context of the class students could be working on functional skills and still get the benefit of [general] classes.

Catherine described her experiences as a liaison to illustrate how important home and community supports are to educational outcomes. She revealed, "So often out-of-district placements happen when there are [challenging] issues at home. Schools seem to be unable or unwilling to be flexible and to get involved to be a change agent around these issues." She noted that it is often difficult for students who require significant physical and/or behavioral supports to receive those supports at home when a family is not able to provide them. Without these accommodations provided at home, Catherine said, it has also been difficult to ensure these students' success at school. Her role as a liaison requires that she be aware of what resources exist in the community and assume responsibility for coordinating these resources.

Catherine offered one example:

A student I support received counseling services, special education services, speech-language [services], and hearing services at school. Her parents also took her to a local clinic in which she received yet another round of therapy. There was no coordination between school and home community services and, unbeknownst to everyone, the school and clinic were working on different goals! As the liaison, I was able to bring this to everyone's attention. Once the family understood that the school was providing those services throughout the course of the day, they were comfortable dropping the after-school therapy and focusing on getting their daughter included in age-appropriate extracurricular activities.

In order to create a wrap-around system of care that coordinates consistent and effective services, an inclusion facilitator's role has evolved to include the responsibility of acting as a liaison between the school, home, and community. Chapter 7 describes in detail an inclusion facilitator's role as an information and community resource broker.

Creating Sustainability

The interviewees provided many recommendations about what it takes to sustain inclusive learning environments. According to Elaine, Sandy, Catherine, and Frank, maintaining an inclusive learning environment requires

- Teachers who are flexible, innovative, and willing to put inclusive ideas into practice
- Teachers who invite inclusion facilitators to share their grade-level planning time and welcome inclusion facilitators and others into their classrooms
- Teachers who see all of the students in their class as their students and not merely visitors
- Teachers and other team members who sustain their own energy and commitment to avoid burnout
- Schools that offer professional development that supports inclusive strategies
- Schools that expect teachers to work as a team and to maintain high expectations for all students

- Schools that emphasize building the trust level among students, parents, and all team members, including the principal and assistant principal

SUSTAINING THE INCLUSION FACILITATOR'S ENERGY AND COMMITMENT BY CELEBRATING SUCCESS

Although the role evolution for inclusion facilitators has not always been easy, celebrating successes is a positive way to maintain one's energy and commitment. Catherine, Elaine, Sandy, and Frank all had stories of celebration that inspire and illustrate their true dedication to inclusive schools.

Catherine revels in the little successes rather than focusing on what has not worked so well. For one of her students with significant disabilities, her team has been able to predict potential challenges and clear expectations ahead of time so that behavioral crises do not occur. As a result of Catherine's leadership, this student has more friends and participates more actively in classroom activities. Another of her students, who has a label of autism spectrum disorder, used to choose picture books to look at rather than books with text to read. Catherine suggested that the paraprofessional and teacher preview the class books and identify questions about the plot and characters that would pique the student's interest. Now, this student is reading text that is grade level and above. Catherine hypothesized,

> He needed a start and a finish to the chapter book, and the comprehension questions gave him a structure and the motivation to engage in reading. People never expected that he could do this, but we figured out what makes him click as a reader, and people could see that he is smart and capable. Before we tried this strategy, no one was sure what he was getting out of it.

Elaine considers the milestones of graduation and the completion of driver's education—activities that some thought particular students would either never have as a goal or be able to achieve—as markers of success. One student who experienced significant behavioral and cognitive disabilities moved into Elaine's former school district from an out-of-state school. In his old school, he was in a self-contained classroom and spent the day working on supposedly functional skills such as sorting, identifying colors, and counting. Elaine recalled with pride,

He is now in tenth grade, attending all general education classes, and being provided with paraprofessional support. He is working on gaining the credits required to graduate. His parents never thought they would see that day, and the whole school community is recognizing and learning from the success. This was a kid who was typically sent home from school because of his behaviors. I get misty eyed when I think of him.

Frank celebrated the close relationships that developed among peers, as well as the creation of teams including students, families, and teachers who shared the same goals. His work with one student led to that student's involvement in the school's booster club and Key Club as well as a summer job alongside another classmate who did not have disabilities. "It made it feel as though you could accomplish anything!" Frank marveled.

Frank also shared the story of Molly's inclusion into a fifth-grade classroom as one of his most challenging, yet satisfying, examples of successful inclusion.

Molly's Story

When Frank met Molly and her parents, she was a resident of a pediatric nursing home, having been placed there by the school district when she was 3 years old. When Molly was approaching her tenth birthday, she and the other students who lived at the facility spent their school day in a small educational program located at the site, engaged in personal care routines, therapy, and preschool activities.

In his role as the elementary school inclusion facilitator, Frank visited Molly a few times a year to ensure that her IEP was being implemented as written, to check on her progress, and to participate in end-of-year program review meetings. He had become convinced that her local school could provide an appropriate and rich education for Molly, and he made it a personal goal to return her to the district. He knew that even if Molly stayed in the pediatric nursing home, he would be busy facilitating successful inclusion for the other seven students on his caseload. Yet, each time he visited her, he knew that he had to advocate for her return as well.

For almost 2 years, Frank broached the idea of moving Molly back to the district with her parents, the district's special education director, and the principal of Molly's neighborhood school, but none of them believed the idea was feasible. Rather than criticize them for their difference of opinion, he acknowledged their concerns and worked to address each and every one in a respectful way.

Then, during Molly's fourth-grade year, the opportunity arose for Frank's school district to be part of the IOD's Statewide Systems Change Project that was focused on building local capacity to educate students with significant disabilities in their home schools. He asked Molly's parents, a team of people from her school, and the family support coordinator from the local developmental service agency if they would like to attend a weeklong summer institute sponsored by the project and then participate in a year's worth of training and technical assistance to help plan Molly's successful transition. The team agreed, as long as members could have the option of making the final decision about Molly's educational program and placement based on her individual needs. Frank was optimistic that everyone's concerns could be addressed, and he welcomed the challenge.

The team did attend the summer institute and left sharing Frank's passion about inclusive education. Although members still had many concerns and questions that needed to be resolved before they would be ready to bring Molly back to the district, their attitude had shifted from "why?" to "how?"

Following the summer institute, Frank and Molly's team met to develop a 12-month plan for Molly's transition that included numerous training opportunities for school staff, Molly's team members, and her future classmates. The team's goal was for Molly to enter fifth grade the following school year. The team decided to visit Molly at the facility, review her IEP, and see how her educational goals and health concerns were being met.

On the way home from the visit, their van buzzed with conversation. The team was unimpressed by the content of Molly's educational program. Even though they weren't really sure about Molly's capacity to learn, they felt sure that their fifth-grade curriculum and classroom would provide a much richer learning environment in which Molly could reach her potential.

Frank was convinced that Molly had greater abilities than she was able to demonstrate. She didn't have a way to communicate but clearly demonstrated an interest in the people and activities around her. Frank remarked that he wouldn't like anyone to try to guess how smart he was if he could not move or speak, and he vowed that he would never make any predictions about what Molly could or could not learn.

Molly's health concerns were substantial and the school, Molly's parents, and team wanted to ensure Molly's safe return to the district by setting standards for her health support. The team determined that Molly would need the services of a paraprofessional with training in cardiopulmonary resuscitation, catheter maintenance, suctioning, and feeding Molly through her gastrointestinal tube. The team's goal was to hire an experienced special education paraprofessional who had Certified Nursing Assistant licensure. Together with the school nurse and occupational therapist, Frank wrote a job description for this person and began interviews about 3 months before the end of that school year.

Frank also worked extensively with Molly's parents and the local developmental service agency to plan for the home supports Molly would need. New Hampshire had recently approved a Medicaid waiver program to provide in-home supports for children with significant health care concerns that was not tied to family income. The family determined that there were architectural barriers that would have to be addressed and that specialized medical equipment and the services of a personal care attendant for several hours of the day were needed to ensure Molly's safety and their family's overall stability. Frank was instrumental in helping the family negotiate the paperwork and regulatory hurdles to obtain those services.

Once the team developed a detailed health and safety plan, it met regularly to discuss how Molly might participate in the fifth-grade classroom and curriculum. Frank spent many hours observing in the fifth-grade class, noting the room's physical layout, the teacher's instructional methods, and the children's interactions. Because Frank had worked with children with significant disabilities for many years, he had developed a file drawer full of lesson plans and creative projects for other students, and the team slowly began to have a vision of how Molly could participate in typical fifth-grade lessons at the same time she was learning the skills on her IEP.

Frank knew Molly's communication barriers would make it difficult to include her in the academic life of the classroom and arranged for her to be assessed by an augmentative communication team from the state's assistive technology center. The team determined that a single-switch communication device would give Molly a way to participate in lessons and that the process of expanding her communication abilities would be a long-term goal.

Every time Frank met with Molly's prospective team, one member or another raised new concerns that had to be addressed. Frank's reassuring manner, his ability to coach the team to voice its concerns, and his years of experience built a real sense of trust within the team. Frank knew that this effort would be successful only if the team was an effective working group, so he developed close relationships with each team member in school and through occasional end-of-the-week get-togethers.

Assisted by Molly's mother, Frank conducted two miniworkshops for the outgoing fourth-grade students because he knew that they would be key in accepting Molly as a valued member of social life in the classroom and school community. Molly's mom shared a scrapbook about Molly with the students. Frank talked openly about her disabilities, but emphasized what Molly and the other students had in common. Toward the end of the school year, the classroom teacher had the students write short notes to Molly telling her all about themselves and their school.

Frank was careful to create a picture of Molly that emphasized her gifts and personality without asking for the students' pity. He knew that some students would take on the role of Molly's helpers, but he talked honestly with them about the need for Molly to feel as if she had something to offer them as well.

As the time for Molly's transition grew nearer, Frank coordinated a half-day visit to the school. Rather than making the event a formal occasion, he and the classroom teacher picked a day during the last month of school when the annual school fair was taking place. Frank, Molly, and her mom sat at a picnic table and introduced Molly to the many children who shyly approached them to find out about the girl whom they had come to know through an occasional videotape or letter.

The transition planning process did not always go as planned. When the fifth-grade teacher who had been part of the planning process announced that she would be going on maternity leave for the first 3 months of the following school year, Frank and the principal worked together to identify another fifth-grade teacher in the building who was open to having Molly in his or her classroom. At first, this change in plans seemed to present an almost insurmountable barrier as the team had invested so much energy in the first teacher. When the team found out that the new teacher had just recently attended a conference on multiple intelligences and was planning to design several multiple intelligences–based units, they felt as if the unplanned change might have unexpected benefits for Molly (Armstrong, 2000).

This description of Molly's transition planning makes it appear as if everything went smoothly, the team members never had a disagreement, and that even the difficulties worked themselves out magically. The reality is far from that. But Frank's disposition and unshakable belief in inclusion provided a sense of steady leadership to the team so that the inevitable problems that arose were addressed in an honest and systematic way. Frank is a good example of the type of professional who holds the beliefs and has the disposition to be a successful inclusion facilitator (see Table 1.1).

Table 1.1.   Beliefs and personality traits of successful inclusion facilitators

Beliefs	Personality traits
Families are central to children's lives.	Committed
Good teaching is good teaching.	Flexible and open-minded
Every person has inherent value.	Collaborative
Every person has competence.	Respectful of others' viewpoints
Diversity enhances community.	Creative
	Friendly
	Optimistic

What about Molly? Her first year in public school was marked by joyous occasions, such as her participation in the holiday concert and her emerging literacy skills. There were also some frustrating moments when people were unsure of what she was communicating or when IEP team meetings were cancelled due to reasons beyond the members' control. But all in all, Molly seemed happy, she was using her communication device, her parents were more optimistic about Molly's future than they had ever been before, and the school moved one step closer to being a true, inclusive community of learners.

CONCLUSION

Although the job title of inclusion facilitator is meant to describe a laudable goal—supporting all students to be successful in the general education classroom and school community—the word *inclusion* has taken on a negative connotation for some people. Language has the power to unite or divide. It can move people forward or backward in the effort to achieve promising practices for students with disabilities. Perhaps the job title of inclusion facilitator is just the "next-best thing," and what really matters most is that all educators promote a vision of an inclusive and just society, hold high expectations for every student, and use effective teaching strategies that result in positive academic and relational outcomes for all students, including those with significant disabilities.

REFERENCES

Armstrong, T. (2000). *Multiple intelligences in the classroom.* Alexandria, VA: Association for Supervision and Curriculum Development.

Brownell, M., Rosenberg, M., Sindelar, P., & Smith, D. (2004). Teacher education: Toward a qualified teacher for every classroom. In A. Sorrells, H. Reith, & P. Sindelar (Eds.), *Critical issues in special education* (pp. 243–257). Boston: Pearson Education.

Education for All Handicapped Children Act of 1975, PL 94-142, 20 U.S.C. §§ 1400 *et seq.*

Erickson, K., Koppenhaver, D., Yoder, D., & Nance, J. (1997). Integrated communication and literacy instruction for a child with multiple disabilities. *Focus on Autism and Other Developmental Disabilities, 12*(3), 142–150.

Falvey, M.A. (1995). *Inclusive and heterogeneous schooling: Assessment, curriculum, and instruction.* Baltimore: Paul H. Brookes Publishing Co.

Fullan, M. (1993). Why teachers must become change agents. *Educational Leadership, 50*(6), 12–17.

Giangreco, M., Reid, R., Dennis, R., & Edelman, S. (2000). Roles of related services personnel in inclusive schools. In R.A. Villa & J.S. Thousand (Eds.), *Restructuring for caring and effective education: Piecing the puzzle together* (2nd ed., pp. 360–388). Baltimore: Paul H. Brookes Publishing Co.

Hardman, M., & Nagle, K. (2004). Public policy from access to accountability in special education. In A. Sorrells, H. Reith, & P. Sindelar (Eds.), *Critical issues in special education* (pp. 277–292). Boston: Pearson Education.

Individuals with Disabilities Education Act (IDEA) Amendments of 1997, PL 105-17, 20 U.S.C. §§1400 *et seq.*

Jorgensen, C. (2003). *Essential best practices in inclusive schools.* Durham: University of New Hampshire Institute on Disability.

Lipsky, D.K., & Gartner, A. (1997). Program implementation. In D.K. Lipsky & A. Gartner (Eds.), *Inclusion and school reform: Transforming America's classrooms* (pp. 117–154). Baltimore: Paul H. Brookes Publishing Co.

Lourie, S., Katz-Levy, J., & Stroul, B.A. (1996). Individualized services in a system of care. In B.A. Stroul (Ed.), *Children's mental health: Creating systems of care in a changing society* (pp. 429–452). Baltimore: Paul H. Brookes Publishing Co.

McSheehan, M., Sonnenmeier, R., & Jorgensen, C. (2002). Communication and learning: Creating systems of support for students with significant disabilities. *TASH Connections, 1*(2), 8–12.

Peterson, M. (1996). Community learning in inclusive schools. In W. Stainback & S. Stainback (Eds.), *Inclusion: A guide for educators* (pp. 271–296). Baltimore: Paul H. Brookes Publishing Co.

Ryndak, D., Clark, D., Conroy, M., & Stuart, C., (2001). Preparing teachers to meet the needs of students with severe disabilities: Program configuration and expertise. *JASH, 26*(2) 96–105.

Stainback W., & Stainback S. (1996). Collaboration, support networking, and community building. In W. Stainback & S. Stainback (Eds.), *Inclusion: A guide for educators* (pp. 193–202). Baltimore: Paul H. Brookes Publishing Co.

Strully, S., and Strully, C. (1989). Friendship as an educational goal. In S. Stainback, W. Stainback, & M. Forest (Eds.), *Educating all students in the mainstream of regular education* (pp. 141–154). Baltimore: Paul H. Brookes Publishing Co.

Thousand, J.S., & Villa, R.A. (2000). Collaborative teaming: A powerful tool in school restructuring. In R.A. Villa & J.S. Thousand (Eds.), *Re-

structuring for caring and effective education: Piecing the puzzle together (pp. 254–292). Baltimore: Paul H. Brookes Publishing Co.

Vandercook, T., & York, J. (1990). A team approach to program development and support. In W. Stainback & S. Stainback (Eds.), *Support networks for inclusive schooling* (pp. 95–122). Baltimore: Paul H. Brookes Publishing Co.

Villa, R., Thousand, J., Paolucci-Whitcomb, P., & Nevin, A. (1990). In search of new paradigms. *Journal of Educational and Psychological Consultation, 1*(4), 279–292.

Wehmeyer, M.L., Sands, D.J., Knowlton, E.H., & Kozleski, E.B. (2002). *Teaching students with mental retardation: Providing access to the general curriculum.* Baltimore: Paul H. Brookes Publishing Co.

Weiner, H. (2002). A matter of confidence and meaningful support: Teachers' perception of their personal impact on teaching and learning. *Focus on Teachers Newsletter.* Retrieved August 21, 2004, from http://www.teachersmind.com/weiner

Ten Promising Practices in Inclusive Education

The Inclusion Facilitator's Guide for Action

Cheryl M. Jorgensen

The Education for All Handicapped Children Act of 1975 (PL 94-142) first guaranteed universal access to free appropriate public education for students with disabilities through mandated procedures and processes. Although the authors of that law presumably believed that these regulated procedures would result in positive educational and life outcomes for students with disabilities, those outcomes were not specified, nor was accountability expected. With each successive reauthorization of the law, however, there has been an increased emphasis on both results and accountability. Committee reports generated during the reauthorization of the Individuals with Disabilities Education Act Amendments of 1997 (IDEA 1997, PL 105-17) stated that "the primary purpose of all these amendments is to go beyond mere access to the schools and secure for every child an education that actually yields successful education results" (Gilhool, 1998, p. 5). To secure these results, legal provisions are now in place (e.g. IDEA 1997; Individuals with Disabilities Education Improvement Act of 2004 [IDEA 2004, PL 108-446]) to ensure that children with disabilities make progress within the general education curriculum based on learning objectives that are, to the maximum extent appropriate, the same for all children. States must not only measure the learning results of children with disabilities; they must also publish them in the same way as they publish results for

Preparation of this chapter was supported in part by a grant from the U.S. Department of Education, Office of Special Education Programs, #H324M020067.

children without disabilities. IDEA 1997 also includes provisions
that all school districts must disseminate and implement "promising educational practices—systems of teaching and learning that have
a record of success" (Gilhool, 1998, p. 5).

Because Congress did not specify in much detail the practices
that qualify as "promising," practitioners must look to the professional literature for guidance. This chapter describes 10 values and
research-based promising practices that, combined with characteristics typically associated with a good general education, define a quality education for students with significant disabilities (Jorgensen,
McSheehan, & Sonnenmeier, 2002a, 2002b). These include

1. Policies and practices based on the least dangerous assump-
    tion and high expectations

2. Membership and full participation in general education classes

3. Family and school partnerships

4. Collaborative teaming

5. Planning and implementing of supports

6. Appropriate augmentative and alternative communication
    (AAC)

7. Friendship facilitation

8. General and special education reform

9. Encouragement of self-determination

10. Person-centered planning

Each section in this chapter defines a promising practice, offers
an example of its use, and describes both positive and negative
exemplars. It is incumbent on an inclusion facilitator to understand
the rationale for each promising practice and to use his or her leadership, teaching, and administrative skills to embed them into
every student's educational program.

POLICIES AND PRACTICES BASED ON THE LEAST
DANGEROUS ASSUMPTION AND HIGH EXPECTATIONS

Imagine that the following description applies to a student who has
a label of severe mental retardation. Her academic records contain
the results of intelligence tests and adaptive behavioral evaluations
that assign her an IQ score of 36 and a developmental age of 18–24

months. She experiences seizures and sensory impairments, and evaluators believe that she lacks intentional movement. This student has no conventional way of communicating and does not appear able to read. Most people assume that she does not know much and cannot learn much.

How would this information affect decisions about this student's educational program? Should it be assumed that these test results and labels are accurate representations of her current abilities and future learning potential? Alternatively, is there another way of thinking about this student that can lead to the creation of an educational program based on expectations that are very different from her reported test results?

Let us consider two completely different approaches to this dilemma. In the first scenario, we assume that the student is not "smart"—that she does, in fact, have *mental retardation*, defined as significantly subnormal intelligence and ability to learn. How might she be treated? First, we would not try to teach her to read. Second, we would speak to her in language more appropriate to a very young child. Third, this student would probably spend her educational career being taught functional skills such as dressing, eating, shopping, cooking, and cleaning. In most states, she would be educated in a separate classroom alongside other students who also have significant disabilities. If she did join the rest of the student body, it might only be during lunch or perhaps a class such as music or art. If we did address her communication skills, the vocabulary and messages that we would make available to her would correspond to our assessment of her intelligence and relate to the functional skills we were teaching her. We would not encourage her to participate in the school's social life because we would assume that her disabilities were too significant for her to enjoy the same activities as her classmates; interactions between her and other students would be limited to their volunteering to be her peer buddy or helper. Perhaps she might participate in Special Olympics a couple of times a year.

As she approached the end of her school career, the possibility of her attending college would not even be considered. Instead, we would plan for her to move into a group home, attend a day habilitation program or work in a sheltered environment, and pursue specialized leisure and recreational opportunities with other adults who have similar disabilities. We would not expect her to have opinions about world events, her future, love, or anything else considered to be complex.

Now, imagine that it is several years in the future. A remarkable discovery has made it possible to determine without question how smart someone is through a simple brain scan. The brain scan results show, surprisingly, that this young woman has an IQ score of 120. She does not have mental retardation. What have been the consequences of our original assumption of mental retardation being wrong? Has any harm been done?

Next, consider another scenario involving the same young woman with the same history of intelligence tests that indicate she has mental retardation. She is still unable to tell us much about what she is thinking and learning, or what she knows because she does not have an effective means to communicate. But in this second scenario, we operate from a different set of assumptions. This time, we treat her as if she is "smart" because we distrust the validity of her test results in light of her communication and movement difficulties. We enroll her in general academic classes, try to teach her to read, and support her with adapted materials and instructional supports. We talk with her about current events and make sure that her AAC device includes words and concepts that are commensurate with someone who can think about current events, love, relationships, and her future. We offer postsecondary education as a graduation option in addition to the possibility of moving into an apartment, working at a real job, or traveling. We also assume that she is capable of, and interested in, making friends—both with and without disabilities.

Once again, many years in the future a new and more accurate brain scan is invented. This time when it is used, however, it shows that she has an IQ score of 40. What have been the consequences of our original assumption of intelligence that has now been proven wrong? Has any harm been done?

These scenarios illustrate the principle of the "least dangerous assumption" that was first described by Anne Donnellan. She proposed that when educational decisions must be made without conclusive information about a person's abilities or intelligence, we ought to work from the assumption that will have the least dangerous consequences should that assumption ever be proven wrong (Donnellan, 1984). Thus, for Donnellan, the least dangerous assumption when working with individuals with significant disabilities is to assume that they are competent because to do otherwise would result in fewer educational opportunities, omitted literacy instruction, a segregated education, and an adult life with fewer choices.

When Donnellan originally proposed the least dangerous assumption principle, few research studies showed that the abilities of people labeled as having mental retardation might be greater than suggested by traditional test results. Since the article was published in 1984, however, AAC, literacy, and special education literature has documented a growing number of examples in which students demonstrated unexpected literacy skills when they were held to high expectations, included in general education classrooms, and/or provided with adequate AAC and instructional supports (Biklen & Cardinal, 1997; Erickson, Koppenhaver, & Yoder, 2002; Erickson, Koppenhaver, Yoder, & Nance, 1997; Koppenhaver, Erickson, Harris, McLellan, Skotko, & Newton, 2001; Ryndak, Morrison, & Sommerstein, 1999).

How to Know It When You See It

When people do **not** assume that students with disabilities are competent and able to learn, educational programs have the following characteristics:

- Participation of students with disabilities in the general education curriculum focuses on learning access or functional skills rather than on acquiring ideas, content knowledge, and related literacy skills.

- Students with disabilities may not be included in general education classrooms, or if they are, they may participate in functional portions of instructional routines but not in the discussion of ideas or content knowledge; in many instances, they will be given different materials and resources than those given to the rest of the class.

- People converse with students with disabilities as if they are talking with a much younger child, and social and academic vocabularies are geared to students' perceived "developmental levels" or IQ scores as measured by traditional assessments.

- Students with disabilities are not supported to engage in social activities with same-age peers because those activities are deemed inappropriate or too advanced.

- Planning for the futures of students with disabilities does not typically include the choice of a postsecondary education; instead, career options are geared to lower-skilled jobs rather than to ones that require higher-order thinking or literacy skills.

When schools follow policies and practices based on the least dangerous assumption and high expectations, the following statements are true:

- "Person-first" language is used so that people say *students with autism*, not *autistic students*.

- Language that classifies students based on their functioning or developmental levels is not used; rather, descriptions of students focus on their abilities and needs.

- Annual goals on individualized education programs (IEPs) reflect content standards from the general education curriculum.

- Students with disabilities are seen as capable of learning; educators do not predict that certain students will *never* acquire certain knowledge or skills.

- People speak directly to students with disabilities rather than speaking to students through a buffer supplied by paraprofessionals or others.

- People use age-appropriate vocabulary, topics, and inflection when talking to students with disabilities.

- In order to respect privacy, staff members discuss the personal care, medical needs, and other sensitive issues of students with disabilities out of earshot from others and only with those people who genuinely need the information.

MEMBERSHIP AND FULL PARTICIPATION
IN GENERAL EDUCATION CLASSES

The second promising practice in inclusive education is for all students with disabilities to be full-time members of general education classes. This practice defines the term *inclusion* (Stainback, Stainback, & Forest, 1989), and a look back in history illustrates how inclusion evolved in response to new research on outcomes and new attitudes toward diversity.

After the first U.S. special education law was passed in 1975, most students with significant disabilities were educated in separate, self-contained classrooms located in general education schools, in regional collaborative programs such as the Board of Cooperative Education Services (BOCES) in New York State, in private educational facilities, or in separate facilities operated by organizations such as Easter Seals.

By the late 1970s, *mainstreaming* had become popular, defined as students with disabilities visiting a general education class or activity such as circle time, art, music, or physical education, primarily for the purpose of socialization. When students were mainstreamed, they were still members of self-contained classrooms, where they received most of their academic instruction.

In the mid-1980s, the practice of *integration* evolved, where students with disabilities were placed in general education classes for part of the day (Calculator & Jorgensen, 1994). Students integrated into a general education classroom, it was thought, might learn skills such as communication or appropriate behavior, along with some of the content of the general education curriculum. Integrated students still received some academic instruction and related services outside of the general education class.

By the late 1980s, parents, researchers, and progressive educators had shifted the paradigm to *inclusion,* which assumes that students are full-time members of general education classes rather than visitors or part-time members. These students' educational programs are based within general education classrooms, and students are provided with the supports they need to ensure their success in that typical environment. The physical space, materials, instruction, and supports are universally accessible to all, not simply modified for some students. As author and community-builder John O'Brien has noted,

> It is simple to state the meaning of inclusion but difficult to set and hold it in place as a context for goal setting and problem solving. Because inclusion happens when communities shift their boundaries and practices to make room for and support people with disabilities, its advocates have more to do than simply change the practice of special educators or human services providers. (2000, p. xii)

Benefits of General Education
Class Membership and Full Participation

National experts and family advocates encourage placing students with significant disabilities in inclusive settings (Biklen, Ferguson, & Ford, 1989; Brown et al., 1989; Giangreco, Cloninger, & Iverson, 2000; Lipsky & Gartner, 1989; Stainback & Stainback, 1990; Villa, Thousand, Stainback, & Stainback, 1993). A variety of rationales support such inclusive placements.

Students with Significant Disabilities Learn More in Inclusive Classrooms A metareview of research on inclusion outcomes

indicated that students with disabilities learn more social skills, develop closer relationships with peers who are typically developing, acquire a greater repertoire of functional skills, and develop better communication skills in inclusive environments than in segregated settings (McGregor & Vogelsberg, 1999).

Students who are well supported in general education classrooms also learn the "hidden curriculum," consisting of expectations, routines, behaviors, relationships, and culture, which is significantly different from that of the special education classroom (Apple, 1979).

Students with Significant Disabilities Can Learn Academic Curriculum Content   The reauthorization of the Individuals with Disabilities Education Act (IDEA) of 1990 (PL 101-476) in 1997 introduced into federal law a requirement that all students with disabilities have access to the general education curriculum, reflecting the growing body of research suggesting that many students previously thought to be unable to learn academics are, in fact, capable of developing literacy and other content knowledge (Biklen & Cardinal, 1997; Erickson et al., 1997; Erickson et al., 2002; Koppenhaver et al., 2001; Ryndak et al., 1999).

Mindful of this research that casts doubt on previously accepted definitions of disability and mental retardation, J. David Smith, Provost and Senior Vice Chancellor at the University of Virginia's College at Wise proposed that the Council on Exceptional Children (CEC) eliminate the phrase "mental retardation" from the title of its Mental Retardation and Developmental Disabilities division. He argued that the term is "scientifically worthless and socially harmful" (Smith, 2002, p. 7). This debate about terminology is related to a growing belief in the field of developmental disabilities that schools should apply the least dangerous assumption about students' potential literacy capabilities and provide all students with access to the general education curriculum and its associated vocabulary. IEP teams should not try to determine a student's intelligence or competence until that student has had access to the general education curriculum and consistent and quality instructional and other supports, and until educators have helped the student to develop an effective means of communication (McSheehan, Sonnenmeier, & Jorgensen, 2002).

Functional Skills Can Be Taught within the Context of Regular Routines and Lessons   Important functional skills can be taught within the context of regular routines and lessons in a general education class and throughout the school community without segregating students. Students should learn these skills in the same contexts and environments as classmates without disabilities (Tashie, Jorgensen, Shapiro-Barnard, Martin, & Schuh, 1996). During the late 1970s and 1980s, the field of special education for students with significant disabilities shifted from a developmental to a functional model. Practitioners recognized that adherence to a purely developmental model of education, in which students were required to pass certain developmental milestones (e.g., identification of shapes) before moving on to higher level skills (e.g., letter identification), locked students into a "pre- means never" mode. Many students often left school at age 21 still working on stacking, color identification, sorting, and so forth (Brown, Branson, Hamre-Nietupski, Pumpian, Certo, & Gruenewald, 1979). In contrast, the functional skills model suggested that all students could learn functional skills in natural contexts, given the right instruction and supports, regardless of their measured developmental levels.

In the late 1980s, another shift occurred in what constituted best practices for students with significant disabilities. Researchers, parents, and educators began to understand that students with significant disabilities need a well-balanced educational experience, not just a functional one. Students need instruction in core academic skills (e.g., reading, writing, using a computer); exposure to content knowledge; and the opportunity to develop dispositions and skills related to responsible citizenship such as effective communication, cooperation, persistence, and work-related skills. Furthermore, research on students enrolled in functional skills curricula showed that although they did, in fact, learn valuable self-help and community-referenced skills in those programs, their social lives were barren: They spent most of their time with paid caregivers and other people with significant disabilities, and they missed out on valuable academic and life-lessons by being out of the school building during the day.

Educators became more sophisticated in their understanding of what functional skills truly contributed to a student's or adult's productive membership in the community. Setting the table, making a bed, and doing laundry came to be seen as less important than reading a newspaper, voting in an election, supervising one's own personal care attendant, remembering a friend's birthday with a card, and finding a ride to a social event (Shapiro-Barnard et al., 1996).

Classmates' Education Is Not Adversely Affected by the Presence of Students with Disabilities   A variety of studies have demonstrated that 1) the development of preschool children who are typically developing does not decelerate when a diverse array of children are in the classroom (Odom, Deklyen, & Jenkins, 1984); 2) academic achievement of elementary age students is not compromised by the presence of students with disabilities in the classroom (Sharpe, York, & Knight, 1994); 3) there is no difference in the amount of attention teachers give to students without disabilities in inclusive classrooms (Hollowood, Salisbury, Rainforth, & Palombaro, 1994/1995); and 4) students without disabilities do not model or copy inappropriate behavior from students with disabilities (Staub, Schwartz, Gallucci, & Peck, 1994).

Diversity Enhances Communities   Schools that value collaboration and diversity create classrooms in which all students are valued for their unique characteristics and talents (Sapon-Shevin, 1998). When students with disabilities are separated from their classmates who are typically developing, all students come to understand that people who are different do not belong. Students in the early elementary grades begin to adopt this attitude when their classmates with disabilities come and go throughout the day to receive services outside the general classroom.

In a landmark study by Schnorr (1990), first-grade students were interviewed on their perceptions of a student with Down syndrome who attended their class on a part-time basis. Most first-grade students did not consider this student to be a member of their class, even though he had a desk and other membership symbols (e.g., cubby) in the room. They saw him as younger and smaller than they were, even though he was the same age and size. They also viewed him as coming to school to play while they worked on academics. Finally, they did not see him as socializing with anyone in their class. This research on a student who was included part-time in a general education classroom has worrisome implications for the development of social relationships between students with and without disabilities and for children's evolving views on diversity.

In studies of fully inclusive classrooms and schools, students who are typically developing report an increase in their own self-concept, growth in social cognition, and reduced fear of human differences (Peck, Donaldson, & Pezzoli, 1990). Jorgensen's research conducted in a fully inclusive high school found that students who are typically developing viewed their classmates with significant disabilities as being "just one of the guys" and "just like us" (Jorgensen, Mroczka, & Williams, 1998).

"Value-Added" Contribution Exists for a Diverse School Community   Although a growing body of research demonstrates the benefits of inclusive education for students, their peers, and families, some research studies suggest that the education of both students and their peers has been compromised rather than enhanced by inclusion (Baker & Zigmond, 1995). These studies postulate that the lack of adequate resources has negatively affected teachers' attitudes toward both special education and inclusion.

Fisher and colleagues offer an alternate paradigm that the presence of students with disabilities offers an added value to a classroom and a school. They suggest that the sum total of the resources that flow into an inclusive environment will "turn out to be 'in the black' rather than 'in the red'" (Fisher, Sax, Rodifer, & Pumpian, 1999, p. 256). These researchers studied an inclusive urban high school in which all students—including 34 students with significant disabilities—were included in general education classes. Semistructured interviews were conducted with 23 members of the teaching staff. Results from qualitative analysis of the interviews indicated that teachers who had taught students with significant disabilities in their classes increased their tolerance and understanding of human differences. Teachers also reported that inclusive education encouraged them to view all of their students in new and individualized ways and increased their understanding of individual learning style differences and the need for differentiated instruction. Finally, this study and others have found that inclusion provides opportunities for teachers to introduce broader "equity" topics into curriculum areas such as science, American government, literature, child development, and even technology.

When Students with Disabilities Are Taught Well, All Students Are Taught Better   When students with disabilities are educated outside the general classroom—thereby decreasing the classroom's diversity—teachers become even less willing and able to teach diverse students. Conversely, teachers who feel confident about their ability to teach students with disabilities report that they feel more competent to teach a wider variety of students (Giangreco, Dennis, Cloninger, Edelman, & Schattman, 1993).

Laws Such as IDEA Put a Presumptive Value on Inclusive Placement   With each successive reauthorization of IDEA, education in the general classroom has been given a greater value. IDEA 1997 stated that to the maximum extent appropriate, children with disabilities are educated with children who are not disabled. Furthermore, the law declares that school districts cannot use a lack of adequate personnel or resources or the challenge of coordinating services as excuses for failing to make a free appropriate public education in the least-restrictive environment available to students with disabilities.

Kluth, Villa, and Thousand (2002) identified three common misunderstandings about inclusive placement decisions. First, parents and schools sometimes think they need to justify why a student should be included, when in fact the opposite is true. Denying a student access to inclusion is only acceptable in rare instances. IDEA 1997 stated that students with disabilities may be removed from the regular education environment only when the nature or severity of the disability is such that education in regular classes with the use of supplementary aids and services cannot be achieved satisfactorily. If schools can successfully educate a student with disabilities in general education settings with peers who do not have disabilities, then the student's school must provide that experience.

The second misunderstanding about inclusive placement is the belief that students need to be able to keep up with the curriculum in order to benefit from inclusion. According to Kluth et al.,

> Students with disabilities . . . do not need to keep up with students without disabilities to be educated in inclusive classrooms; they do not need to engage in the curriculum in the same way that students without disabilities do; and they do not need to practice the same skills that students without disabilities practice. Learners need not fulfill any prerequisites to participate in inclusive classrooms. (2002, p. 26)

Finally, some courts have challenged the assignment of students to disability-specific programs and schools. In *Roncker v. Walter*, the judge stated,

> It is not enough for a district to simply claim that a segregated program is superior. In a case where the segregated facility is considered superior, the court should determine whether the services that make the placement superior could be feasibly provided in a non-segregated setting. If they can, the placement in the segregated setting would be inappropriate under [IDEA]. (1983, p. 1063)

Negative Effects Are Associated with Separating Students from their Peers

Researchers and others have found certain negative consequences of educating students with significant disabilities in separate classes, including 1) poorer quality IEPs (Hunt & Farron-

Davis, 1992); 2) lack of generalization of learning to environments outside of the separate classroom (Stokes & Baer, 1977); 3) disrupted opportunities for sustained interactions and social relationships with students without disabilities (Strully & Strully, 1992); 4) a decrease in the confidence that general class teachers have for teaching diverse learners (Giangreco et al., 1993); and 5) absence of appropriate behavior and role models.

How to Know It When You See It

When schools are **not** committed to the true meaning of inclusion, or actively work against it, educational practices have the following characteristics:

- The establishment of an inclusion program, an inclusion classroom, and inclusion students; an inclusive school does not need to specify which classrooms are inclusive or which students are included.

- Separate classrooms and programs are reserved for students with significant disabilities.

- Disproportionate numbers of students with disabilities are in certain classrooms.

- A lack of ownership exists on the part of general education teachers for students with disabilities rather than collaborative teaming to benefit all students.

- Students with disabilities go out into the community to learn in groups that do not include students without disabilities.

- Students with disabilities participate in only a limited number of extracurricular activities, such as the Special Olympics.

- Students with disabilities are always on the receiving end of help (e.g., special buddy programs) rather than engaging in reciprocal relationships that benefit both students with and those without disabilities.

- Students with disabilities have no social life outside of school.

When schools truly understand inclusion and the meaning of full membership and participation, the following statements are true:

- Students with disabilities are members of age-appropriate general education classes.

- Students with disabilities attend the same school that they would be attending if they did not have disabilities.

- Students with disabilities progress through grade levels according to the same pattern as students without disabilities.

- Students with disabilities participate in the graduation ceremony at the same average age as their classmates without disabilities.

- Students with disabilities receive a diploma when they are discharged from special education.

- Students with disabilities learn in outside-of-school, age-appropriate, and inclusive environments after the age of 18 (before they receive their high school diploma or are discharged from special education programs).

- Students with disabilities are not removed from general education classes for academic instruction.

- Related services are delivered to students with disabilities primarily through consultation in the classroom and in typical, inclusive environments.

- No places or programs in the school are reserved just for the use of students with disabilities.

- Students with disabilities comprise about 12% of the enrollment (i.e., a natural proportion) in classes, courses, clubs, and extracurricular activities.

- The names of students with disabilities are included on all class lists, job lists, and other groups listed on blackboards and bulletin boards.

- Instructional materials are universally accessible to all students.

- Students with disabilities participate in classroom and school routines in typical locations, such as saying the Pledge of Allegiance, performing jobs and errands, and eating lunch in the cafeteria.

- Students with disabilities ride the same school buses as their classmates without disabilities.

- Students with disabilities participate in classroom instruction in similar ways as do students without disabilities.

- Students with disabilities participate in school plays, field trips, and community service activities.

- Schools are physically accessible to all students.

- Schools accommodate all students' sensory concerns.

FAMILY AND SCHOOL PARTNERSHIPS

The third promising practice in educational programs for students with significant disabilities is mutually beneficial family and school partnerships. When families and schools work together to create quality inclusive educational experiences for students with significant disabilities, they do not always agree about every decision, but they hold a common vision and make a commitment to work together even when differences of opinion exist (Sommerstein & Wessels, 1996).

The following experience of Beth Dixon and her son, Andrew, exemplifies the kind of collaborative partnership that can be forged between families and schools.

Andrew's Story

When her son, Andrew, was in preschool, Beth Dixon attended the New Hampshire Leadership Series sponsored by the Institute on Disability (IOD) at the University of New Hampshire. For three weekends, parents of students with significant disabilities came together to articulate a vision for their children's futures, learn about current best practices in education, and develop skills in community organizing. At the end of the series, Beth said that she had totally changed her vision of what Andrew's schooling and future should look like. She no longer felt that Andrew was "broken" or "needed to be fixed" before he could be a part of a mainstream classroom and school community. So, for the next 10 years, Beth worked to share her vision with the school and enlist its help to give Andrew a typical education with the supports and services he needed in order to be a full participant.

In the early years of Beth and Andrew's journey, she recalls team meetings in which professional after professional would read reports summarizing Andrew's "deficits" and then make recommendations for therapy or remedial services to eradicate them. During these meetings, there were always many reasons given for why Andrew was not ready for the general education classroom, such as the severity of his disabilities. Beth recalled one meeting when Andrew's elementary school principal, who was very wary of Andrew's entry into first grade, summarized the whole team's feelings.

He asked, "Beth, I just can't imagine what you think Andrew will get out of coming to school here. What do you really want for him?"

Without a moment's hesitation, she said, "I really want him to get invited to a birthday party. I want other kids not to be afraid of him in the grocery story. I want him to be able to go to our neighborhood school just like my other kids did."

A look of relief passed over the principal's face, and he smiled. "Well, you know, Beth, I think we can do that here."

By the time Andrew was in high school, the initial resistance had turned into planning for how, not why. Every 6 weeks or so, Beth and Andrew would sit down with a couple of key team members and talk about Andrew: his likes and dislikes, his interests and passions, his temperament and communication style, and the supports he needed in order to have a typical high school experience. The partnership they developed over the years was not always harmonious, but overall, Beth felt that her wishes for Andrew were honored and that the school did its best to provide the supports Andrew needed for a typical high school education. Likewise, Beth treated the school team members as allies and made it a point to acknowledge their hard work, their commitment to Andrew, and their willingness to push through difficult problems to reach a win-win situation for both the family and school.

Beth and the members of Andrew's school team did not arrive at this partnership by accident. Beth took an active role in Andrew's education and used her knowledge of community organizing to enlist the school's support of her vision for Andrew. She found in-service training workshops and attended them with Andrew's team. She contacted the IOD and took the lead on securing long-term technical assistance for Andrew's team. She encouraged other parents in her district to attend the Leadership Series so that they, too, would develop new visions for their children. Years later, Beth expanded her commitment to advocacy when she became the coordinator of the Leadership Series, helping more than 400 families create their vision of inclusive education for their children.

How to Know It When You See It

When the relationship between a family and a school has soured, the following scenarios are all too frequent:

- The school neither listens to nor supports the family's vision for their child, but rather promotes its own view of what the child's education should be like and where he or she will go in the future.

- IEPs are developed by the school team and then presented to parents for their signatures without the parents' having any chances to offer their input.

- The family assumes negative intentions on the part of the school and creates an antagonistic atmosphere in every interaction.

- The family and team members only meet when legally required to do so.

- Communication between the family and the team is spotty and focuses primarily on legal documents and formalities.

When a family and a school work collaboratively toward a common vision for a student with disabilities, as in the story of Beth and Andrew Dixon, the following statements are true:

- School staff members respect the family's cultural background when developing and implementing the student's educational program.

- The family's priorities are reflected in annual goals on the student's IEP.

- The family acknowledges the teachers' efforts on behalf of their child.

- The family knows about resources for building their own leadership and advocacy skills relative to their child's education.

- The family attends case-management meetings or curriculum planning meetings on a regular basis.

COLLABORATIVE TEAMING

Team collaboration, the fourth promising practice, has always been the cornerstone of effective inclusive education for students with significant disabilities. Thousand and Villa (2000) defined collaborative teams as those that coordinate their work to achieve at least one common goal; hold in common a belief that all team members have unique and needed expertise; demonstrate parity, alternatively engaging in the dual roles of teacher and learner, expert and recipient, consultant and consultee, mentor and protégé; distribute leadership functions; and employ collaborative teaming processes.

A collaborative team must include the right people: those who are essential to the team in order to ensure the student's success as well as those who want to be members of the student's team. Each person sees his or her role as supporting inclusive and effective education for all students. There is a "we are all in this together" feeling among team members. Members of the team possess the disciplinary expertise unique to their professions and use effective interpersonal and communication skills, including problem-solving, decision-making, long-range planning, and conflict-resolution techniques.

Villa and Thousand (1996) also noted that involving classmates without disabilities and siblings on a student's educational team is too often overlooked; they suggested that peers and siblings can serve as useful resources for good ideas, energy, and information about what constitutes a typical school experience.

It is essential for an effective collaborative team to have frequent face-to-face interactions to celebrate and socialize, engage in programmatic planning and evaluation, and raise and resolve problems and concerns. The team uses formal meeting processes that produce a written record of discussions, decisions, and action plans. To support its continued growth, the collaborative team periodically evaluates the quality of its collaboration and engages in professional development activities related to teaming.

A collaborative team goes through many stages of development. It will begin with the team's formation and initial trust building, and ideally, it will culminate with a high level of team functioning in which strategies are in place to deeply reflect on its practices and resolve conflicts (Thousand & Villa, 2000). Within a collaborative team, all members take responsibility for creating a classroom environment in which all students are members and can participate fully. The specific roles and responsibilities of each team member are identified, and there is considerable overlap between the responsibilities of the classroom teacher and the special education professionals.

How to Know It When You See It

When teams are in disarray or are otherwise unable to collaborate effectively, they often have the following characteristics:

- General and special educators do not share responsibility for all students' success; instead, there is an attitude among members of the team of "my students" versus "your students."

- Special education staff members only serve students with disabilities, oftentimes in segregated environments.

- Roles are not clearly defined among team members: Sometimes no one is accountable for an important task; other times several team members work on the same task at cross purposes or there is outright conflict among team members regarding role definitions or educational practices.

- Little collaborative planning time is available for team members.

- Communication among team members is spotty, and important information is not shared in a timely manner.

- No agreed-on process exists to make decisions or resolve conflicts.

- Follow-through is inconsistent and accountability systems are not in place to ensure that tasks are completed in a timely fashion.

When teams are collaborative, the following statements are true:

- The roles and responsibilities of all teachers and staff reflect the commitment and skills needed to teach all students, including those with disabilities.

- Special education staff work within the general education classroom as co-teachers, team-teachers, small group instructors, or one-to-one support teachers for all students in the class.

- The roles and responsibilities of special education teachers, paraprofessionals, and related-services providers reflect the provision of supports and services that enable students with disabilities to participate in and benefit from the general education curriculum and enable teachers to effectively teach heterogeneous classes.

- Collaborative planning time is provided during the school day for general and special education teachers and related-services providers.

- Teams use formal processes to conduct meetings, problem-solve, make decisions, and evaluate their effectiveness.

PLANNING AND IMPLEMENTING OF SUPPORTS

Many parents and educators believe that the performance of students with significant disabilities is more closely related to the quality of supports provided to them than it is to their disability labels. The fifth promising practice is that students should be provided with supports that enable them to fully participate in and make progress within the general education curriculum and other inclusive academic and social interactions, activities, and environments. A combination of natural and specialized supports should be considered effective when they serve to maximize learning, self-determination, inclusion, and reciprocal relationships between students and their peers.

Creating a School Culture that Celebrates Diversity

What does a school's culture have to do with supports for students with significant disabilities? When a school says "all children belong here" and breaks down attitudinal, architectural, and instructional barriers for students with disabilities, the need for specialized supports for those students decreases (Sapon-Shevin, 1998). In an inclusive and accessible school, all educators embrace a shared responsibility to create a schoolwide culture that naturally encompasses all students, including those with disabilities. Disability is not a unique difference, but a natural part of the human experience (Snow, 2001). In such a school, differences among all children are made ordinary by

- Embedding social justice topics into the general education curriculum (Fisher, Sax, & Jorgensen, 1998)

- Establishing schoolwide celebrations of diversity (Sapon-Shevin, 1998)

- Abandoning labels and attitudes that reflect *handicapism*, a "set of assumptions and practices that promote the differential and unequal treatment of people because of apparent or assumed physical, mental, or behavioral differences" (Bogdan & Biklen, 1977, p. 69)

- Helping students understand their own strengths and needs by respecting and accommodating different learning styles, talents, and intelligences (Gardner, 1983)

- Designing curriculum and instruction right from the start to naturally include students with different learning and communication styles, different temperaments, and different ways of "showing what they know" (Onosko & Jorgensen, 1998)

- Eliminating tracking, whole class ability grouping, and separate special education classrooms and programs (Jorgensen, Fisher, Sax, & Skoglund, 1998)

- Giving out awards based on personal best achievement

Inclusion facilitators model these values through their language and practices. In addition, they often serve in leadership roles within their schools to implement reforms related to these practices through professional development and school improvement.

Planning Supports

When a student with significant disabilities needs additional supports in order to fully participate and learn, the student's instructional team shares this responsibility, with the inclusion facilitator providing leadership, offering expert knowledge, and facilitating the participation of other team members. "Big picture" planning for student supports happens at the annual IEP meeting, but the real work of planning supports occurs through regularly scheduled team meetings that consider upcoming lessons, activities, and events. During these instructional planning meetings, specific supports can be identified to enable a student to participate and learn, and the team should carefully plan the resources and assistance that are necessary in order to accurately and reliably deliver the student's supports (McSheehan et al., 2002). Student plans should describe the supports needed, who will provide them, when they will be provided, and the preparation required ahead of time in order for the provider to be ready when the support is needed.

The first level of supports that ought to be considered are those that can be provided by someone who will be in close proximity to the student during the identified activity. This person might be a classmate, a classroom volunteer, a classroom teacher, or another member of the school community who will be involved in the activity. A member of the student's educational team such as a paraprofessional, speech-language pathologist, occupational therapist, or special education teacher often provides the second level of supports. When a balance between natural and specialized supports is achieved, students are less likely to develop an overreliance on paraprofessionals, and students are more likely to develop connections to their classmates (Giangreco, Edelman, Luiselli, & MacFarland, 1997).

Implementing Supports

Implementing supports requires a commitment to the plan agreed to by the team, expertise in many areas (e.g., AAC, movement and sensory differences, reading instruction), and flexibility to adjust the plan when an unexpected situation arises. Supports for students with significant disabilities have been described and categorized in many ways by various authors (Falvey, 1995; Giangreco et al., 2000; Onosko & Jorgensen, 1998; Weymeyer, Sands, Knowlton, & Kozleski, 2002). A framework that blends elements of all of these models (i.e., supports for students with significant disabilities) is available in Appendix B.

Evaluating Supports

In day-to-day practice, a discrepancy often exists between the supports that were planned and those that are actually delivered (McSheehan et al., 2002). It is unfair to render judgment of student performance unless quality supports have been provided. Therefore, an integral part of the evaluation process must include a careful assessment of the quality of supports. Inclusion facilitators should ask, "Did we provide the supports we said we would?" "How accurately were supports provided?" "Did we provide them in the right situations?" "Did we back away when we should have?" "How might we do better next time?" and "How will we know?" Teams should be mindful that the most prudent course of action to take when trying to assess students with significant disabilities is to postpone judgment until the actual supports that are delivered better match those that were planned.

How to Know It When You See It

When supports are **not** being provided or are being provided ineffectively, the following indicators are all too common:

- Students with disabilities are sitting idle when a paraprofessional is not right at their desks.

- Students with disabilities are seated away from their classmates.

- Paraprofessionals physically serve as buffers between students with disabilities, the classroom teacher, and other classmates.

- Adults serve as conversational go-betweens rather than students interacting with one another.

- The academic performance of students with disabilities is poor.

- The behaviors of students with disabilities are inappropriate.

When supports are provided to students according to these promising practice guidelines, the following statements are true:

- Students with disabilities are being called on in class—and in response, they answer questions and make comments.

- Students with disabilities are provided with academic materials with which to work at the same time as their classmates.

- Students with disabilities talk directly with the classroom teacher and their classmates.

- Students with disabilities are busy at the same times as their classmates.

- Support personnel help all students in the class.

APPROPRIATE AUGMENTATIVE AND ALTERNATIVE COMMUNICATION

The sixth promising practice in inclusive education is to provide students with a means to communicate about academic and social topics that are relevant to their classmates without disabilities. Philip's story illustrates the impact that appropriate communication supports can have on a student's entire educational experience.

Philip's Story

Philip was in fourth grade at his neighborhood elementary school and had been included in general education classrooms since first grade. On his IEP, Philip had been given the label of autism. Philip communicated using some signs, gestures, and a Go Talk device (Attainment Co.). In addition, Philip used some signs, natural gestures, and a number of differentiated vocalizations.

Even with these communication skills and supports, Philip was not able to participate fully in his general education classroom, nor was he able to communicate with classmates about the things that 9-year-old boys talk about. It is not surprising that Philip's most recent 3-year evaluation stated that he had moderate mental retardation because, of course, he did not perform well on tests that required communication skills!

When his team became part of the IOD's Beyond Access Model Demonstration Project, it worked to enhance Philip's communication system. It expanded his communication options to include general messages that could be used in a variety of situations (core vocabulary) as well as content-specific messages that would allow Philip to participate in classroom lessons and topic-specific conversation (Sonnenmeier, McSheehan, & Jorgensen, 2005).

The team decided to explore the use of symbols other than the Picture Communication Symbols that were available in Mayer-Johnson's Boardmaker software on the district's computers. In addition, the team included text on his devices. A 40-item communication board was designed to include frequently occurring core vocabulary, selected based on a review of a list of functional words that were being taught in the classroom and a review of standardized lists of core vocabulary

(Bruno, 1999). Additional communication boards for sentence fill-in activities were made for specific lessons, and a desktop computer was programmed to use Speaking Dynamically Pro with Boardmaker color symbols.

Within 2 months of the introduction of the new communication supports, data indicated that Philip did indeed have a valid and consistent yes/no response—a goal that had been included on his IEP since he was 3 years old! A year later, Philip had access to an expanded vocabulary set of 80–100 messages available on a DynaMyte, a desktop computer, and on communication boards.

Philip developed an ability to communicate with words using AAC. He learned to use some single words and word combinations to make requests for desired items, actions, and locations when provided with modeling and physical support as needed. In addition to using words functionally, Philip demonstrated an increased ability to recognize words in print.

Philip's story exemplifies what progress can be made when a team understands the essential role of appropriate communication supports to facilitate participation and meaningful inclusion.

How to Know It When You See It

When a student with disabilities is **not** provided with appropriate or effective communication supports, the following scenarios are all too common:

- The student with disabilities does not have a means to communicate all of the time.

- The communication system of the student with disabilities reflects outmoded assumptions about cognitive prerequisites and does not allow the student to communicate about age-appropriate academic curriculum or to participate in age-appropriate social interactions with classmates.

- The communication system of the student with disabilities is designed by the speech-language pathologist without input from the student, parents, or other team members.

- People talk for the student with disabilities rather than supporting the student's communication.

- People talk to the support staff rather than directly to the student with disabilities.

- No training is made available for classmates, family members, or general education teachers on how to use the communication system of the student with disabilities.

- The communication supports being provided to the student with disabilities are dictated by the school district's budget rather than the student's needs.

When a student with disabilities is effectively supported to communicate, the following statements are true:

- The student with disabilities has a means to communicate all of the time.

- The student with disabilities communicates for a variety of purposes.

- Although the student with disabilities may have multiple ways of communicating, a primary means of communication is identified.

- The communication system of the student with disabilities is programmed with messages to demonstrate learning of age-appropriate core academics, commensurate with his or her age-appropriate classmates.

- The communication system of the student with disabilities is programmed with messages for social communication that promote his or her participation in school and community extracurricular activities with peers without disabilities.

- The AAC system provided enables the student with disabilities to communicate for the purposes of self-determination and futures planning.

- The student with disabilities, his or her family members, and classmates without disabilities participate in the selection of messages programmed into the AAC system.

- People who are acting as communication facilitators for the student with disabilities clearly engage in a supportive role and do not actively participate in the content of the interaction between the student and his or her conversational partners.

- Classmates and adults who converse with the student with disabilities utilize information provided by facilitators to converse directly with the student, not just with or through the facilitator.

- The student with disabilities is provided with the training and support to use the AAC system in the contexts and routines in which the student will communicate.

- Training and support to use the AAC system is provided to the team, including classmates, in the contexts and routines in which the student with disabilities will communicate.

- The AAC supports of the student with disabilities take into consideration the communicative functions of any challenging behavior.

- A variety of funding sources and streams (e.g., Medicaid, Medicare, private insurance, school funding) are utilized to acquire and maintain assistive technology and AAC systems and to support training for the student with disabilities, his or her family, classmates, and support personnel.

FRIENDSHIP FACILITATION

The first essential condition for friendship is full inclusion. When students with disabilities are kept apart from the mainstream of school life, they have few opportunities to develop friendships (Martin, Jorgensen, & Klein, 1998). When students are educated in separate classrooms, their relationships tend to be based on benevolence rather than shared interests and respect for one another's diversity (Kunc, 1992). Sharing recess, lunchtime, and extracurricular activities are recognized as the key ingredients to forming friendships. Students who experience significant disabilities should be members of sports teams, perform in band and choral groups, and perform in school plays. Accessible transportation and staff support must be provided when necessary to enable students to participate successfully. Many students with significant disabilities need the support of individuals and policies that will intentionally facilitate social relationships (Forest, Pearpoint, & O'Brien, 1996). Making a commitment to facilitating students' social relationships is the seventh promising practice of inclusive education.

Brian's story is not front-page news, nor would it win any awards as a shining example of a great friendship program. Yet, it contains lessons about the importance of friendship in students' lives.

Brian's Story

After spending his entire educational career at a segregated special education school, Brian made the transition back to his own school district as a ninth-grade student. He was a student who would not typically be the most popular kid in school. To some of the students, he was just a kid with a bad haircut; others noticed that his eyes were crossed, his facial features were irregular, he had significant physical disabilities, he did not talk, and he sometimes scratched himself or others around him.

With assistance from a model demonstration project that focused on inclusion and school reform, the school did an excellent job of supporting Brian's inclusion into typical academic classes (Crowder, 1994). But by the end of his sophomore year, it was clear that something was missing. Unlike some of the other students at his school who experienced significant disabilities and yet were able to make extracurricular and social connections, Brian still spent most of his day surrounded by adults. When he went home after school, he spent the evening in his room by himself watching television. Brian began to communicate that he was lonely and wished that other students were not afraid of him and would take the time to talk to him.

Since entering school, Brian's educational plan had focused on his acquisition of the skills people thought he would need in order to be successful in school and in the community. He had mastered some of these skills, but still, he had no friends. His IEP team began to understand that friendships are more than a nice benefit of an education. In fact, according to Strully and Strully, "Relationships, including friendships, are at the very heart of what is needed to ensure a high quality of life for each of us" (1992, p. 165). So Brian's team decided that in order for him to form and sustain friendships, they would have to intentionally work toward that goal.

Over the next 2 years, Brian's team struggled to figure out what friendship was really about for Brian. Throughout this time, Brian's family, a dedicated group of professionals, and one other student remained stable in his life. The other classmates who entered into his social circle changed frequently. His team learned that friendships couldn't be forced, bribed, or achieved through special friendship programs. They learned that sustaining work around friendships requires at least one committed adult in a student's life who is in it for the long haul. They also learned that many students were interested in getting to know Brian but needed some support to figure out how to be his friend without falling into the trap of just being his helper or special buddy.

How to Know It When You See It

When a student with disabilities has few friends and is **not** supported to develop authentic friendships, the following indicators are all too common:

- The student with disabilities is always on the receiving end of support, in the position of being helped.

- The student with disabilities forms friendships only with other students with disabilities.

- The student with disabilities only participates in leisure, sport, and recreational activities that are specialized (e.g., Special Olympics).

- The student with disabilities spends most of his or her in- and out-of-school time with professionals or family members.

When a student with disabilities is socially included, the following statements are true:

- The student with disabilities has the same variety of social networks as students without disabilities: close friends, acquaintances, and kids with whom they share activities.

- The student with disabilities participates in the same variety of inclusive and typical extracurricular activities as students without disabilities.

- Adults facilitate the building of social networks for the student with disabilities when necessary.

- Physical, emotional, and instructional supports are provided by classroom teachers, librarians, classmates, office personnel, or volunteers—not special educators—whenever possible.

- The student with disabilities has opportunities to provide as well as receive support and assistance.

GENERAL AND SPECIAL EDUCATION REFORM

Administrative leadership is necessary to align general and special education reform in order to create a community of learners that includes students with significant disabilities. This commitment to effective and inclusive education for all students is the eighth promising practice (Lipsky & Gartner, 1997).

The stories that follow of two contrasting high schools illustrate many differences when inclusion *is* or *is not* a part of overall school improvement and reform.

An Inclusive, Restructuring School

Souhegan High School opened in 1992 as a member of the Coalition of Essential Schools, a national school reform network (Jorgensen, 1998).

Approximately 550 students from three rural towns came together in this very differently organized high school. At the ninth- and tenth-grade levels, students and teachers were members of small learning teams, although the eleventh and twelfth grades were organized more traditionally. Although the administrative team considered a plan to open the school with more traditional self-contained classrooms and resource rooms and then work toward integrating students, they eventually decided to "start where we want to end up" and include all students as full-time members of heterogeneous general education classrooms.

The school did not practice tracking or ability grouping, and all ninth- and tenth-grade students took the same English, history, science, and math classes. The school's curriculum was based on several key ideas. Essential questions (e.g., Can you be free if you are not treated equally?) formed the foundation of all units of study (Cushman, 1990). Teachers used differentiated instructional strategies that addressed students' varied learning styles. Assessment was based on some traditional measures such as homework and tests, but at the end of major units of study, students were asked to demonstrate what they had learned through public, performance-based exhibitions.

The roles of general and special education teachers had a great degree of overlap with respect to responsibilities for students with and without disabilities. General education teachers were primarily responsible for curriculum design, instruction, and assessment of all students. Special education teachers, called *learning specialists,* were full-time members of the ninth- and tenth-grade teaching teams, and the whole team met for 90 minutes a day for curriculum planning and to discuss instructional and classroom management. In the eleventh and twelfth grades, the learning specialists were members of either the humanities team (English, psychology, arts, history) or the combined math, science, and technology team. The role of the special education teachers included co-teaching, small group instruction, one-to-one assistance to any student who needed it, and instructional support provided in the school's Learning Center.

The Learning Center was staffed throughout the day by both general and special education teachers. Students with and without disabilities went to the center during their free periods to get help with homework, study skills, or large class projects.

Four students with significant disabilities (with labels of mental retardation and autism) who had been educated in out-of-district special education programs were returned to the high school, and a special education teacher was designated as their inclusion facilitator. This teacher's role consisted of case management, coordinating each student's services, acting as a liaison with parents, developing adapted curriculum materials, and supervising student-specific paraprofessionals. The inclusion facilitator sat in on teachers' curriculum planning meetings so that he would know about upcoming lessons, but he was not generally involved in delivering whole class instruction.

Students with significant disabilities at Souhegan were involved in many different extracurricular activities, including sports teams, computer club, recycling club, and the school's Community Council. Their postsecondary school plans were individualized. Some went on to supported work, and some went on to a combination of postsecondary education and work.

A Noninclusive, Traditionally Structured High School

Granite State High School was a traditional high school in its general and special education philosophies, structures, and practices. There were seven levels of classes in most subject areas, including honors classes; two levels of college preparatory classes; three levels of general, noncollege preparatory classes; and basic skills classes reserved for students with disabilities. Because of scheduling difficulties, a student who was placed in a basic skills class for history could not take a higher level English class, even if the student's team believed that he or she could handle the curriculum's demands. Many students with disabilities were in classes that did not teach to the New Hampshire Curriculum Framework Standards. Instead, they studied a special education curriculum consisting of language arts and math skills in addition to functional life skills such as cooking, doing laundry, and using money.

Special education teachers taught the basic skills classes and had little time available to consult with general education teachers who had students with disabilities enrolled in their classes. General and special education teachers attended different professional development workshops, with general education teachers learning about teaching innovations in their subject area and special education teachers learning about changes in special education law or how to write better IEPs.

At Granite State High School, students with significant disabilities were educated in the school's basement. They did not participate in extracurricular activities or serve on the student council. Their post–high school education plans were characterized by placement in sheltered workshops, and many did not receive services because of a long waiting list for state-funded services.

The school's administrative leadership team was sharply divided along traditional general education and special education lines. The special education building coordinator was actually housed in a different building several miles away from the high school campus. Many times both the principal and special education coordinator said that, although their school might eventually become more inclusive, they were committed to *never* including students with significant developmental disabilities within the mainstream of school life.

Mirroring their administrators' views and practices, special education teachers held monthly faculty meetings separate from their general education colleagues. Several years previously, a progressive assistant principal tried to institute changes in the tracking system to collapse the three, noncollege preparatory levels into one heterogeneous level. Despite bringing in resources for long-term professional development and teacher consultation, he encountered significant resistance from teachers who believed that some students would never master high curriculum standards and that it was impossible to teach a diverse classroom of learners.

The educational programs of students with significant disabilities are significantly different at Granite High School compared to Souhegan High School. The Granite High School Vice Principal's goal of reducing the number of tracked classes and integrating some students with disabilities into more heterogeneous courses was not successful because it ran contrary to the teachers' long-held view that tracking was effective for students and manageable for teachers. The change was not seen as a logical extension of the faculty's philosophy about student learning and effective teaching. At Souhegan, the proposal to include students with significant disabilities in general education classes was successful because it was viewed as a natural extension of their emerging philosophy of quality education for all students.

How to Know It When You See It

When a school only gives lip service to inclusive education, actively discourages it, or treats inclusion as a special education initiative, the following indicators are all too common:

- The school community does not espouse the values of diversity and inclusion.

- The school does not publicly support inclusive education but reluctantly endorses the least-restrictive environment requirements of the special education law.

- The school views efforts to improve general education and special education as separate initiatives, and staff members from one area do not generally participate in reform efforts for the other.

When a school is truly inclusive, the following statements are true:

- The values of diversity and inclusion are evident in the school's mission statement.

- General and special education administrators promote the values and benefits of inclusive education at meetings; in conversations; in school improvement plans; and in annual reports, school newsletters, and web sites.

- General and special education personnel participate together in schoolwide improvement and reform efforts that benefit students with and without disabilities.

ENCOURAGEMENT OF SELF-DETERMINATION

In its earliest conceptualization, *self-determination* referred to the inherent right of individuals with disabilities to assume control of and make choices that affect their lives (Nirje, 1972). Self-determination is characterized by personal attitudes and abilities that facilitate an individual's identification and pursuit of meaningful and self-identified goals. It is reflected in personal attitudes of empowerment, active participation in decision-making, and self-directed action to achieve personally valued goals. "An individual is self-determined if his or her actions reflect four essential characteristics: autonomy, self-regulation, psychological empowerment, and self-realization" (Wehmeyer, 1996, p. 116). Promoting all students' self-determination is the ninth promising practice in inclusive education.

Amro's Story

When Amro Diab first came to Souhegan High School in Amherst, New Hampshire, he put his head down on the desk if adults spoke to him and hugged the wall in the hallway as he walked to class. By the time he had graduated 4 years later, he had played in several high school football games (kicking off at the beginning of each quarter), been voted Senior Prom King by his classmates, received the Souhegan Saber Award as the student who best exemplified the school's mission statement, and gave his senior project presentation on "My School to Work Transition." In most schools, Amro would not likely have been given the opportunity to develop his self-determination skills; many people believe that individuals with significant cognitive disabilities are unable to make responsible decisions, need protection or legal guardianship, and are too vulnerable to be exposed to the kinds of typical life experiences from which self-determination grows (Wehmeyer, 1996).

The development of Amro's self-determination occurred as a result of many interrelated experiences throughout his high school years. Perhaps the most significant was that Amro was fully included in a typical array of general high school classes at Souhegan, and he was *not* educated in the restrictive environment of a self-contained classroom. Amro rode on the school bus with his general education peers in the morning. He passed from class to class unassisted. During unstructured time in the classroom, he received most of his support from other students. He used a letter communication board for both social communication and to support his participation in academic lessons. He became a member of the football team his freshman year and gradually moved from the position of assistant manager to occasionally participating in games.

Amro had a unique personality. On one hand, he loved being in social situations and could give and take good-humored ribbing just like his classmates. On the other hand, he could be extremely shy and reticent in new situations. Instead of making decisions for him when he was uncertain, his support staff encouraged him to try out several different alternatives (e.g., school clubs), and then they coached him to make decisions based on these trial experiences.

Amro had the opportunity to give several presentations about school inclusion before the local school board, the New Hampshire State School Board, and conference audiences comprised of educators and parents from all over the United States eager to learn about inclusive education and school reform. Over time, the young man who had cowered in the hallway during his first week in an inclusive school situation learned to stride confidently up to the podium at the IOD's Equity & Excellence conference. He used his letter board to answer questions from the audience about his high school experiences (Diab, 1996).

Within everyday interactions both in and outside of the classroom, Amro was supported to make choices about class projects, extracurricular activities, and work opportunities. Every summer, he worked alongside a classmate who did not have disabilities, gaining experience in heating and air-conditioning repair, house painting, packing groceries, and retrieving shopping carts at a local store. He attended his own IEP meetings, and during his senior year, he focused his senior graduation project on making a postgraduation plan. Between the ages of 18 and 21, when he was still receiving special education services, he explored a number of other jobs including working at a candle factory and at a restaurant. By the time he left the educational system, he was working about 30 hours a week, living at home with his family, working out at a fitness club, and exploring the possibility of opening a family-run business.

Amro's life changes quite frequently, just like the lives of other young men in his community. His quality high school education and growing self-determination skills help him deal with change, and with the support of his family and the people that he has come to know in his community, he has a full life.

How to Know It When You See It

When self-determination is **not** a priority for a student with disabilities, the following indicators are all too common:

- Adults make all decisions about the student's education and future; the student with disabilities is not asked to express preferences nor involved in decision making.

- The student with disabilities does not attend meetings at which his or her education or future is discussed.

- The student's IEP does not reflect choice and control issues.

When the life of a student with disabilities is self-determined, the following statements are true:

- The student with disabilities communicates his or her own thoughts, concerns, opinions, and wishes, with support from augmentative communication, friends, family, and educators.

- The student with disabilities has control in decision making that affects his or her life.

- The student with disabilities participates in IEP meetings from junior high or middle school through graduation.

- The student with disabilities is encouraged to join organizations that promote self-determination and to design a postgraduation futures plan based on his or her wishes, interests, and talents.

- The student with disabilities has the opportunity to participate in peer mentor programs both as a mentor and as a protégée.

- The student with disabilities has access to and interactions with adult role models with and without disabilities.

- The student with disabilities has the opportunity to fail and learn from mistakes.

PERSON-CENTERED PLANNING

The tenth promising practice in inclusive education is the use of *person-centered planning strategies.* These strategies help students and their families articulate a vision for an inclusive life in the school and community and help build the relationships, supports, and resources necessary to reach that vision (Mount, 2000). Personal futures planning was first developed "between 1973 and 1986 among people from across North America who shared a passion for understanding and teaching how the principles of normalization might be applied to improve the quality of services to people with disabilities" (O'Brien & Lyle-O'Brien, 2000, p. 3; see also Forest et al., 1996).

The different versions of personal futures planning all share the following characteristics:

1. The individual and sometimes the person's family controls the decisions that will be made, defined by the outcomes desired by them.

2. Planning is not a one-meeting event but rather a long-term commitment and process that evolves over time.

3. Planning is not a formula for service planning but rather a creative process through which "a group's ability to create meaningful opportunities and supports emerges as people develop the skills to think strategically together" (Cotton, 2003, p. 16).

The first person-centered planning sessions were held with adults who were considering moving out of institutions into the community, but person-centered planning is now a strategy used with school-age students at various points in their educational careers.

How to Know It When You See It

When person-centered futures planning is **not** utilized, the following indicators are all too common:

•   The student with disabilities and his or her parents are not asked about their vision for the student's education or future adult life.

•   Although a plan is developed, there is no effort to identify the supports that will be needed in order for the student with disabilities to achieve the plan's goals.

- Untrained and/or uncommitted people are in charge of futures planning for the student with disabilities, and there is no accountability to the student or the family for the plan's success.

- Futures planning includes only paid professionals rather than the student's friends, family, classmates, co-workers, or other individuals who are not paid to be in the student's life.

When person-centered planning guides a student's school program and postsecondary school plans, the following statements are true:

- As soon as the student with disabilities is school age, a person-centered planning process is used to plan critical transitions in the student's school career (e.g., entry into preschool, first grade, middle school, high school, graduation planning).

- A person-centered plan includes specific strategies to maximize the control of the student with disabilities over both personal and publicly funded resources.

- A person-centered plan utilizes natural and generic supports to the maximum degree possible, supplemented by specialized supports.

REFERENCES

Apple, M. (1979). *Ideology and curriculum.* Boston: Routledge Kegan Paul.

Baker, J., & Zigmond, N. (1995). The meaning and practice of inclusion for students with learning disabilities: Themes and implications from the five cases. *Journal of Special Education, 29,* 163–180.

Biklen, D., & Cardinal, D. (Eds.). (1997). *Contested words, contested science.* New York: Teachers College Press.

Biklen, D., Ferguson, D.L., & Ford, A. (1989). *Schooling and disability: Eighty-eighth yearbook of the National Society for the Study of Education.* Chicago: University of Chicago Press.

Bogdan, R., & Biklen, D. (1977). Handicapism. *Social Policy, 7*(3), 14–19.

Brown, L., Branson, M., Hamre-Nietupski, S., Pumpian, I., Certo, N., & Gruenewald, L. (1979). A strategy for developing chronological age-appropriate and functional curriculum content for severely handicapped adolescents and young adults. *Journal of Special Education, 13*(1), 71–90.

Brown, L., Long, E., Udvari-Solner, A., Schwartz, P., VanDeventer, P., et al. (1989). The home school: Why students with severe intellectual disabilities must attend the schools of their brothers, sisters, friends, and neighbors. *Journal of The Association for Persons with Severe Handicaps, 14*(1), 1–7.

Bruno, J. (1999). *Gateway to language and learning: Application program for the DynaVox and DynaMyte communication devices.* Pittsburgh: DynaVox Systems.

Calculator, S., & Jorgensen, C. (1994). *Including students with severe disabilities in schools: Fostering communication, interaction, and participation.* San Diego: Singular Publishing Group.

Cotton, P. (2003). *Elements of design: Frameworks for facilitating person-centered planning.* Durham: Institute on Disability at the University of New Hampshire.

Crowder, R. (1994). Inclusion. *Equity and Excellence, 2,* 9–10.

Cushman, K. (1990). Performance and exhibitions: The demonstration of mastery. *Horace, 6*(3), 101.

Diab, A. (1996, June 26). *My experiences at Souhegan High School.* Presentation at the Equity & Excellence Conference, Portsmouth, NH.

Donnellan, A. (1984). The criterion of the least dangerous assumption. *Behavioral Disorders, 9,* 141–150.

Education for All Handicapped Children Act of 1975, PL 99–142, 20 U.S.C. §§ 1400 *et seq.*

Erickson, K., Koppenhaver, D., & Yoder, D. (2002). *Waves of words: Augmented communicators read and write.* Toronto: ISAAC Press.

Erickson, K., Koppenhaver, D., Yoder, D., & Nance, J. (1997). Integrated communication and literacy instruction for a child with multiple disabilities. *Focus on Autism and Other Developmental Disabilities, 12*(3), 142–150.

Falvey, M.A. (Ed.). (1995). *Inclusive and heterogeneous schooling: Assessment, curriculum, and instruction.* Baltimore: Paul H. Brookes Publishing Co.

Fisher, D., Sax, C., & Jorgensen, C.M. (1998). Philosophical foundations of inclusive, restructuring schools. In C.M. Jorgensen, *Restructuring high schools for all students: Taking inclusion to the next level* (pp. 29–48). Baltimore: Paul H. Brookes Publishing Co.

Fisher, D., Sax, C., Rodifer, K., & Pumpian, I. (1999). Teachers' perspectives of curriculum and climate changes: The added value of inclusive education. *Journal for a Just and Caring Education, 5*(3), 256–268.

Forest, M., Pearpoint, J. & O'Brien, J. (1996). MAPS, Circles of Friends, and PATH: Powerful tools to help build caring communities. In S. Stainback & W. Stainback (Eds.), *Inclusion: A guide for educators* (pp. 67–86). Baltimore: Paul H. Brookes Publishing Co.

Gardner, H. (1983). *Frames of mind: The theory of multiple intelligences.* New York: Basic Books.

Giangreco, M.F., Cloninger, C.J., & Iverson, V.S. (2000). *Choosing outcomes and accommodations for children (COACH): A guide to educational planning for students with disabilities* (2nd ed.). Baltimore: Paul H. Brookes Publishing Co.

Giangreco, M., Dennis, R., Cloninger, C., Edelman, S., & Schattman, R. (1993). I've counted Jon: Transformational experiences of teachers educating students with disabilities. *Exceptional Children, 59*(4), 359–373.

Giangreco, M.F., Edelman, S., Luiselli, T.E., & MacFarland, S.Z. (1997). Helping or hovering? Effects of instructional assistant proximity on students with disabilities. *Exceptional Children, 64*(1), 7–18.

Gilhool, T. (1998). A Q & A on IDEA '97 with Tom Gilhool. *TASH Newsletter, 23/24*(12/1), 5–7, 14.

Hollowood., T., Salisbury, C., Rainforth, B., & Palombaro, M. (1994/1995). Use of instructional time in classes serving students with and without severe disabilities. *Exceptional Children, 61*(3), 242–253.

Hunt, P., & Farron-Davis, F. (1992). A preliminary investigation of IEP quality and content associated with placement in general education versus special education classes. *Journal of The Association for Persons with Severe Handicaps, 17,* 247–253.

Individuals with Disabilities Education Act Amendments of 1997, PL 105-17, 20 U.S.C. §§ 1400 *et seq.*

Individuals with Disabilities Education Act of 1990, PL 101-476, 20 U.S.C. §§ 1400 *et seq.*

Individuals with Disabilities Education Improvement Act of 2004, PL 108-446, 20 U.S.C. §§ 1400 *et seq.*

Jorgensen, C.M. (1998). *Restructuring high school for all students: Taking inclusion to the next level.* Baltimore: Paul H. Brookes Publishing Co.

Jorgensen, C.M., Fisher, D., Sax, C., & Skoglund, K. (1998). Innovative scheduling, new roles for teachers, and heterogeneous grouping: The organizational factors related to student success in inclusive, restructuring schools. In C.M. Jorgensen, *Restructuring high schools for all students: Taking inclusion to the next level* (pp. 49–70). Baltimore: Paul H. Brookes Publishing Co.

Jorgensen, C., McSheehan, M., & Sonnenmeier, R. (2002a). *Best practices that promote learning of general education curriculum content for students with the most significant disabilities.* Durham, NH: Institute on Disability at the University of New Hampshire.

Jorgensen, C., McSheehan, M., & Sonnenmeier, R. (2002b). *Essential best practices in inclusive schools.* Durham, NH: Institute on Disability at the University of New Hampshire.

Jorgensen, C.M., Mroczka, M., & Williams, S. (Producers). (1998). *High school inclusion: Equity and excellence in an inclusive community of learners* [Video]. (Available from Paul H. Brookes Publishing Co., P.O. Box 10624, Baltimore, MD 21285)

Kluth, P., Villa, R., & Thousand, J. (2002, December/January). Our school doesn't offer inclusion and other legal blunders. *Educational Leadership,* 24–27.

Koppenhaver, D., Erickson, K., Harris, B., McLellan, J., Skotko, B., & Newton, R. (2001). Storybook-based communication intervention for girls with Rett syndrome and their mothers. *Disability and Rehabilitation, 23,* 149–159.

Kunc, N. (1992). The need to belong: Rediscovering Maslow's hierarchy of needs. In R.A. Villa, J.S. Thousand, W. Stainback, & S. Stainback, *Restructuring for caring and effective education: An administrative guide to creating heterogeneous schools* (pp. 25–39). Baltimore: Paul H. Brookes Publishing Co.

Lipsky, D.K., & Gartner, A. (1997). *Inclusion and school reform: Transforming America's classrooms.* Baltimore: Paul H. Brookes Publishing Co.

Lipsky, D.K., & Gartner, A. (Eds.). (1989). *Beyond separate education: Quality education for all.* Baltimore: Paul H. Brookes Publishing Co.

Martin, J., Jorgensen, C.M., & Klein, J. (1998). The promise of friendship for students with disabilities. In C.M. Jorgensen, *Restructuring high schools for all students: Taking inclusion to the next level* (pp. 145–182). Baltimore: Paul H. Brookes Publishing Co.

McGregor, G., & Vogelsberg, R.T. (1999). *Inclusive schooling practices: Pedagogical and research foundations: A synthesis of the literature that informs best practices about inclusive schooling.* Baltimore: Paul H. Brookes Publishing Co.

McSheehan, M., Sonnenmeier, R., & Jorgensen, C.M. (2002). Communication and learning: Creating systems of support for students with significant disabilities. *TASH Connections, 28*(5), 8–13.

Mount, B. (2000). *Person-centered planning: Finding direction for change using personal futures planning.* New York: Graphic Futures.

Nirje, B. (1972). The right to self-determination. In W. Wolfensberger (Ed.), *Normalization* (pp. 176–200). Ottawa, Canada: National Institute on Mental Retardation.

O'Brien, J. (2000). Foreword. In J. Nisbet & D. Hagner (Eds.), *Part of the community: Strategies for including everyone* (p. xii). Baltimore: Paul H. Brookes Publishing Co.

O'Brien, J., & Lyle-O'Brien, C. (2000). *The origins of person-centered planning: A community of practice perspective.* Georgia: Responsive Systems Associates.

Odom, S., Deklyen, M., & Jenkins, J. (1984). Integrating handicapped and non-handicapped preschoolers: Developmental impact on non-handicapped children. *Exceptional Children, 5*(1), 41–48.

Onosko, J., & Jorgensen, C.M. (1998). Unit and lesson planning in the inclusive classroom. In C.M. Jorgensen, *Restructuring high schools for all students: Taking inclusion to the next level* (pp. 71–105). Baltimore: Paul H. Brookes Publishing Co.

Peck, C., Donaldson, J., & Pezzoli, M. (1990). Some benefits adolescents perceive for themselves from their social relationships with peers who have severe disabilities. *Journal of The Association of Persons with Severe Handicaps, 15*(4), 241–249.

Roncker v. Walter, 700 F.2d 1058 (6th Cir. 1983).

Ryndak, D., Morrison, A., & Sommerstein, L. (1999). Literacy before and after inclusion in general education settings: A case study. *Journal of The Association for Persons with Severe Handicaps, 24*(1), 5–22.

Sapon-Shevin, M. (1998). *Because we can change the world.* Boston: Allyn & Bacon.

Schnorr, R., (1990). "Peter? He comes and goes . . ." *Journal of The Association for Persons with Severe Handicaps, 15*(4), 231–240.

Shapiro-Barnard, S., Tashie, C., Martin, J., Malloy, J., Schuh, M., Piet, J., et al. (1996). *Petroglyphs: The writing on the wall.* Durham: Institute on Disability at the University of New Hampshire.

Sharpe, M., York, J., & Knight, J. (1994). Effects of inclusion on the academic performance of classmates without disabilities. *Remedial and Special Education, 15*(5), 281–287.

Smith, J. (2002). Abandoning the myth of mental retardation: Carefully constructing developmental disabilities. *MRDD Express, 12*(3), 1.

Snow, K. (2001). *Disability is natural.* Woodland Park, CO: BraveHeart Press.

Sommerstein, L., & Wessels, M. (1996). Gaining and utilizing family and community support for including schools. In S. Stainback & W. Stainback

(Eds.), *Inclusion: A guide for educators* (pp. 365–382). Baltimore: Paul H. Brookes Publishing Co.

Sonnenmeier, R., McSheehan, M. & Jorgensen, C.M. (2005). A case study of team supports for a student with autism's communication and engagement within the general education curriculum: A preliminary report of the Beyond Access Model. *Augmentative and Alternative Communication, 21*(2), 101–115.

Stainback, S., & Stainback, W. (Eds.). (1990). *Support networks for inclusive schooling: Interdependent integrated education.* Baltimore: Paul H. Brookes Publishing Co.

Stainback, S., Stainback, W., & Forest, M. (Eds.). (1989). *Educating all students in the mainstream of regular education.* Baltimore: Paul H. Brookes Publishing Co.

Staub, D., Schwartz, I., Gallucci, C., & Peck, C. (1994). Four portraits of friendship at an inclusive school. *Journal of The Association for Persons with Severe Handicaps, 19*(4), 314–325.

Stokes, T., & Baer, D. (1977). An implicit technique of generalization. *Journal of Applied Behavior Analysis, 10*(2), 349–367.

Strully, J., & Strully, C. (1992). The struggle toward inclusion and the fulfillment of friendship. In J. Nisbet (Ed.), *Natural supports in school, at work, and in the community for people with severe disabilities* (pp. 165–178). Baltimore: Paul H. Brookes Publishing Co.

Tashie, C., Jorgensen, C.M., Shapiro-Barnard, S., Martin, J., & Schuh, M. (1996). High school inclusion: Strategies and barriers. *TASH Newsletter, 22*(9), 19–22.

Thousand, J.S., & Villa, R.A. (2000). Collaborative teaming: A powerful tool in school restructuring. In R.A. Villa, & J.S. Thousand (Eds.), *Restructuring for caring and effective education: Piecing the puzzle together* (2nd ed., pp. 254–291). Baltimore: Paul H. Brookes Publishing Co.

Villa, R.A., & Thousand, J.S. (1996). Student collaboration: An essential for curriculum delivery in the 21st century. In S. Stainback & W. Stainback (Eds.), *Inclusion: A guide for educators* (pp. 171–191). Baltimore: Paul H. Brookes Publishing Co.

Villa, R.A., Thousand, J.S., Stainback, W., & Stainback, S. (Eds.). (1993). *Restructuring for caring and effective education: An administrative guide to creating heterogeneous schools.* Baltimore: Paul H. Brookes Publishing Co.

Wehmeyer, M.L. (1996). Self-determination for youth with significant cognitive disabilities: From theory to practice. In L.E. Powers, G.H.S. Singer, & J. Sowers, *On the road to autonomy: Promoting self-competence in children and youth with disabilities* (pp. 115–134). Baltimore: Paul H. Brookes Publishing Co.

Wehmeyer, M.L., Sands, D.J., Knowlton, H.E., & Kozleski, E.B., (2002). *Teaching students with mental retardation: Providing access to the general curriculum.* Baltimore: Paul H. Brookes Publishing Co.

Transforming Hearts and Minds
The Inclusion Facilitator's Role as a Change Agent

Cheryl M. Jorgensen

A 1913 version of Webster's dictionary defines transformation as "a change in disposition, heart, character, or the like" in which heart is meant as "the seat of the affections or sensibilities . . . the better or lovelier part of our nature; the spring of all our actions and purposes; the seat of moral life and character" (*Webster's Revised Unabridged Dictionary*). This chapter is about the inclusion facilitator's role in helping to transform others' beliefs about inclusive education and students with significant disabilities. Changing people's core values and beliefs about inclusion is essential, as "a teacher's self-knowledge of what he or she stands for is the most important gyroscope a professional educator has to maintain a steady course through the bumpy shoals of life in school" (Garmston & Wellman, 1999, p. 25). The chapter focuses on "the 'human face' which embraces the emotion, feelings, needs and perceptions of teachers and leaders as well as their roles and beliefs and/or pedagogical assumptions" (Norman, 2001, p. 1). It is grounded in the professional literature on general and special education reform and high-quality professional development, but, above all, it reflects the 20 years of experience the author of this chapter has educating preservice teachers, providing student-specific consultation, and working with numerous school districts on inclusive education systems change projects.

This chapter is also about changing beliefs. It is about changing the beliefs of paraprofessionals who support students so that these paraprofessionals see their role as learning and social facilitators rather than as helpers who hover over students every minute of the day (Giangreco, Cloninger, & Iverson, 2000). It is about changing general education teachers' beliefs so that they hold the least dangerous assumption about students' capabilities and have high expectations for student achievement (Donnellan, 1984). It is about changing related-services professionals' understanding of their primary contribution to students' teams from that of providing direct service to supporting students' communication, behavior, and movement within typical routines and lessons. Finally, it is about helping parents recapture their lost dreams so that they believe once again that their children deserve an enviable future as a respected member of the community.

Chapter Organization

The chapter is organized in four parts, which can be read consecutively or by particular sections in order to fill the gaps in current understanding and experience. First, the notion of change agentry is introduced. Second, three characteristics of an effective change agent (i.e., guiding principles, a belief in personal efficacy, specific intervention skills) are elaborated. Third, a perspective is described through which inclusion facilitators can understand the personal identities or traits of their colleagues that influence their behaviors. These identities include bottom-line values, concerns about inclusion, and personality types. The fourth and final section presents a detailed case study of an inclusion facilitator's experience with a school struggling with the philosophy and practice of inclusion.

CHANGING INDIVIDUALS

If you pick up any book about education that has been written since 1980, the focal point for reform is the group and the system (and in particular, the culture of the system) rather than the individual. The author of this chapter acknowledges the critical need for systems thinking within educational reform efforts (see required reading such as Fullan, 2001; Garmston & Wellman, 1999; Jorgensen, 1998; Sarason, 1996; Senge, Kleiner, Roberts, Ross, & Smith, 1994; Sizer, 1992; Villa & Thousand, 2000), but she has chosen to focus this chapter on the often neglected topic of changing the individuals who comprise the educational systems, who must have their own self-interests resolved before they can truly show concern for the organization (Hall & Loucks, 1978). The author's decision to focus on changing individuals acknowledges that there are many special education teachers who work in very traditional (or dysfunctional) school systems but are committed nonetheless to including their students and want to know how they can begin the process of inclusion in the absence of a reform-minded culture.

This chapter describes the characteristics of and strategies used by inclusion facilitators who want to be effective change agents. The Concerns-Based Adoption Model (CBAM) is presented, which can help an inclusion facilitator answer the following questions about each person (e.g., paraprofessional, general education teacher, related-services professional, parent) that he or she deals with and then use the answers to plan strategies for transforming that person's beliefs and practices:

1. What does this person **value**?

2. What are this person's **concerns** about inclusion?

3. How might this person's **personality type** affect the best way to communicate and work with him or her?

Limitations of This Model

This model is not without its limitations. First, no one paradigm explains everything about human behavior. Organizations and change are complex. Many theories of motivation, individual behavior, group behavior, and systems theory have been postulated to explain why educators do one thing versus another.

A second limitation is that the elements of the model described in this chapter are not mutually exclusive. The theoretical underpinnings of research on personality types, concerns, and value systems have many common ancestors in the fields of philosophy and psychology. Thus, the inclusion facilitator should not consider the strategies described in this chapter as part of a cookbook recipe, but rather, as an interesting lens through which to view the challenge of transforming people's core beliefs and related actions.

Third, change agents themselves are as varied as the individuals or systems they wish to change. Some are charismatic; others have modest personalities. Some are new to the profession; others have many years of experience. Some start with quiet grassroots efforts; others give eloquent speeches that rally thousands to action. One does not need to become a Martin Luther King, Jr., or a Mother Teresa in order to be an effective inclusion facilitator change agent, although learning from the histories of these leaders can help to enhance anyone's effectiveness.

Finally, although each element of the model described herein has research supporting its effectiveness in specific situations, no body of research has demonstrated the efficacy of using the described strategies in the way that they are organized together in this chapter. The usefulness of this paradigm will be judged through the experiences of those who try it in their own schools and then reflect on their experiences with professional colleagues from other schools, each with their own unique histories and personalities. The authors of this book welcome this friendly criticism and believe that this kind of professional dialogue rooted in real-life practice will move us all forward in our quest for understanding what creates and sustains an inclusive school.

CHANGE AGENTRY

In Jan Nisbet's introduction to this book, she cites a variety of terms that have been used to describe people who see themselves as change agents, including *linker* (Havelock, 1971), *community organizer,* and *bridge-builder* (McKnight, 1995). A *change agent* is anyone, in any position or at any level, who is focused on the continual, constructive, reinvention of a system. He or she is always scanning for ideas, potential applications, needs, synergies, or emerging markets and is ready to move on anything promising. The change agent is nimble and strives to build flexibility in the surrounding system. He or she works the system, pulling in others and creating a movement around his or her mission. Change agents possess a clear understanding of themselves and their role (Center for Critical Impact, n.d.).

Teachers as Change Agents

In schools, the role of change agent has traditionally been assigned to the principal, the superintendent, or an outside consultant hired by the district to work on its long-range plan. Fullan recommended that teachers become agents of change because "to have any chance of making teaching a noble and effective profession . . . teachers must combine the mantle of moral purpose with the skills of change agentry" (1993, p. 12). Although having a moral purpose keeps teachers focused on the needs of their students, "change agentry causes them to develop better strategies for accomplishing their moral goals" (p. 13). Fullan described a "new conception of teacher professionalism that integrates moral purpose with change agentry, one that works simultaneously on individual and institutional development" (p. 13). To the extent that inclusion facilitators are charged with the moral purpose of creating classroom and school communities in which diversity is celebrated, Fullan's call speaks directly to them.

Characteristics of Effective Inclusion Facilitators/Change Agents

Inclusion facilitators who are effective as change agents are guided by strong principles related to working with others, are confident about their own efficacy, and possess a broad repertoire of skills for working with diverse individuals in a variety of situations.

Principles To be effective change agents, inclusion facilitators must embody many important working principles, but the three that will serve them particularly well in their efforts to change others' hearts and minds about students with disabilities are their commitment to inclusiveness, their presumption of positive intentions, and their ability to balance inquiry and advocacy (Garmston & Wellman, 1999). Ironically, some advocates of inclusive education have not shown respect for opinions other than their own, leading to accusations that they are zealots who care more about their cause than about the feelings or concerns of others (Fuchs & Fuchs, 1994). When the cause is the inclusion of diverse students within the classroom and school community, an inclusion facilitator's attitude of "my way or the highway" can destroy credibility and hurt the very cause being promoted. Thus, the hallmark of an effective inclusion facilitator is the ability to be clear about one's values yet able to acknowledge the rights of others to disagree without making moral judgments.

How many of us have left a difficult meeting saying, "I don't trust Ms. X! She clearly has a hidden agenda—she probably doesn't even like kids with disabilities and unless we uncover her ulterior motives, we won't be able to gain control of this situation." Garmston and Wellman suggested that presuming positive intentions is a more effective way to approach individuals with whom we disagree or have conflict.

> Assuming that others' intentions are positive encourages honest conversations about important matters. . . . Positive presuppositions reduce the possibility of the listener perceiving threats or challenges in a paraphrase or a question. . . . [When people presume positive intentions in one another] the emotional processors in the brain hear the

positive intention and open up access to higher level thinking [which can lead to more effective and inclusive solutions]. (1999, pp. 45–46)

The third working principle of effective inclusion facilitators is the commitment to balancing advocacy and inquiry. As an inclusion facilitator who may feel that inclusion is a moral imperative, it is tempting to see one's role as advocate and, therefore, perceive that articulating and arguing for inclusion is the right thing to do. Achieving a balance between articulating one's opinions and inquiring into the beliefs of others results in "more creative and insightful realizations that occur when people combine multiple perspectives" (Ross & Roberts, 1994, p. 253). The Skills section presents specific scripts that illustrate how to achieve this balance between advocacy and inquiry.

Self-Efficacy   Self-efficacy is the belief in one's capabilities to organize and execute the sources of action required to manage prospective situations. In plain language, "perceived self-efficacy is concerned not with the number of skills that you have, but with what you believe you can do with what you have under a variety of circumstances" (Bandura, 1997, p. 37). Inclusion facilitators come to believe in their ability to make a difference through personal experiences and identification with others who have accomplished similar efforts. Inclusion facilitators with a well-developed sense of efficacy

- Approach tasks as challenges to be mastered rather than situations to avoid

- Set challenging goals for themselves

- Maintain their commitment to those goals even after experiencing failure

- Attribute any lack of success to insufficient or ineffective effort on their part rather than to uncontrollable outside influences

These individuals persevere in the face of rejection, manage their stress in difficult situations, and use self-talk productively rather than in ways that hinder their continued effort.

Skills   Effective inclusion facilitators have a repertoire of skills and strategies that helps them influence the beliefs and actions of others in one-to-one or group situations. They know how to 1) maintain a healthy balance between advocacy and inquiry, 2) teach adult learners, 3) mediate individuals' learning over time, 4) negotiate "win-win" or "both/and" solutions, and 5) monitor and incorporate evidence into decisions about future actions.

Balancing Inquiry and Advocacy An inclusion facilitator with well-developed advocacy and inquiry skills can begin to change educational practices for students with significant disabilities by approaching individual teachers or parents, by working with groups such as students' individualized education program (IEP) teams, or through broader systems-focused efforts such as curriculum committees or a strategic planning task force. Practitioners who support inclusive education are often more skilled in advocating than in using inquiry as a means of engaging with others who do not share their values or experiences. Although expanding one's skills in inquiry does not mean abandoning the right to share one's strongly held viewpoint, such expansion can also broaden one's repertoire of dialogue that can be adapted to particular situations or individuals.

Dialogue is distinguished from discussion or debate by a focus on "reflective learning . . . in which group members seek to understand each other's viewpoints and deeply held assumptions" (Garmston & Wellman, 1999, p. 55). When individuals or groups enter into dialogue with one another, they deepen their understanding of one another's perspectives, are more likely to examine and alter their beliefs, and strengthen their relationships.

According to Sparks (2004), dialogue is characterized by a "suspension of judgment, release of needs for specific outcomes, an inquiry into and examination of underlying assumptions, authenticity, a slower pace with silence between speakers, and listening deeply to self, others, and for collective meaning." The following example demonstrates how an inclusion facilitator can balance advocacy with dialogue and inquiry.

Marie Thibideaux (pseudonym) is an inclusion facilitator who provides support to 20 students with significant disabilities who attend six schools in a large rural school district. Each week, she spends about 2 hours in each school, attending team meetings or meeting with the students' general education teachers and administrators. Marie has learned how to balance advocacy with inquiry and has positive relationships with each member of the student's team, even though they don't always agree on every issue. Recently, a student named Cameron moved from a small elementary school to a larger middle school, and Marie was involved in planning his transition. At the first meeting of Cameron's sixth-grade team, the math teacher made the following comment:

> *To be honest, I don't think that this student is appropriate for my math class. We are already starting to get into algebra,*

*and from what I have read in his records, he has an IQ score
of only 40. Wouldn't he be better off if he spent time learning the functional uses of money and time?*

Marie could have responded with traditional advocacy statements,
such as

- "IQ scores aren't a reliable measure of a student's intelligence.
  We need to have the highest expectations for Cameron despite
  what his test results say."

- "Cameron's IEP specifies that he will be in a general education
  math class. We don't really have a choice here."

- "I have known many students like Cameron who have surprised
  us with their knowledge once we gave them a chance in general
  classes."

The math teacher might then have made some retort such as, "I
don't really think that we should be doing something for our students just based on unfounded 'hope' that they will benefit. I need
evidence."

Marie's initial response has set up a *she said, he said* debate, in
which both sides provide increasingly vehement arguments for
their point of view, with no likelihood that any resolution will ever
be found. Perhaps if Marie tried an advocacy or inquiry approach,
using different language to respond to her colleague's comments,
her efforts would have been more successful.

Advocacy: "I can understand your concern. I have worked with
Cameron since he was in preschool. Would you be
interested in hearing about some of the strategies
teachers have used to successfully include him in challenging academic classes?

Inquiry: "Could you give me a little background on the experiences you've had with students like Cameron?"

Advocacy: "My experience, particularly with students with significant disabilities like Cameron's, is that IQ scores
have little relationship to what they can actually learn
in classes. Is that your experience, or do you have a different take on this?"

Inquiry: "I wonder if you could share your thinking behind your
recommendation that Cameron should learn money
skills and time management as opposed to algebra?"

If Marie takes this revised approach, she shows that she has an open mind about the teacher's viewpoints, she models the behavior of questioning assumptions, and she will find out more information about the math curriculum and the teacher's approach to instruction. In addition, she has preserved her relationship with the teacher whom Cameron will have for an entire academic year.

In *The Fifth Discipline Fieldbook* (Senge et al., 1994), Ross and Roberts shared protocols for improved advocacy and inquiry. They recommended that individuals practice using sample statements that serve the following purposes:

- To make one's thinking process visible

- To test one's conclusions and assumptions

- To ask others to make their thinking visible

- To compare one's assumptions to theirs

- To deal with someone who disagrees with one's point of view

- To cope with an impasse that seems to have stalled discussion

Many conversations about inclusion seem to present as an impasse right from the start. The natural reaction is for people to continue to articulate their beliefs, raise their voices with each successive volley, agree to disagree, or finally, call for an administrator to make the decision.

Ross and Roberts offered other options that can lead people away from the perceived impasse to a point in which they can calmly consider alternative options or enter into a data-gathering phase of the problem-solving process. They suggested that change agents or facilitators use phrases such as

- What do we know for a fact?

- What do we agree on, and what do we disagree on?

- Perhaps we might state the assumptions behind our opinions.

- It seems as if we aren't going to reach a mutually agreeable decision today. What might we each do before we come back to the table to continue this discussion?

Rather than inflaming the participants' emotions, these statements serve to diffuse the situation, asking each person to use a different part of his or her brain to explore possibilities while showing a commitment to working out a win-win solution.

Teaching Adults   Acting in the role of change agent, an inclusion facilitator has many opportunities to teach others about students with significant disabilities and inclusive education. Most general education teachers have never had a student with significant disabilities in their class before, and it is unlikely that they had any preparation during college to address the needs of students who use augmentative communication, experience significant physical challenges, or have sensory differences such as blindness or deafness. Teaching other adults can take many forms, but these methods should not include lecturing or simply presenting people with facts.

Some adults may be open to listening to stories about other students that illustrate broad concepts that can be applied to a new student. Inclusion facilitators typically have strong skills in this area because they themselves were probably deeply moved by the personal stories of students and their families. The skilled inclusion facilitator walks a fine line between proselytizing and telling stories from which larger values or lessons can be learned. Other individuals may want to read about inclusive education first and then have a one-to-one discussion over coffee about the implications for their classrooms. Still others may need to see a teaching strategy demonstrated, try it themselves, and then talk about the outcome with a valued colleague.

This last teaching and learning method—giving teachers the opportunity to learn by doing and then reflect on their experience—is supported by research on innovation diffusion, reflective practice, and professional development (Hole & McEntee, 1999). Pfeffer and Sutton (2000) coined the term the *knowing–doing problem* to describe the gap between what teachers know how to do and what they actually do. They suggested that the most effective way to bridge the knowing–doing (or research-to-practice) gap is to emphasize teacher learning within the context of teaching actual lessons rather than focusing on more formal, didactic training programs. Thus, inclusion facilitators should focus on coaching others to try out new practices in their classrooms and then should spend time with them reflecting on the process and outcomes, rather than relying on presenting a workshop on the theoretical rationale for inclusive education. Table 3.1 depicts the many opportunities that inclusion facilitators have to teach others about best practices, utilizing effective professional development and change techniques.

Mediating   Inclusion facilitators have a powerful tool for effecting changes in beliefs and attitudes through their roles as medi-

Table 3.1. Opportunities for inclusion facilitators to teach others about inclusive education

Topic	Audience	Venue
Evidence-based rationale for inclusion	Teachers	Staff development workshops Readings distributed in mailboxes Study groups
Value of diversity	Students Teachers Parents	Classroom/hallway bulletin boards Assemblies that feature panels of people with disabilities and their parents Personal stories shared with others
Augmentative and alternative communication (AAC)	Speech-language pathologists Occupational therapists Paraprofessionals	Team meetings Staff development workshops After-school demonstrations Opportunities within the classroom with a specific student AAC conferences or workshops attended with other staff members
Models that support inclusive education	Administrators	School improvement committee/task force meetings One-to-one meetings Meetings between administrators from different schools
Curriculum adaptations and modifications	Teachers Related-services staff	Staff development workshops State teachers' conferences Individualized education program team meetings Instructional planning meetings
Strategies for helping to support students without hovering	Paraprofessionals	Before- or after-school workshops Opportunities in the classroom when modeling is appropriate
Curriculum creation based on principles of universal design for instruction	Teachers	Study circles, reflective practice groups, or graduate classes held at the school Curriculum committees
Classroom and behavioral support strategies	Teachers Paraprofessionals	Opportunities in the classroom when modeling is appropriate Collaborative planning time

ators or coaches who shine a "judgment-free flashlight, illuminating internal or external data, the examination of which may lead to self-directed learning" (Garmston & Wellman, 1999, p. 177). As a form of coaching, mediating incorporates all of the skills of good group facilitation such as paraphrasing, probing for specificity or understanding, inquiring, and presuming positive intentions (Garmston & Wellman, 1999). Inclusion facilitators who enter into long-term professional relationships with other teachers in a school go beyond fulfilling their own roles as teachers. Over time, they will mediate the other teachers' growing understandings about inclusive education by comparing and contrasting the teachers' past and present experiences, positing new norms and testing them against traditional ones, sharing research-based information about inclusion, and addressing the teachers' practical concerns about how inclusion will affect day-to-day life in the classroom or school.

Negotiating   In the ideal world, every teacher and related-services provider along with every parent, teacher, school board member, administrator, and public policy maker would enthusiastically support the goals of inclusive education and fund schools adequately. The inclusion facilitator could wave a magic wand, and doubters would become believers, resisters would cast aside their objections, and fiscal and structural barriers would be considered mere nuisances instead of roadblocks to innovation. In the real world, however, inclusion facilitators must be skilled negotiators at the same time that they are building others' support for inclusion.

Negotiation with respect to inclusion can be a tricky business. Saying, "If you agree to have this student in your class, I will bake you brownies every Friday" does not reflect the valued place that we think students with disabilities should have in general education. However, asking, "What support would you need in order for Jim to be successful in your social studies class?" acknowledges the teacher's concerns, does not forsake the idea that Jim has the right to be in a social studies class, and still underscores the collaborative nature of supports for inclusion.

Here is another effective negotiation that respects a teacher's concerns:

> *I know that you have some concerns about whether this will work for you. Would it work for you to identify your concerns about Jim being in your class so that we can address as many as we can right now? Then, perhaps we can try it out for a few weeks and come back together after that to talk about what's been working and what still needs to be done to support Jim's success in your classroom.*

The goal of all negotiation should be to craft win-win solutions. Fisher, Ury, and Patton (1991) called this *principled negotiation,* in which the interests of conflicting parties are taken into consideration to craft solutions that are acceptable to both sides—in effect *both/and* rather than *either/or solutions.* Chapter 4 provides additional strategies to help inclusion facilitators deal with conflict within teams; these same strategies work equally well when the conflict is between individuals.

Monitoring The last intervention strategy is for inclusion facilitators to serve as the monitors of their students' progress and thereby help teachers or other educators make new decisions based on sound data as well as values and beliefs (Garmston & Wellman, 1999). Particularly in the current atmosphere that values evidence-based practice (e.g., Individuals with Disabilities Education Improvement Act of 2004 [PL 108-446]), inclusion facilitators must be able to gather and help interpret outcome data in a way that is meaningful to classroom teachers, parents, and administrators. In other words, when a teacher shares a belief or concern that the student "won't learn anything in my class," it is a call to an inclusion facilitator to work with the rest of the team to provide consistent and accurate supports for the student and to collect data on student learning.

DISCOVERING IDENTITIES TO PLAN INTERVENTION STRATEGIES

So what strategies should an inclusion facilitator use to influence a given individual in a given situation? The authors of this book suggest that inclusion facilitators discover what comprises each person's identity with respect to inclusion across three dimensions

- Bottom-line values
- Concerns about inclusive education
- Personality type

Bottom-Line Values

It is likely that some individuals with whom inclusion facilitators may work will value the students' development of self-esteem or self-actualization above everything else. These teachers would probably support constructivist, experiential teaching. Some teachers may believe that the central role of education is passing down time-honored knowledge, focusing on covering the breadth of the curriculum rather than exploring a few ideas in depth. Others feel that the role of school is to teach students how to learn, given the pace at which new knowledge is outpacing present-day knowledge. Some school personnel may hold core values about evidence-based practice, valuing only those pedagogies that have evidence of effectiveness over time. Still other individuals may think that the purpose of schooling is to right societal wrongs and to prepare students to take an active role in a democracy. These individuals might construct curriculum around a set of provocative essential questions or problems and emphasize students' growing moral consciousness to global issues.

In their work with schools in New Hampshire and other states since the mid-1980s, the authors of this book have noticed that people's bottom-line values tend to cluster within one of four dimensions (i.e., expedience, authority, altruism, social justice) that are expressed either to satisfy an ego need (*self*) or to satisfy someone else's need (*other*). Table 3.2 correlates these four value dimensions with their *self* or *other* expressions. The authors hypothesize that these are the most enduring values about inclusion—the ones that will keep people committed when the wisdom of inclusion is challenged.

Expedience   Expedience guides some people's decisions about their professional behavior. The principal who acts out of concern for expedience—who makes the decision that will be easy for him- or herself—may be an initial supporter of inclusion, on the one hand, because he or she believes it will satisfy the group of parents who are ready to bring a due process claim against the school if their children are not included in general education classes. On the other

Table 3.2.   How an individual's primary values affect his or her focus on "self" and "other"

Primary value	Focus on self	Focus on other
Expedience	"I'll do whatever is easiest for me and causes the least conflict."	None
Authority	"I want to live up to my own professional expectations and how I was trained."	"I'll do whatever is proven through research, whatever the law requires, or whatever my boss mandates."
Altruism	"I fear what having a disability means and would like it to be eradicated."	"I want to make life easier for people with disabilities who are less fortunate than I."
Social justice	"I want to be valued for my unique gifts and welcomed into my community and my world."	"I want everyone to be valued for their unique gifts and welcomed into our community and world."

hand, that same principal may be as easily swayed against including students because he or she envisions the extra time and effort that will have to be devoted to staff development, meetings, and one-to-one conversations that will be necessary if a change in philosophy or programs is introduced. This value dimension tends to be all about one's concern for one's self and less about concern for others.

Authority   The second value dimension is that of authority, which is either internalized or externally imposed. Many veteran educators and related-services providers have strongly developed professional identities that function as internal voices of authority. These people make decisions based on their notions of what they should do as professional speech-language pathologists (SLPs), psychologists, or occupational therapists. For example, Diane is an SLP in an urban elementary school. For 20 years, she has provided articulation therapy to students with significant disabilities, and the suggestion that she change her practice to focus on students' functional communication abilities rattles the core of her identity as a competent SLP. She identifies herself as an articulation therapist, and her allegiance to the value of authority comes from within.

Other professionals who value authority are influenced by external rules in the form of law, regulations, and research. They seek to understand exactly what is expected of them from a higher authority and will not challenge their supervisor or a piece of research from a prestigious university. For example, Marsha, a special education case manager in a large high school, follows her teacher's contract or what her boss tells her during her monthly supervision meetings as the letter of the law to guide every decision she makes.

Altruism   The third dimension of values around inclusion centers on people's expressed desire to be altruistic—to demonstrate their unselfish concern for the welfare of others. Altruism toward people with disabilities is rooted in the self as an expression of fear about people with disabilities (or about being disabled themselves) or in feelings of benevolence toward others who are perceived as needing one's help or charity. Each expression of this value is harmful toward many people with disabilities who "no longer see their physical or mental limitations as a source of shame or as something to overcome to inspire others" (Shapiro, 1993, p. 4).

In his landmark investigative study of the disability rights movement in the United States, *U.S. News and World Report* reporter Joe Shapiro interviewed hundreds of people with disabilities throughout the country, many who were active in the movement as well as those who did not consider themselves to be at all political. The resounding message he received was that the vast majority of people with disabilities do not want pity or charity because they do not see any tragedy in having a disability but rather view "society's myths, fears, and stereotypes [as making] being disabled difficult" (Shapiro, 1993, p. 5).

Although most people without disabilities would not recognize it, some argue that fear is the root of compassion toward people with disabilities. Robert Murphy, an anthropologist with a disability, wrote

> We are subverters of the American Ideal just as the poor are betrayers of the American Dream. The disabled [sic] serve as constant, visible reminders to the able-bodied [sic] that the society they live in is a counterfeit paradise, that they too are vulnerable. (1993)

This reminder of vulnerability often gets turned outward and expressed as concern or benevolence toward people with disabilities. To some, programs and events such as the Jerry Lewis Muscular Dystrophy Telethon, The Walk to Cure Autism, and the donation cups at local convenience stores to raise money for a segregated school for children with disabilities express the belief that disability should be eradicated because having a disability is a horrible existence, barely worth living (McBryde Johnson, 2003).

Norman Kunc (1995), a social activist who experiences a disability, described four levels of society's perceptions about and response to disability, including

- Disability as deviance, expressed as extermination, aggression, segregation, and avoidance

- Disability as deficit, expressed through rehabilitation, remediation, and assimilation

- Disability as tragedy, expressed as tolerance, patronization, and charity

- Disability as diversity, expressed as respect, appreciation, equal worth, and inclusion

Kunc and others who have first-hand experience with disabilities embrace only the last perspective and demand that having a disability be considered to be a natural part of the human experience. They argue that people with disabilities should be given choice and control over their lives (as exemplified by the precept "Nothing about us without us") and that they should be guaranteed full access to education, employment, housing, medical care, recreation, and relationships (Charlton, 1998; Snow, 2000).

Social Justice   The value of social justice represents both self-interest and a legitimate interest in the rights and opportunities of others. Thus, it is a powerful value for inclusion facilitators to promote toward students with disabilities or any other difference.

Kunc (2003) has pointed out that "inclusion is in everyone's self-interest." He illustrated that point with a parable called "The Story of the Stranger." In this parable, the star of the basketball team is riding a wave of adulation from his peers, his coaches, his teachers, and the community because he has led the team to the state championship. During the week before the big game, pep rallies celebrate his skills, cheerleaders chant his name when he comes up to the podium during an assembly, and the local newspaper asks, "Can Scott lead the Panthers to their first state championship since 1954?"

Kunc then asked a provocative question: As Scott dribbles the ball toward the basket during the final seconds of play when the score is tied, is he thinking, "I'm the big man on campus; the world is my oyster; I really have it made?" Kunc's answer helps us understand that Scott's experience is really no different from that of the kid with Down syndrome who wishes he could be on the basketball team. Scott fears that his value to the team and the school hangs in the balance because if he doesn't make the basket, he is no longer the golden boy. People won't remember his previous 3 years of success but instead will remember the newspaper headline proclaiming that the Panthers went down in defeat in the final seconds because he failed to make the shot.

Kunc argued that all students—Scott, the prom queen, the valedictorian, and the kid with Down syndrome who is teased on the bus—want to live in a society in which they are accepted for who they are as people, not for what they look like, the score they got on their SATs, or their prowess on the basketball court. Kunc said that one of the strongest arguments for social justice for *others* is that in a just society—one that "recognizes inalienable rights and adheres to what is fair, honest, and moral" (Cunningham, Cunningham, & Saigo, 2003)—each of us can be confident that the world will be just toward *us* as well.

Concerns About Inclusive Education

Highly experienced and respected teachers may have reservations about inclusive education. One English teacher revealed during a team meeting that his reticence about having a particular student in his class really centered on what this decision would mean for his day-to-day responsibilities. He expressed general support for the philosophy of inclusion but was deeply concerned about the extra planning time required, the effect that this student would have on his usual teaching methods, and the challenge of classroom management. In this type of situation, the school's inclusion facilitator needs to take this teacher's concerns into consideration before expecting him to be on board with an inclusion decision or to invest his energy in its implementation.

The ability to address the concerns of others about an innovation has long been recognized as being an essential skill of effective change agents. In 1973, Hall, Wallace, and Dossett first wrote about the developmental stages of the process of adopting educational innovations that they called the CBAM. Their model included three dimensions: the concern that potential users express about the innovation, how the innovation is used, and the ways that the innovation can be adapted to the needs and styles of different people. Hall and Loucks (1978) applied the work of Hall and colleagues to the challenge of designing staff development based on teacher concerns. There are lessons in their work for inclusion facilitators in their role as change agents.

Hall and Loucks identified several assumptions about adopting innovations that have relevance to inclusive education, such as

- Change is a process, not an event; it takes time and is achieved in stages.

- The individual must be the primary target of interventions designed to facilitate change.

- Change is a highly personal experience, with the personal dimension being more important to address than the organizational one.

- Individuals go through many stages during the adoption of the innovation, and change agents must accommodate their strategies to each stage, constantly assessing each individual's perceptions relative to the movement of the whole organization.

Research on the CBAM has identified seven stages of concern about an innovation, depicted in Table 3.3. These stages of concern about inclusion are represented by the following statements:

- "I'm not really familiar with the term *inclusion.*" (*Awareness*)

- "I think that we are going to be talking about that in a class that I'm taking toward my master's degree." (*Informational*)

- "I've got so much on my plate now that I don't think that I really have the time to invest in this effort right now." (*Personal*)

- "The planning time required is really more than I can handle, and I'm not sure if it makes sense for me to devote so much time and energy to one student." (*Management*)

- "Things seem to be going all right, but I wonder how this is going to affect my students' grades this semester." (*Consequences*)

- "Maybe if we met less frequently, but for a longer block of time, it would be more efficient and effective for everyone on the team." (*Collaboration*)

- "This just makes so much sense for all students. Can we talk to the Curriculum Committee about introducing some of the things we are doing in other classes?" (*Refocusing*)

Inclusion facilitators who take individuals' concerns into consideration recognize that "since change is brought about by individuals, their personal satisfactions, frustrations, concerns, motivations, and perceptions generally all play a part in determining the success or failure of a change initiative" (Hall & Loucks, 1978, p. 38).

Table 3.3.   Stages of concern about an innovation

Stage number	Stage or level of concern	Characteristics demonstrated by individuals
0	Awareness	Little concern about or interest in the innovation
1	Informational	More interest in learning about the innovation, such as the general characteristics, effects, and requirements for its use
2	Personal	Uncertainty about the demands of the innovation, one's capacity to make the innovation work, and one's role in the process
3	Management	Focus on the innovation's effects on specific tasks, efficiency, scheduling, time, and energy
4	Consequences	Beginning of consideration of the impact of the innovation on students
5	Collaboration	Eagerness to work with others who are involved in the same innovation
6	Refocusing	Openness to implementing new programs to replace the old

Source: Hall, Wallace, and Dossett (1973).

Personality Type

The third component of identity that inclusion facilitators need to take into consideration is a person's basic personality type. Numerous models of personality typing have been described (Myers & McCaulley, 1985), but one that has been used successfully by the author of this chapter is the Enneagram (Riso & Hudson, 2003). The *Enneagram* is a dynamic personality system that is founded on a number of ancient traditions originally synthesized by Oscar Ichazo and describes nine distinct patterns of thinking, feeling, and acting (Ichazo, 1982). Each of the patterns is based on a perceptual filter that determines what people pay attention to and how they direct their energy. Each pattern is supported by a basic proposition about what is needed for survival and satisfaction. Thus, understanding individuals' personality types can be a powerful tool in learning *what* motivates them, *where* their attention goes during stress, *how* to effectively communicate with them, and *how* to maximize group development and manage conflict.

The Enneagram is based on a number of assumptions about personality typing:

1. People have a dominant type that does not change from one situation to another.

2. The personality types are universal, applying equally to men and women from diverse cultures.

3. People fluctuate among healthy, average, and unhealthy expressions of their dominant type.

4. No type is inherently better or worse than any other, each having capacities and limitations.

5. The purpose of the using the Enneagram is not to change people's personality types, but rather, to enable them and others to use the healthy behaviors of each type in the appropriate situation.

Assessing people's personalities using the Enneagram is easily accomplished by having each person take an inexpensive on-line assessment available at http://enneagraminstitute.com. Staff members and teams that have used this personality test have found that it gave them insights into their interactions with other personality types.

The nine personality types are described as follows:

- *The Reformer*—a rational and idealistic type who is principled, purposeful, self-controlled, and perfectionistic

- *The Helper*—a caring and interpersonal type who is generous, demonstrative, people pleasing, and possessive

- *The Achiever*—a success-oriented and pragmatic type who is adaptable, excelling, driven, and image conscious

- *The Investigator*—an intense and cerebral type who is perceptive, innovative, secretive, and isolated

- *The Loyalist*—a committed and security-oriented type who is engaged, responsible, anxious, and suspicious

- *The Enthusiast*—a busy and fun-loving type who is spontaneous, versatile, acquisitive, and scattered

- *The Challenger*—a powerful and dominating type who is self-confident, decisive, willful, and confrontational

- *The Peacemaker*—an easygoing, self-effacing type who is receptive, reassuring, agreeable, and complacent

In addition to describing individuals' dominant personality types, the Enneagram also accounts for each person's second side of his or her personality, which can either complement the dominant type or contradict it; level of development along a healthy-average-unhealthy continuum; tendencies when feeling secure or threatened; and basic instincts that lie at the heart of the quest for survival.

Using the Enneagram to understand personality type is far more complex than taking a 10-question magazine quiz titled "What Kind of Person Are You?" Change agents may find the Enneagram approach to be a powerful tool, however, as they strive to understand the most effective ways to work with the diverse individuals on a student's team.

APPLYING THE MODEL

The following case study illustrates how an inclusion facilitator might use the model described in this chapter to engage with others in the school community to promote inclusive values and beliefs.

The School

Lakeside Middle School houses approximately 1,200 students in fifth through eighth grades. All students are organized into teams—consisting of instructors in core academic areas, guidance counselors, and special educators certified in mild disability areas—within each grade level. Faculty in the arts, health, physical education, and information technology teach students across all grade levels.

The service delivery model for students with disabilities is best described as a traditional least restrictive environment model. Most students with learning disabilities are part of heterogeneous social studies, science, and related arts classes but are taught language arts and math in pull-out classes by teachers certified in learning disabilities. Students with serious emotional disabilities or those with significant cognitive disabilities are educated primarily in self-contained classrooms and mainstreamed for one or two periods a day into arts or physical education classes.

Within the last few years, a few students with significant disabilities have been included in more general education classes, but there is no schoolwide vision for full inclusion. The teacher who instructs students with severe disabilities and the districtwide inclusion facilitator are philosophically supportive of inclusive education and see themselves as the change agents of the school.

The Student and Parent

Student   Ben is a 13-year-old student at Lakeside Middle School who has autism.

Parent   Hillary, Ben's mother, is concerned primarily with her son's learning vocational skills. She works as a paraprofessional in another school in the Lakeside school district and is not supportive of Ben's full inclusion in general education.

The Staff

Inclusion Facilitator   David is the districtwide inclusion facilitator and was a general education classroom teacher until his career switch 3 years ago. David provides assistance to six schools across the district and spends approximately 2 days a week at Lakeside Middle School. David sees himself as an inclusion advocate who aggressively pursues ongoing professional development to improve his skills. He has an adult son, Pete, with a developmental disability who lives and works in the community.

Principal   Steve is a veteran educator who has spent nearly 20 years at Lakeside Middle School. He has instituted a number of reforms at the school within the last 5 years, including advisory groups, a service learning requirement, interdisciplinary teaching of English and social studies, and an alignment of the school curriculum to comply with state standards. He is concerned because his school has been notified that it is in need of improvement because of the low statewide assessment scores of its students who are receiving special education services.

Special Education Coordinator   Kevin is in his second year as the coordinator of special education at the middle school and has been a special educator for 18 years. He reports to the principal and to the district special education director. Most of the staff members he supervises in his new role as coordinator were peer colleagues before he was promoted.

Special Education/Severe Disabilities Teacher   Jeff has been a special educator for 22 years and has worked for most of his career in self-contained classrooms for students with significant cognitive disabilities. Three years ago, his job was changed to include both teaching students with moderate and significant disabilities in a pull-out classroom and planning and collaborating with general and special education team members.

Science Teacher   Dan is a sixth-grade science teacher who has been with the school for 8 years. He has no training in special education but prides himself on his creative teaching methods. He is one of the most popular teachers in the school. He has never had a student with significant disabilities in his class.

Paraprofessional   Delores is a one-to-one paraprofessional who supports Ben in his participation on a part-time basis during science and social studies in sixth-grade classes. Delores does not have any training in special education although she worked for many years in a group home for adults with disabilities. She is not particularly supportive of Ben's inclusion into general education classes. She has a close personal relationship outside of school with Ben's mother, Hillary.

Speech-Language Pathologist   Deborah is a veteran speech-language pathologist who has worked in schools providing pull-out speech services to students for approximately 20 years. She has a caseload of approximately 60 students, including 3 who have significant disabilities and are candidates for augmentative communication.

Life Skills Teacher   Maxine is a special education teacher who provides classroom life skills and community-based instruction to students with significant disabilities. She has been in the field for approximately 25 years.

Assessing Staff Identities

In his role as the district inclusion facilitator, David is committed to fully including all students in age-appropriate general education classes in their neighborhood schools. He is responsible for providing expert facilitation to teams across the district. His students include those who qualify for the state's alternate assessment, those who have significant physical and sensory disabilities, and those who could benefit from augmentative and alternative communication (AAC). David understands that Ben's team is very diverse, not only in terms of their professional roles but also, presumably, in their values, concerns, and personality styles. He has a number of tools at his disposal to assess the team members across these identity dimensions, including conversational and observational assessments, informal assessments conducted via written surveys, and other valid and reliable assessment instruments.

Assessing Values   Assessment of a person's values about students with significant disabilities and inclusion is best accomplished by getting to know him or her as an individual. This is best accomplished by paying attention to conversations in team meetings and informal chats in the hallway, and by observing the person's interactions. Does the person talk to the student with a disability as if the student understands what is being said, or does the person use baby talk or talk about the student as if he or she were not present? Does the person speak about a future life for the student that is characterized by college, work, and community living, or does the person assume that the student will live in a group home or in an institutional setting? Does the person describe the student in person-first language, emphasizing his or her gifts and talents and unique personality traits and characteristics, or does the person focus on the student's impairments, using phrases such as "low functioning," "severely involved," or "wheel-chair bound." An inclusion facilitator should not make assumptions based on only one or two conversations but should attempt to find out the basis of the person's assumptions.

Jorgensen, McSheehan, and Sonnenmeier (2002) described indicators of positive values toward students with disabilities within a larger document that lists essential best practices in inclusive schools. One method of uncovering beliefs and assumptions might be to ask team members to read this document and then discuss it through open dialogue.

Assessing Concerns   Assessing concerns about inclusion can be accomplished by asking team members an open-ended question, "What concerns you about including Ben?" or by creating an informal survey such as that depicted in Figure 3.1. An inclusion facilitator should not use the ratings from this instrument as if they were scores on a statistically valid and reliable instrument, but the ratings can illustrate the approximate level of concern expressed by the different members of a student's team.

The most formal and precise measure of stages of concern is the SoC (Stages of Concern) Questionnaire (Hall, George, & Rutherford, 1977). This questionnaire, which assesses concern about any innovation (not specifically inclusion), is psychometrically rigorous and can provide the inclusion facilitator with meaningful data for planning his or her change strategy.

Results of Team Member Identity Assessments

David decided to use a combination of strategies to identify the values, concerns, and personality types of Ben's team members. He used his own observational and conversational assessment of their values, surveyed the team for their concerns using the questionnaire depicted in Figure 3.1, and had each staff member take the on-line Enneagram test. Table 3.4 depicts the results of these assessments. Examining this team's identities yields several interesting observations.

1. Four members' primary values lie in authority—what they judge has been proven by data or what their supervisor mandates.

2. The **inclusion facilitator** and the **special education teacher** could be natural allies because they both value social justice and are at levels 5 and 6 on the concerns scale. They must be cautious about moving too far ahead of the other team members, however, because most of them are concerned about the personal and management impact of inclusion and will need to have those concerns addressed before they will be open to rethinking their assumptions or adjusting their values.

3. The **parent** is the only person on the team who is a *Challenger*. The **special education coordinator** and **life skills**

Concerns About Inclusive Education Questionnaire

Directions: This is an anonymous questionnaire. Please read each statement below and then rate each statement according to the following scale:

1 = It is unlikely that I would make this statement.
2 = It is somewhat likely that I would make this statement.
3 = It is very likely that I would make this statement.

____ 1. I don't think inclusion will work in my class. I don't have any training in special education or experience working with students who have significant disabilities.

____ 2. I know our school has been doing some inclusion, but I'm not really sure how it would affect me.

____ 3. I'm going crazy with all these meetings and adapting all these teaching materials. I find that I am spending too much time on the one or two students in my classroom who have significant disabilities.

____ 4. I wonder if we could have more informal discussions about inclusion with other teachers. I know it would help me do a better job if I could hear what is working for them.

____ 5. So far, having a student with disabilities in my class is working out fine. The other students seem to be eager to work with him or her, but I wonder how this will affect his or her learning and theirs?

____ 6. I think we've made a good start with a few students who have been included. I think that now we need to take a look at all the students with more significant disabilities and develop a schoolwide plan for including them.

____ 7. Inclusion? I think that there are some students who will always be best served in a self-contained classroom.

____ 8. Being in class with a student who has a significant disability has helped my students become more tolerant. Still, I wonder how my attention to this student has affected their mastery of the curriculum.

____ 9. It's been great to have the special education teacher meet with me to do lesson planning for one of my students with significant disabilities. Do you think that we could have more common planning time so that we could develop whole units based on differentiated instruction?

____ 10. I think I understand the concept of inclusion—it's really for social reasons, isn't it? I'm not really sure what it means in terms of academic learning, though.

____ 11. Other: _____

Figure 3.1.   Concerns about inclusive education questionnaire.

teacher are *Peacemakers* who will be reticent to challenge Ben's mom.

4.   The **special education coordinator** is primarily concerned with making his job easy and with not "rocking the boat." He will not be eager to take a stand for inclusion unless his values change or unless it can be proven that his job will actually be easier if students are included.

Table 3.4   Results of team member identity assessment

Team member	Primary values	Major concerns	Personality type
David (inclusion facilitator)	Social justice, self, others	*Stage 6 (refocusing)*— concerned with persuading others to replace current programs and practices with full inclusion	*Helper*—caring, interpersonal, generous, demonstrative, people pleasing, possessive
Steve (principal)	Authority, self, professional competence, others, evidence-based practices	*Stage 4 (consequences)*— concerned with considering the impact of inclusion on student learning	*Investigator*—intense, cerebral, perceptive, innovative, secretive, isolated
Kevin (special education coordinator)	Expedience, self, "making it easy for me"	*Stage 3 (management)*— concerned with focusing on the effects of inclusion on time, schedules, and staffing	*Peacemaker*— easygoing, self-effacing, receptive, reassuring, agreeable, complacent
Jeff (special education teacher)	Social justice, others, equity for students with disabilities	*Stage 5 (collaboration)*— concerned with the effects of inclusion relating to his ability to work with others	*Loyalist*—committed, security-oriented, engaged, responsible, anxious, suspicious
Dan (science teacher)	Altruism, others, benevolence toward students with disabilities because they are less fortunate than others	*Stage 3 (management)*— concerned with focusing on the effects of inclusion on time, schedules, and staffing	*Enthusiast*—busy, fun loving, spontaneous, versatile, acquisitive, scattered
Hillary (parent)	Altruism, others, benevolence toward students with disabilities because they are less fortunate than others	*Stage 4 (consequences)*— concerned with worrying about Ben's skill acquisition	*Challenger*—powerful, dominating, self-confident, decisive, willful, confrontational
Delores (paraprofessional)	Authority, others, whatever her boss or Ben's mother tells her to do	*Stage 2 (personal)*— concerned with worrying about her role in the middle between the school and the parent	*Helper*—caring, interpersonal, generous, demonstrative, people pleasing, possessive
Deborah (speech-language pathologist)	Authority, self, professional competence	*Stage 4 (consequences)*— concerned with worrying about Ben's skill acquisition	*Achiever*—success-oriented, pragmatic, adaptable, excelling, driven, image-conscious

(continued)

Table 3.4. *(continued)*

Team member	Primary values	Major concerns	Personality type
Maxine (life skills teacher)	Authority, others, following the orders of the special education coordinator	*Stage 3 (personal)*— concerned with worrying about the demands on her time and on her relationship with her boss	*Peacemaker*— easygoing, self-effacing, receptive, reassuring, agreeable, complacent

Note: Although only the dominant personality types are reported here, effective use of the Enneagram requires consideration of the entire assessment that includes a person's secondary type, instincts, and level of development within the type.

Planning the Inclusion Facilitator's Strategy

After about the first month of school, David feels as if he has enough information about Ben's team members to begin to work with each of them through a balanced advocacy and inquiry approach and to address their concerns about Ben's inclusion. First, however, he needs to look inward to understand his own values, concerns, and personality type.

David's values are grounded in a wish for social justice and equity for all people. He does not feel sorry for the students with significant disabilities that he supports, and he works toward their full participation and learning instead of toward remediating their impairments. He changed careers a few years ago and earned an additional teaching certification in severe disabilities just so that he could be part of the movement to include all students in the mainstream of general education. Because his values are grounded in his own personal life experience as a parent of a child with a disability, David has credibility with the team and with other parents of children with disabilities. His easygoing *Helper* personality indicates that he forms relationships easily and understands the importance of strengthening the relationships among Ben's team members. He is accepting of others' viewpoints and life experiences and does not judge them harshly if they differ from his own; however, he must be careful not to let his tendency to please others get in the way of expressing his own viewpoints or engaging others in conversations that challenge assumptions.

The major foci of his work with each team member are described next.

Principal   Steve is primarily motivated by what research says will improve all students' performance in his school. Because his personality type is that of an *Investigator,* he will respond well to information from the research literature on the outcomes of inclusion for students with and without disabilities. David might share with Steve excerpts from three research syntheses: McGregor and Vogelsberg's (1999) *Inclusive Schooling Practices: Pedagogical and Research Foundations,* Ryndak and Fisher's (2003) *A Compendium of Articles on Effective Strategies to Achieve Inclusive Education,* and Fisher and Ryndak's (2001) *The Foundations of Inclusive Education: A Compendium of Articles on Effective Strategies to Achieve Inclusive Education.* Steve might also be interested in reading a book on school reform and inclusive education, such as Lipsky and Gartner's (1997) *Inclusion and School Reform: Transforming America's Classrooms.* Because Steve is very busy, David might put together a brief annotated bibliography summarizing some key books and journal articles. Steve might also support David's starting of an action research group at Lakeside to study research on various instructional and support strategies. Finally, because Steve will likely be paying close attention to how well students with significant disabilities do on the statewide assessment, David tells Steve about another student with significant disabilities who was one of only seven sixth-grade students to score in the advanced category of the assessment during the previous year.

Special Education Coordinator   Kevin's values play out in his wish to keep the status quo so as not to do anything that will make his job more difficult. Kevin will respond best if David can present a well-thought-out plan for how including all students will favorably affect each and every staff member, their planning time, their relationships with students' parents, and Kevin's role during the change process. Kevin might benefit from visiting other middle schools and talking with their special education coordinators. Because David is part of a statewide network of parents and educators who meet regularly to talk about inclusion, he could invite Kevin to a meeting of that group, facilitate a visit to another school, and invite one of Kevin's peers to visit Lakeside.

Special Education Teacher   Jeff is David's closest ally on the special education staff, and David should enlist him as a partner in the inclusion change process. Because Jeff's dominant personality type is that of a *Loyalist,* David will have to provide close support and mentoring to Jeff so that the stresses of the change process do not push him to express the unhealthy sides of his *Loyalist* personality (i.e., anxiety, suspicion). David would be well served to meet with Jeff on a weekly basis to discuss issues that are surfacing within Ben's team. Jeff is anxious to learn new skills, and the meetings with David could focus on discussing student supports and on strategies for getting Ben's team to work together in a more effective and efficient way.

Science Teacher   Dan has the potential to be a great teacher for all students. His lack of experience with students with significant disabilities makes him feel incompetent, however, and he is therefore likely to assert, "I don't think Ben belongs in my class." Because he is an *Enthusiast,* he teaches in a very active, yet spontaneous way; this teaching style might be challenging for Ben if he doesn't have the right supports in place. Dan's concerns center on the management of inclusion, and he asks questions such as

- "Do I have to design a special lesson just for Ben?"

- "What will happen when we use the lab equipment? I like to give my kids quite a bit of freedom, but I still need to be real cautious about safety issues."

- "It's kind of hard for me to predict exactly where I'll be in my curriculum on any particular day. It's important to me that I am able to change my lesson plan at the last minute to capitalize on something that happened on the news the night before or on a question that a student has asked. If Ben is there, will that restrict my ability to be flexible?"

David should focus on giving Dan just the amount of information that he is asking for and not overwhelming him with details. David must address Dan's concern about his creative teaching style and assure him that he will not have to miss any teachable moments just because Ben is in the class. The most effective collaboration strategy with Dan will be for David to ask him about the big themes of upcoming units, the instructional routines that Dan uses regularly, and the materials that the students will be using during those routines. Trying to pin Dan down to find out exactly what lesson he will be teaching on a certain day just will not work; therefore, to fit in with Dan's teaching style, David will have to provide extensive support to Delores (paraprofessional) so that she learns to use a repertoire of support strategies that will work across many different lessons or routines.

If David can show Dan that Ben is more similar to his other students than he thought, Dan will be able to welcome Ben into his class and provide him with a rich science learning experience.

Parent Hillary is potentially one of David's strongest allies for Ben's inclusion, but at the present time her energies are focused on assuring that Ben acquire traditional functional skills. She wants Ben to learn to dress himself; eat appropriately; and perform repetitive tasks such as sorting, which she believes will help Ben get a job someday. Hillary does not believe that Ben has the capacity to learn academic content and frequently refers to him as "low functioning," "retarded," and "still my little baby." Her vision for Ben's adult life is that he will live at home after high school and then move to a group home in his mid-20s. She envisions him being surrounded by human services workers and has never imagined that he might travel, go to college, fall in love, or exercise control over his own destiny. Therefore, David's primary goal with Hillary should be to expand her idea of what is possible for her son and what his school experience should look like given these new possibilities. David should also be conscientious about including Hillary in all decisions regarding Ben's educational program and especially in discussions of Ben's successes within those general education classes in which he is enrolled.

Hillary has expressed that she is open to finding an adult mentor for Ben, someone who has a disability who could take Ben under his wing, so to speak, and help him make the transition from school to adult life. David's son, Pete, might be a perfect candidate because he experiences some of the same challenges as Ben and also was not expected to learn much in school. Pete is now living with a roommate in the community, working two jobs, and enjoying an active social life. In fact, Pete recently celebrated his 30th birthday by taking a hot air balloon ride and then going out dancing with his friends. Linking David's son with Ben would provide opportunities for David to get to know Hillary outside of the formal school environment. It would also allow Hillary to see the positive and challenging sides of Pete's life in the community, so she would have a better understanding of what Ben's life might be like. Finally, it would also be good for David to see the positive and challenging sides of his son's life.

Another strategy for working with Hillary would be to suggest that she attend their state's Partners in Policymaking Leadership Series (see http://partnersinpolicymaking.com). Established in Minnesota by the Governor's Council on Developmental Disabilities in 1987, Partners is an innovative, competency-based leadership training program for adults with disabilities and parents of children with developmental disabilities. It is designed to help individuals and parents expand their vision of what is possible, learn about best practices, and acquire competencies for influencing public officials through personal action and community organizing.

Because Hillary is a very involved community member who values good works, this might be a productive outlet for her leadership that might change her assumptions about Ben's education and life after high school. In New Hampshire's Partners series, for example, participants have heard such speakers as Norman Kunc (a social activist who experiences a disability), Jeffrey Strully (a parent of three adult children with disabilities and a nationally known author and speaker), other adults with disabilities who moved from institutional to community life, and other parents whose children have been successfully included.

Paraprofessional Helping Delores change her views may well be the most difficult challenge facing David. Delores' dominant personality type is that of a *Helper*, and she has a long history in the human service industry working with adults with disabilities who live rather restrictive lives. Like many school paraprofessionals, she works 29.5 hours per week—just under the 30 hours that would make her eligible for benefits—so she is not eligible for school-funded professional development. Delores is very attached to Ben, and David wonders about the likelihood of her shifting her role from providing for most of Ben's needs to that of facilitating natural supports for Ben from other adults and his classmates.

David's most powerful strategy might be to connect Delores with other paraprofessionals who are supporting students who are fully included. He could accomplish this by finding a substitute aide and some discretionary funding so that Delores could attend a three-session workshop series on "The Role of the Paraprofessional in the Inclusive Classroom" being offered by the state's Parent Information Center. In this setting, Delores would be among her peers, no administrators would be present, and she could relate to the instructors, who themselves had been paraprofessionals with students whose challenges were similar to Ben's.

If Delores would be open to reading or watching a video about inclusion and the paraprofessional's role, David might lend her his book by Mary Beth Doyle (2002) titled *The Paraprofessional's Guide to the Inclusive Classroom* or a video such as *High School Inclusion: Equity and Excellence in an Inclusive Community of Learners* (Institute on Disability, 1999), *Petroglyphs* (Institute on Disability, n.d.), or *Voices of Friendship* (Institute on Disability, n.d.).

Speech-Language Pathologist Although Deborah appears to be working against Ben's inclusion—by focusing her services on pull-out articulation and language therapy—she is actually another potential ally for David if she adopts a new role on Ben's team. She has a strong work ethic, takes her professional role very seriously, and could be an important key to Ben's inclusion in the general education classroom.

Because he is not an SLP, David is not positioned to influence Deborah's professional identity; still, he might be well advised to bring an outside expert in augmentative communication into Ben's team to help with Ben's 3-year reevaluation. This expert could share with Deborah some of the latest research on AAC and related recommendations from national professional organizations, for example

- "Guidelines for Meeting the Communication Needs of Persons with Severe Disabilities" (National Joint Committee on the Communication Needs of Persons with Severe Disabilities, 1992)

- *Communication Supports Checklist for Programs Serving Individuals with Severe Disabilities* (McCarthy et al., 1998)

- "Augmentative and Alternative Communication Knowledge and Skills for Service Delivery" (American Speech-Language-Hearing Association, 2002)

Life Skills Teacher Although Ben attends Maxine's self-contained life skills class one period per day for cooking instruction, she has no interest in exploring the possibility of Ben's being included in the regular sixth-grade consumer and family sciences class. Maxine learns best when she can see specific alternatives to her present practices. Therefore, David might decide to sit down with Maxine to plan for Ben's participation in a cooking lesson within a general education class and then model the process of providing supports for Ben in another class in which Ben is included. Because Maxine has never served in the role of team teacher or inclusion facilitator, she would need to talk through what that role shift would mean for her, the implications for her schedule, and the reaction of Jeff, the special educator, to a change in Maxine's responsibilities.

A Final Word About Social Justice and Transforming Hearts and Minds

Each of the members of Ben's team and the whole school staff would benefit from exploring how the concept of social justice aligns with the practice of inclusive education so that they might develop enduring values that can withstand the challenges experienced during any innovation. Years ago, it was common practice for schools to host a Disability Awareness Day that featured exploration activities such as having students without disabilities use a wheelchair for a day, smearing a pair of eye glasses with Vaseline and then trying to read, or trying to write while making small circles with one's foot. These experiences were supposed to heighten awareness of the struggles that children with disabilities face, leading to greater empathy and tolerance for their presence in schools and communities. The impact of these activities was often short-lived, however, and they did not lead to more reciprocal relationships between students or to a change of heart about people with disabilities or inclusive education.

David might try a host of different strategies to focus the students and staff on issues of equity and social justice for students with disabilities. First, David might join the school's committee that is addressing issues of school culture and safety. As a member of that committee, he could share resources with the other members, including books such as *No Pity* (Shapiro, 1993) and *You Can't Say You Can't Play* (Paley, 1993). The committee might be interested in thinking about how to embed consideration of diversity into the curriculum through readings in popular literature (e.g., *The Curious Incident of the Dog in the Night-Time* [Haddon, 2003]), by addressing the civil rights issues of people with disabilities in social studies (e.g., by contrasting the Americans with Disabilities Act of 1990 [PL 101-336] with Civil Rights legislation), and by asking students to wrestle with dilemmas in science (e.g., Would the world be a better place if we could genetically engineer the "perfect" person?).

If David could partner with his state's Developmental Disabilities Council, Parent Information Center, or University Center for Excellence in Disability, they might sponsor a school assembly with a nationally known speaker such as Norman Kunc, Jeffrey Strully, or Jamie Burke (a young man with autism). Having a follow-up panel presentation by local self-advocates could provide a powerful glimpse into the lives of people who have discarded Kunc's "disability as deviance" paradigm for one that recognizes that

If we are to achieve a richer culture, rich in contrasting values, we must recognize the whole gamut of human potentialities, and so weave a less arbitrary social fabric, one in which each diverse human gift will find a fitting place. (Mead, 2001, p. 300)

REFERENCES

American Speech-Language-Hearing Association. (2002). Augmentative and alternative communication knowledge and skills for service delivery. *ASHA, 22,* 97–106.

Americans with Disabilities Act of 1990, PL 101-336, 42 U.S.C. §§ 201 *et seq.*

Bandura, A. (1997). *Self-efficacy: The exercise of control.* New York: W.H. Freeman.

Center for Critical Impact. (n.d.). *Definitions.* Retrieved October 3, 2004, from http://www.centerforcriticalimpact.com/definitions.htm

Charlton, J. (1998). *Nothing about us without us.* Los Angeles: University of California Press.

Cunningham, W., Cunningham, C., & Saigo, B. (2003). *Environmental science: A global concern. Glossary.* McGraw-Hill Online Learning Center. Retrieved October 4, 2004, from http://highered.mcgrawhill.com/sites/0070294267/student_view0/glossary_s-z.html

Donnellan, A. (1984). The criterion of the least dangerous assumption. *Behavioral Disorders, 9,* 141–150.

Doyle, M.B. (2002). *The paraprofessional's guide to the inclusive classroom: Working as a team* (2nd ed.). Baltimore: Paul H. Brookes Publishing Co.

Fisher, D., & Ryndak, D. (2001). *The foundations of inclusive education: A compendium of articles on effective strategies to achieve inclusive education.* Baltimore: TASH.

Fisher, R., Ury, W., & Patton, B. (1991). *Getting to yes: Negotiating agreement without giving in* (2nd ed.). New York: Penguin Books.

Fuchs, D., & Fuchs, L. (1994). What's special about special education? A field under siege. *Phi Delta Kappan, 76*(7), 522–530.

Fullan, M. (1993). Why teachers must become change agents. *Educational Leadership, 50*(6), 12–17.

Fullan, M. (2001). *The new meaning of educational change.* New York: Teachers College Press.

Garmston, R., & Wellman, B. (1999). *The adaptive school: A sourcebook for developing collaborative groups.* Norwood, MA: Christopher-Gordon Publishers.

Giangreco, M.F., Cloninger, C.J., & Iverson, V.S. (2000). *Choosing outcomes and accommodations for children (COACH): A guide to educational planning for students with disabilities* (2nd ed.). Baltimore: Paul H. Brookes Publishing Co.

Haddon, M. (2003). *The curious incident of the dog in the night-time.* New York: Doubleday.

Hall, G., George, A., & Rutherford, W. (1977). *Measuring stages of concern about the innovation: A manual for the use of the SoC questionnaire.* Austin, TX: Southwest Educational Development Laboratory.

Hall, G., & Loucks, S. (1978). Teacher concerns as a basis for facilitating and personalizing staff development. *Teachers College Record, 80*(1), 36–53.

Hall, G., Wallace, R., & Dossett, W. (1973). *A developmental conceptualization of the adoption process within educational institutions.* Austin: University of Texas Research and Developmental Center for Teacher Education.

Havelock, R. (1971). *Planning for innovation through dissemination and utilization of knowledge.* Ann Arbor: University of Michigan Institute for Social Research.

Hole, S., & McEntee, G. (1999). Reflection is at the heart of practice. *Educational Leadership, 56*(8), 34–37.

Ichazo, O. (1982). *Interviews with Oscar Ichazo.* New York: Arica Institute Press.

Individuals with Disabilities Education Improvement Act of 2004, PL 108-446, 20 U.S.C. §§ 1400 et seq.

Institute on Disability at the University of New Hampshire. (Producer). (1999). *High school inclusion: Equity and excellence in an inclusive community of learners* [Video]. (Available from Paul H. Brookes Publishing Co., P.O. Box 10624, Baltimore, MD 21285)

Institute on Disability at the University of New Hampshire. (Producer). (n.d.). *Petroglyphs* [Video]. (Available from Inclusion Press, 24 Thorne Crescent, Toronto, ON M6H2S5 Canada)

Institute on Disability at the University of New Hampshire. (Producer). (n.d.). *The voices of friendship* [Video]. (Available from http://iod.unh.edu)

Jorgensen, C.M. (1998). *Restructuring high schools for all students: Taking inclusion to the next level.* Baltimore: Paul H. Brookes Publishing Co.

Jorgensen, C.M., McSheehan, M., & Sonnenmeier, R. (2002). *Essential best practices in inclusive schools.* Durham: Institute on Disability at the University of New Hampshire.

Kunc, N. (1995). *The right to be disabled.* British Columbia, Canada: Axis Consultation and Training.

Kunc, N. (2003, October). *The right to be disabled.* Presentation at the New Hampshire Leadership Series, Hampton Beach, NH.

Lipsky, D.K., & Gartner, A. (1997). *Inclusion and school reform: Transforming America's classrooms.* Baltimore: Paul H. Brookes Publishing Co.

Mead, M. (2001). *Sex and temperament in three primitive societies.* New York: Harper Collins.

McBryde Johnson, H. (2003, February 16). Unspeakable conversations: The case for my life. *New York Times Magazine.*

McCarthy, C.F., McLean, L.K., Miller, J.F., Paul-Brown, D., Romski, M.A., Rourk, J.D., & Yoder, D.E. (1998). *Communication supports checklist for programs serving individuals with severe disabilities.* Baltimore: Paul H. Brookes Publishing Co.

McGregor, G., & Vogelsberg, R.T. (1999). *Inclusive schooling practices: Pedagogical and research foundations: A synthesis of the literature that informs best practices about inclusive schooling.* Baltimore: Paul H. Brookes Publishing Co.

McKnight, J. (1995). *The careless society: Community and its counterfeits.* New York: Basic Books.

Murphy, R. (1993). *The body silent.* New York: W.W. Norton.

Myers, I., & McCaulley, M. (1985). *Manual: A guide to the development and use of the Myers-Briggs type indicator.* Palo Alto, CA: Consulting Psychology Press.

National Joint Committee on the Communication Needs of Persons with Severe Disabilities. (1992). Guidelines for meeting the communication needs of persons with severe disabilities. *Asha, 34*(Suppl. 7), 2–3.

Norman, S. (2001). The human face of school reform. *National Forum of Educational Administration and Supervision Journal, 18E*(4), 1–6.

Paley, V. (1993). *You can't say you can't play.* Boston: Harvard University Press.

Pfeffer, J., & Sutton, R. (2000). *The knowing–doing gap: How smart companies turn knowledge into action.* Cambridge, MA: Harvard Business Press.

Riso, D., & Hudson, R. (2003). *Discovering your personality type: The essential introduction to the Enneagram* (Rev. ed.). Boston: Houghton Mifflin.

Ross, R., & Roberts, C. (1994). Balancing inquiry and advocacy. In P. Senge, A. Kleiner, C. Roberts, R. Ross, & B. Smith, *The fifth discipline fieldbook* (pp. 253–259). New York: Doubleday.

Ryndak, D., & Fisher, D. (2003). *The foundations of inclusive education: A compendium of articles on effective strategies to achieve inclusive education* (2nd ed.). Baltimore: TASH.

Sarason, S. (1996). *Revisiting the culture of the school and the problem of change.* New York: Teachers College Press.

Senge, P., Kleiner, A., Roberts, C., Ross, R., & Smith, B. (1994). *The fifth discipline fieldbook.* New York: Doubleday.

Shapiro, J. (1993). *No pity.* New York: Times Books.

Sizer, T. (1992). *Horace's school: Redesigning the American high school.* Boston: Houghton Mifflin.

Snow, K. (2000). *Disability is natural: Revolutionary common sense for raising successful children with disabilities.* Woodland Park, CO: Braveheart Press.

Sparks, D. (2004, March). Dialogue deepens understanding and strengthens relationships. *Transformational Professional Learning,* 1–5. Retrieved October 9, 2004, from http://nsdc.org/library/publications/transformational/index.cfm

Villa, R.A., & Thousand, J.S. (Eds.). (2000). *Restructuring for caring and effective education: Piecing the puzzle together* (2nd ed.). Baltimore: Paul H. Brookes Publishing Co.

Webster's Revised Unabridged Dictionary. (1913). Springfield, MA: C. & G. Mirriam.

Participatory Decision Making
The Inclusion Facilitator's Role
as a Collaborative Team Leader

Cheryl M. Jorgensen

When special education teachers begin to act as inclusion facilitators, their roles in their schools change—sometimes in modest ways and sometimes radically. This is especially true in situations in which an inclusion facilitator serves as a school's collaborative team leader. The competencies reflected within this role are depicted in Table 4.1 and are a subset of the inclusion facilitator competencies found in Appendix A.

Although inclusion facilitators no longer have classrooms of their own, they still teach both children and adults. Inclusion facilitators must be able to model good inclusive teaching in the general education classroom so that others may learn how to do it. Inclusion facilitators must be skilled participant-observers—sitting in on classroom lessons, using their expertise to see what is working well and what needs to be changed in order to provide more effective supports for all students. They occasionally provide direct instruction and support in the general education classroom to particular students to gather information about that student's learning. Inclusion facilitators teach children with and without disabilities to understand, respect, and celebrate diversity.

Inclusion facilitators also educate other adults who teach students with significant disabilities, taking into consideration the different learning styles and needs of adult learners. Effective inclu-

Preparation of this chapter was supported in part by a grant from the U.S. Department of Education, Office of Special Education Programs, #H324M020067.

Table 4.1.   Competencies reflected in the collaborative team leader role

Assessment of the student and the learning environment

Identifies opportunities for learning and communication in a variety of inclusive
    environments, including general education classrooms, typical school routines and
    activities, extracurricular activities, the community, and the home

Assesses students' learning and communication styles, strengths, and needs using a
    variety of authentic assessment strategies such as criterion-based assessments,
    ecological inventories, futures planning assessments, and other classroom or typical
    activity-based strategies

Assesses factors that affect learning and communication, such as the physical and sensory
    environments, the curriculum, instructional methods, and classmates' and teachers'
    attitudes

Design of educational programs and supports

Collaborates with others to develop students' educational programs that reflect
    individualized goals based on the content of the general education curriculum,
    including 1) subject matter knowledge, 2) literacy, 3) social skills, 4) career skills,
    5) community service learning, 6) skills for independent living, and 7) general learning
    habits and behaviors

Designs and coordinates individualized natural and specialized supports in the
    classroom, school, and community in the areas of curriculum, instruction,
    communication, assistive technology, and medical and related services

Supports graduation planning that leads to students' participation in a variety of typical
    adult roles and inclusive environments such as postsecondary education, work, and
    community living

Promotes the use of a variety of augmentative communication symbols, modes, aids, and
    techniques (e.g., letters, words, graphic language symbols, sign/gesture symbols,
    posture and gaze, communication boards and books, electronic and nonelectronic
    communication devices) that support students' active participation, learning, and
    communication in the general education curriculum, during typical school routines,
    and in the community

Understands the unique nature of communication by students who use augmentative and
    alternative communication and uses advanced assessment and problem-solving skills to
    enhance their interactions with others

Demonstrates awareness of appropriate seating, positioning, personal care, eating, and
    mobility principles, strategies, and equipment and collaborates with others to provide
    these supports to students

Collaborates with others to secure funding for augmentative communication and other
    learning aids and assures their optimal functioning through regular maintenance and
    service

Social relationships

Identifies barriers (e.g., attitudes, educational practices, communication supports,
    transportation) to the development of students' social relationships and develops
    strategies for avoiding and/or overcoming them

Facilitates interactions between students with disabilities and their age-appropriate
    classmates in order to develop, maintain, and enhance social and communicative
    relationships

Identifies opportunities and facilitates support for students' participation in typical extra-
    and co-curricular activities, based on students' interests and desires

Positive approaches to behavioral support

Understands the complex interrelationships among behavior, communication, and
    sensory and movement differences

Conducts comprehensive functional behavior assessments

Designs positive approaches to challenging behavior and supports teams to implement individualized student support plans

Evaluation of learning and communication outcomes

Develops meaningful documentation procedures to evaluate students' learning and communication skills and provides this information for general education and alternate assessment purposes

Evaluates educational programs in order to improve team collaboration, enhance the effectiveness of supports, and maximize student achievement

---

sion facilitators respect their colleagues' current understandings, validate their concerns and consider themselves to be fellow learners rather than experts who have all the answers.

When acting as a team leader, an inclusion facilitator's job is to help teams work effectively to design and implement practices that lead to quality inclusion and positive learning outcomes for students with significant disabilities. An inclusion facilitator believes in and models the values of inclusive education, has the skills to work with people who oftentimes hold very different sets of beliefs and experiences, and is knowledgeable about current and emerging practices that are effective in inclusive settings. An inclusion facilitator has strong leadership skills but understands that shared leadership and participatory decision making will be most effective over the long term.

DEFINITION, RATIONALE, AND CHARACTERISTICS OF COLLABORATIVE TEAMS

A *collaborative team* is a group of people who 1) coordinate their work to achieve at least one common goal, 2) hold a belief system that all members of the team have unique and needed expertise, 3) demonstrate parity by alternatively engaging in the dual roles of teacher and learner, 4) distribute leadership functions, and 5) employ a collaborative teaming process (Thousand & Villa, 2000). It is the most effective way for teachers and other professionals to work together to support the inclusion of students with significant disabilities. Collaborative teams empower the people closest to a student to make decisions that affect the student, family, and team members. Such teams are based on the maxim that "two heads are better than one" and the idea that student outcomes will be better when people representing diverse viewpoints and skills work together. Service delivery and supports to students are more efficient when everyone buys into decisions and is held accountable for tasks and outcomes.

Effective collaborative teams that work well together have the following characteristics: 1) the team is composed of people with the right constellation of skills related to each student's needs; 2) team members have the optimal level of skill in their profession; 3) team members have high-quality interpersonal and communication skills; 4) team members use effective structures and processes when they meet, such as a standardized agenda, distributed leadership, problem-solving strategies, consensus-building techniques, accountability structures, and conflict-resolution tools; and 5) the team periodically assesses its own effectiveness in relation to how well students are learning (Thousand & Villa, 2000).

Collaborative teams are not simply a group of people who sign the same individualized education program (IEP) once a year. They are complex social units that go through many phases of development, including stages of forming, functioning, formulating, and fermenting (Thousand & Villa, 2000). Teams in the *forming* stage are engaged in the initial trust building and role clarification needed to establish a collaborative team. Healthy teams then move into a second phase called *functioning*, in which members develop the communication and leadership skills that help manage and organize team activities so that tasks are completed and relationships are maintained. The third stage of team development, *formulating*, occurs when team members develop the skills needed to stimulate creative problem solving and decision making and to create deeper comprehension of unfamiliar information. The last stage of team development, *fermenting*, occurs when team members develop the skills needed to manage controversy and conflict, search for more information, and become reflective practitioners.

Table 4.2 depicts the activities that are characteristic of each stage of team development. The inclusion facilitator provides opportunities for teams to develop the skills that compose each level of team performance and helps teams be mindful of their own strengths and needs for improvement.

THE INCLUSION FACILITATOR'S ROLE AS A COLLABORATIVE TEAM LEADER

The inclusion facilitator is responsible for helping teams reach their optimal potential through advocating and modeling effective practices, facilitating decision making, coaching and mentoring other team members, and continuously promoting the team's professional development. The inclusion facilitator should assess each of his or her teams to answer the following questions:

Table 4.2.   Activities associated with different stages of team development

Forming	Establish group norms.
	Share background and philosophies.
	Socialize.
	Do "getting to know you" exercises.
	Read about collaborative teaming, and set team learning goals.
	Adopt meeting agenda and minutes format.
	Distribute leadership functions and roles.
Functioning	Run meetings efficiently within time limits.
	Read about collaborative teaming and problem-solving strategies.
	Complete peer–peer observations.
	Celebrate together.
	Attend workshops with other team members.
Formulating	Go to workshops on creative problem solving and teaming.
	Engage a consultant to do individualized training with teams.
	Seek feedback on personal communication skills.
	Evaluate team effectiveness, and develop a plan for improvement.
	Celebrate together.
Fermenting	Conduct miniseminars for team members in one's area of expertise.
	Seek training in conflict resolution.
	Celebrate together.
	Try new ways to work together.
	Mediate difficulties through an outside consultant or critical friend.
	Evaluate effectiveness and plan for improvement.

- Who are the members of this student's team? How are their roles and responsibilities articulated with respect to this student's educational program?

- What are the individual team members' professional skills relative to this student's needs?

- How well does this team work together to plan, implement, and evaluate the student's educational programs? How well do team members solve challenging problems? How do they deal with conflict or discord within the team?

- In what areas do team members need additional professional development relative to meeting this student's needs?

- What professional development does the whole team need in order to improve its work?

- What resources does this team need in order to provide the supports that the student needs?

- How does the team evaluate its own effectiveness relative to student performance (e.g., if the student performs poorly, have the right supports been offered)?

An inclusion facilitator engages in several information-gathering processes to answer these questions. First, he or she asks questions about team collaboration, roles, and the need for professional development as part of a team member interview (see the team member interview questions provided in Table 6.1 of Chapter 6). Second, with input from each team member, the inclusion facilitator develops a list of each person's role and responsibilities. Third and last, the inclusion facilitator observes team members as they work with students or with each other to identify the members' use of promising practices in instruction and collaborative teaming.

When the team's current skills are compared with the promising practices in collaborative teaming, both strengths and needs for improvement will be evident. The remainder of the chapter describes strategies and tools for supporting teams with respect to 1) role clarification, 2) team meeting structures and processes, 3) participatory decision making and problem solving, and 4) conflict resolution.

Role Clarification

General and special education staff who are members of a collaborative team share a number of common roles and responsibilities relative to a student's successful inclusion, including 1) creating a classroom environment in which all students are valued members and participate fully, 2) monitoring and evaluating student learning, 3) creating instructional and assessment materials, 4) developing and implementing student IEPs, 5) delivering student supports, 6) providing individualized instruction, 7) attending team meetings, and 8) engaging in continuous professional development to improve skills related to high-quality inclusive education.

In addition to these common responsibilities, team members have certain specialized roles (see Table 4.3 for a description of the specialized collaborative team roles of general education teachers, special education teachers, paraprofessionals, related-services providers, and administrators). An inclusion facilitator should consider all of these variables in making the decisions necessary to support a collaborative team. Finally, an inclusion facilitator should draft a

Table 4.3   Specialized roles within collaborative teams

General education teacher

Develops the structure of the class, including general education curriculum, discipline policy, physical layout, and materials

Plans major units of study

Plans daily lessons, activities, tests, assignments, and projects

Develops and implements instruction for all students in the class

Co-supervises paraprofessionals in the classroom

Assigns grades

Special education teacher

Provides modified materials for students with extraordinary learning needs (e.g., books on different reading levels, models, videos or audiobooks, modified tests, assistive technology)

Co-supervises paraprofessionals

Coordinates writing of individualized education programs (IEPs)

Coordinates comprehensive evaluations

Communicates with parents of students with disabilities

Co-teaches in the classroom during whole-class instruction

Provides small-group and one-to-one instruction

Paraprofessional

Follows classroom policies that are developed by the general education teacher

Carries out instructional plans and modifications developed by the team

Provides support in a way that promotes students' independence, interaction with other students, and overall membership in the classroom

Teaches the whole class, small groups, or individuals under the supervision of the classroom teacher

Facilitates direct conversation and interaction between students with and without disabilities

Prepares instructional materials under the direction of the classroom or special education teacher

Participates in team meetings

Related-services provider

Provides support to students with disabilities to enable them to participate in the general education curriculum

Writes goals and objectives that are directly related to learning and membership in the general education classroom

Participates in team meetings

Provides in-class support to enable students to better participate and learn in the general education classroom

Trains other staff to implement related-services goals to promote carryover and generalization

Works with small groups of students with and without disabilities

Uses a block-scheduling format to facilitate in-class service delivery

team role matrix that depicts each team member's role, modify it based on members' feedback, and then use the final matrix as a referent when there is confusion regarding any person's role on a particular student's team.

Team Meeting Structures and Processes

Effective meetings are those in which the right people are present, the meetings' purposes are clear, important information is shared, new ideas are discussed, problems are solved, and accountability to tasks and outcomes is monitored. Effective and efficient collaborative teams use a number of structures and processes for managing their meetings, including 1) being clear about the purpose of a meeting, 2) using a standardized agenda format, 3) distributing leadership roles among team members, and 4) using accountability structures for tasks and outcomes.

Meeting Purposes   An efficient team meeting starts with the right people being present for the purpose at hand. Some teams designate three different types of meetings with different members attending each. IEP meetings are formal legal gatherings that require the attendance of all team members, including the student (if middle-school age or older), parents or guardians, general and special education administrators, classroom teachers, special education teachers, related-services providers, and paraprofessionals. Case management meetings are often defined as meetings to discuss services, staff assignments, financial issues, or other administrative tasks and are attended by the inclusion facilitator, case manager, and/or special education teacher. Some schools designate different staff to fulfill the roles of case manager and special education teacher. In others, the same person fulfills both functions.

At instructional planning meetings, teams discuss upcoming lessons, instruction and assessment, materials and assistive technology, other student supports, and the roles of each team member within particular lessons or activities. The classroom teacher, inclusion facilitator, case manager and/or special education teacher, and paraprofessional typically attend these meetings. Related-services staff can attend these meetings on a periodic basis, particularly to discuss augmentative and alternative communication or any other assistive technology supports necessary for students to gain access to the general classroom environment and curriculum. No matter what the purpose, team meetings should be considered as sacred planning time to be interrupted only by true emergencies.

Standardized Agenda   A standardized team meeting agenda, which may be customized to suit each team's purposes and style, is provided in Appendix C. Regardless of the agenda format that is used, time needs to be carefully managed. Careful notes are taken for record keeping, communication, and accountability purposes, and to-do tasks are reviewed regularly.

Distributed Leadership Roles Even though an inclusion facilitator is the designated or assumed collaborative team leader, there is research to suggest that distributing leadership roles periodically improves effectiveness and efficiency and builds the skills of all team members (Thousand & Villa, 2000). The roles that are typically rotated include facilitator, recorder, and timekeeper.

Accountability Structures for Tasks and Outcomes Without an accountability structure, it is likely that many good ideas may never be implemented because of people's busy schedules and multiple responsibilities. Every team meeting should end with a review of the to-do list items, identifying the task to be completed, the name of a single individual who is responsible for making sure the task is completed, and a date by which the task will be completed. One of the easiest and most effective ways to assure that items on the to-do list are accomplished is for the inclusion facilitator to ask, "So, Cheryl, when will you be able to begin that task?" and for the team member to enter into a datebook a specific day and time when the task will be started as well as a notation of when it must be completed.

Participatory Decision Making and Problem Solving

To be effective, an inclusion facilitator must understand collaborative teaming processes, including how groups function and how different facilitation strategies can be used in the right situations. An inclusion facilitator must also be able to teach other team members the value of learning and using systematic collaborative teaming processes. Although there are many teaming and group work models, participatory decision making is a model that is particularly responsive to the characteristics and challenges of education teams and school culture (Kaner, 1996).

Participatory decision making, under the guidance of a skilled facilitator, has probably been used for thousands of years by native Americans and Alaskans and peoples in the Middle East, Far East, and Africa! Beginning in the 1960s, groups of people who were united for social changes (e.g., civil and women's rights, environmentalism) adopted participatory decision-making values and began to hone specific techniques and strategies for planning community and organizational change. Kaner (1996) characterized participatory decision making by four principles:

1. Full participation by everyone in the group

2. Commitment to building a shared framework of understanding

3. Work toward inclusive solutions

4. Shared responsibility for implementation

Today, varieties of participatory decision making are used by large, for-profit corporations to tap into the intellectual talents and energies of all their employees, as well as by local neighborhoods that want to improve their quality of life through health, education, environmental, safety, cultural, or housing initiatives. The school reform movement began to apply some of the lessons about change learned from the broader community and the business world by incorporating the work of Garmston and Wellman (1999), Kaner (1996), and Senge, Cambron-McCabe, Lucas, Smith, Dutton and Kleiner (2000) into their continuous improvement and professional development activities.

When schools use the principles of participatory decision making, every committee or team member participates, not just a vocal few. Members draw each other out with supportive questions such as "Is this what you mean?" and refrain from talking behind each other's backs. A problem is not considered solved until everyone who will be affected by the solution understands the reasoning behind the solution. Participatory decision making takes more time than conventional group decision making, but the hours of time originally spent are saved later by avoiding the misunderstandings, false assumptions, and hard feelings that often occur when a team is working at cross purposes (Kaner, 1996).

According to Kaner, in contrast to decision making by conventional groups and means,

> [Participatory] decision-making remains the best hope for solving difficult problems. There is no substitute for the wisdom that results from a successful integration of divergent points of view. Successful group decision-making requires a group to take advantage of the full range of experience and skills that reside in its membership. This means encouraging people to speak up. It means inviting difference, not fearing it. It means struggling to understand one another, especially in the face of the pressures and contradictions that typically drive group members to shut down. In short, it means operating from participatory values. (1996, p. xiii)

When inclusion facilitators model and teach these participatory values and use the tools associated with group decision making, more sustainable agreements are made, people enjoy working with one another, and, ultimately, students benefit from the improved productivity of their education teams.

Participatory Decision-Making Fundamentals for Inclusion Facilitators   The role of any facilitator is to support everyone to do his or her best thinking. If a school team has a talented, dedicated, and outspoken occupational therapist and a talented, dedicated, and quiet speech-language pathologist who never voices her opinion, that team may not operate to its greatest potential. If the task assigned to IEP teams was to simply share information, then a skilled facilitator might not be needed. If students with significant disabilities had educational issues that were easy to figure out, then teamwork would not be as essential.

Instead, the IEP team members have a challenging task in front of them. They must seek to understand how a student learns when he or she cannot communicate well. They must decide what is most important to teach him or her from among hundreds of possible general education and individualized learning goals. The team must reconcile the varied philosophies and histories of its team members and develop a sustainable agreement about how best to teach and support the student. It must continually integrate new information from research and practice into its working repertoire and engage people outside the team to actively support its work. Even the most congenial team members who have known each other and worked together for years often need someone to help them through these challenges.

To promote effective group functioning, Kaner (1996) suggested that facilitators need a set of fundamental and advanced skills related to building sustainable agreements. Fundamental facilitation skills include

- Listening

- Facilitating open discussions

- Using alternatives to open discussion

- Using chart-writing techniques

- Brainstorming

- Managing long lists

- Dealing with difficult dynamics

- Designing realistic agendas

Although each of these skills is important and will be used by inclusion facilitators in many different group situations, two merit more in-depth discussion: facilitating open discussion and dealing with difficult dynamics. These skills are then used to help teams reach sustainable agreements.

Facilitating Open Discussion   Facilitating open discussion is much more involved than simply posing a question or suggesting a topic and then waiting for everyone to weigh in on it. The facilitator's role is to monitor the speakers, ensure full participation, focus the discussion on topics of most interest, and decide when it would be helpful to switch to a different and more effective way of addressing a topic or issue (e.g., working in smaller groups or using a problem-solving technique; Kaner, 1996). Open discussion in team meetings is important because members often bring issues to the table that call for different perspectives.

When the goal of open discussion is for every team member to understand each other's viewpoint, a facilitator has several tools at his or her disposal. The first commonly used strategy is *stacking,* in which a facilitator explicitly determines the order in which people will speak by saying, "Debra, you go first, then Leigh, and then Jeff." This technique is particularly effective when one team member dominates the conversation by commenting after every other person speaks. This stacking technique communicates, "Everyone will have a turn, but people do have to wait a while before speaking again."

Another technique, called *using the clock,* encourages participation by everyone within a limited period of time. To employ this technique, the facilitator may say, "We have 10 minutes for everyone to weigh in on this issue, and then we'll need to move on to our next topic."

When a team is discussing complex issues such a student's challenging behavior, other techniques known as *calling for themes* and *reframing* can help the group begin to make sense of many streams of thought and prepare to do more convergent thinking. The facilitator might say, "Everyone has shared an anecdote about Philip's behavior from the classroom, the cafeteria, the playground, and the bus. What themes do you hear coming up again and again?" After listening to a few suggested themes, the facilitator might then reframe the conversation by saying, "Now that we have all shared our stories and talked about our theories about why Philip is having such a tough time with transitions, let's go back to our original three questions: What does Philip seem to be communicating? Which of our supports seem to be working well? and What other messages might we put on his communication device to enable him to communicate more effectively in those situations?"

Dealing with Difficult Dynamics   It may be more helpful for inclusion facilitators to view troublesome meetings as representing difficult dynamics rather than involving difficult people (Kaner, 1996). When one person on a team becomes viewed as being difficult, polarization occurs and the inclusion facilitator spends time and energy trying to figure out how to silence that person rather than thinking about how the team could work more effectively.

When difficult dynamics arise, it is almost always a result of the team not having established norms for communication and meeting processes. The three most typical difficult situations would include those in which 1) one individual dominates the discussion, 2) one individual becomes strident in his or her views and is not willing to compromise a position, or 3) one of more people are lax about following through on assignments. All of these situations can be addressed through improved initial agreements about how the team will communicate in meetings, how agendas will be developed and followed, and how decisions will be made.

Even when agreements and norms have been reached, teams may encounter problems on occasion. For example, one person might dominate a particular conversation. An effective facilitation technique in this situation is for the facilitator to invite participation from others who are not talking instead of merely asking that person to stop speaking or announcing that his or her time is up. Likewise, when two people in a group are carrying on a lengthy back-and-forth debate, the facilitator's most effective intervention is to invite others to weigh in on that same issue. If one group member becomes strident about a point of view or issue—refusing to give up his or her advocacy stance—the facilitator's job is to ensure that the person feels heard by each member of the group and to ask the group to step back from the situation and review its previously agreed-on rules for making decisions (Kaner, 1996).

How to Reach Sustainable Agreements   Inclusion facilitators need to know how to coach and support diverse team members to build sustainable agreements. Kaner (1996) suggested that facilitators need five skills to reach this goal, which include the ability to

1.   Gather diverse points of view

2.   Build a shared framework of understanding

3. Develop inclusive solutions

4. Strive toward unanimity

5. Reach closure

Gather Diverse Points of View   During the first stages of group decision making, open discussion is often an effective means of drawing out all of the members' viewpoints. This stage of divergent thinking is necessary and avoids moving too quickly or thoughtlessly into a solution that might not be fully supported by all team members. Once a problem has been well described, members' individual viewpoints shared, and possible solutions generated, however, one of two things generally happens. In the rare instance in which everyone agrees with one possible solution, the team then moves to planning the action steps associated with that solution. Although this scenario describes the ideal, it is much more likely that differences of opinion will surface and the group will struggle a bit toward unanimity and closure. This is the situation in which an inclusion facilitator's help is most needed.

Build a Shared Framework of Understanding   As a collaborative team leader, an inclusion facilitator's job during this period of struggle and confusion is to help team members create a shared context that leads to greater understanding and to strengthen interpersonal relationships on the team. For example, if one team member thinks that a student needs to go outside the general education class to receive instruction because the student is too distracted in the classroom and another team member has seen the student working productively in the classroom, then these individuals need to experience and understand the context within which these opinions were formed and are being held. The inclusion facilitator has several tools at his or her disposal to promote shared context. One way to share another person's context is to role-play being that person. Kaner (1996) called this the *If I Were You* activity. In this activity, the inclusion facilitator suggests a starter sentence, such as "If I were you, I would think that a legitimate reason for pulling a student out of class is . . ." or "If I were you, I would think that the most important rationale for inclusion is . . ." Taking turns, each person in the group looks to a colleague and completes the starter sentence. After the first person finishes the sentence, the person being addressed either agrees with, clarifies, expands, or corrects the statement. This process continues with the whole team. At the end

of the activity, the facilitator asks questions that continue to promote shared understanding, such as "How do our perceptions of one
another's viewpoints influence our work together?" and "How
might we avoid reading one another incorrectly?"

Develop Inclusive Solutions   After team members have a
shared understanding of the issues and perspectives of other team
members, the inclusion facilitator coaches the team to focus on
needs instead of positions or solutions. This strategy is central to
mediation and conflict resolution and can be very helpful when an
argument seems to be going around in circles (Fisher & Ury, 1983).
In this situation, one team member may say, "John really needs to
leave the classroom when he begins to make noise," to which
another member may respond, "We need to support John to stay in
the classroom." The facilitator should coach these individuals to
list their needs pertaining to this situation. Once the individuals
articulate needs such as 1) a learning environment in which students can concentrate well enough to do their work, 2) a classroom
in which every child feels welcome, 3) a means for John to communicate his needs more effectively, and 4) a way for a particular classroom teacher to signal that she needs more help during a stressful
time, then the inclusion facilitator can help the group design a solution that meets this broad range of needs (Kaner, 1996).

Strive Toward Unanimity   After team members have explored
an issue and are sure that they understand one another's points of
view, the inclusion facilitator's job is to support them to explore
possible solutions and develop a sustainable solution to the problem. When those solutions are elusive, teams need to think "outside of the box" and come up with creative solutions that meet
most people's needs. Kaner (1996, p. 187) listed several "out-of-the-
box" solutions that should be explored by inclusion facilitators
when teams get stuck. These include

- Creating more interdependence between the alternatives (e.g.,
  you cut and I choose)

- Shifting from solutions to needs

- Questioning ideas that have been labeled impossible

- Dividing a problem into independent parts and solving each separately

- Searching for resources from unusual sources

- Finding out how others have solved a similar problem

- Challenging fixed assumptions about the ways things have always been done

- Negotiating for more time

One strategy that has been very useful in the inclusive education field is examining case studies to learn how others have developed novel solutions to similar problems. Although the particular solutions developed by others may not offer the exact prescription needed for a school, an inclusion facilitator can coach team members to analyze how others have creatively reframed their problem or designed creative solutions. When team members take a break from thinking about their own dilemma to read about and discuss successful solutions found by others, their own creativity may be primed for returning to their problem with a fresh perspective (Kaner, 1996).

Once a proposed solution is on the table, many teams do not have explicit rules for deciding whether they will adopt the solution or idea. Kaner suggested that groups use a gradient of agreement scale for testing group support for a proposal. Table 4.4 describes the six points on this scale and what they mean. The degree of support for a proposed solution or idea determines whether the inclusion facilitator supports the group to keep wrestling with the issue until greater agreement is reached. The need for enthusiastic support is affected by many factors, including whether the stakes are so high that the consequence of failure would be dangerous, the reversibility of a decision, the number of people who will be affected by the decision, and the dedication required of group members to implement the decision (Nutt, 1992). For example, if a proposal about the color of the tablecloth for the holiday party does not have strong support, the consequences may be minor if an unpopular decision is implemented. In contrast, if a pro-

Table 4.4. Levels of agreement among team members

1. I can say an unqualified yes to the accuracy of this information.
2. I find the summary of the information acceptable.
3. I can live with the summary of this information, but I'm not enthusiastic about it.
4. I do not fully agree with the summary of this information and need to register my view about it. I do not, however, choose to block the process. I am willing to support the team's acceptance of this information because I trust the wisdom of the group.
5. I do not agree with the summary of this information and cannot support moving forward until greater agreement is reached.
6. I feel that we have no clear sense of unity in the group. We need to do more work before consensus can be reached.

Source: Kaner (1996).

posal about restructuring job descriptions does not have strong support but is implemented, the consequences might be disastrous.

Reach Closure   Finally, productive group decision making ends when five steps have been completed:

1. The discussion has ended.

2. The proposal has been stated.

3. Team members have been polled.

4. The group's decision-making rule has been used to reach a final decision.

5. The action plan that has been developed specifies responsibilities and timelines for implementing the decision.

The final decision can be made by a particular level of agreement, by a majority vote, by a person in charge, or even by a flip of a coin! The group must acknowledge how the final decision will be made. In some cases the group itself can set its own decision rule and in other cases someone higher up on the organizational hierarchy may make the decision by fiat.

Conflict Resolution

Few teams operate smoothly without occasional conflict, and manageable conflict within teams can lead to new learning and growth. When conflict gets in the way of providing a quality education to a student or destroys personal relationships, however, intervention is necessary. Team dynamics that can be disruptive include 1) entrenched communication habits such as interrupting, bullying, or monopolizing; 2) the development of team subgroups that sabotage team decisions; and 3) conflicts that go unresolved.

Effective Communication Skills   An inclusion facilitator needs to support his or her teams to set group norms for communication, model effective communication, and coach individuals who have difficulty learning and using the skills. Table 4.5 depicts skills and tasks that assist effective communication. An inclusion facilitator can create opportunities for team members to use and practice the skills described in Table 4.5 by such means as 1) promoting self-reflection through diaries or journals, 2) using outside observers to give feedback, 3) creating audio- or videotapes that can be reviewed, 4) setting individual behavioral goals, and 5) rotating group roles frequently.

Table 4.5.   Communication skills and task functions

Communication skills
Paraphrasing
Describing others' behaviors
Listening actively and reflectively
Using inviting body language
Checking impressions
Maintaining eye contact
Criticizing ideas, not people
Never interrupting
Respecting others' contributions

Task functions
Initiating
Seeking opinions
Clarifying
Summarizing
Reaching a consensus

When individual team members persist in using ineffective or disruptive communication methods, an inclusion facilitator has some choices about how to handle the situation. He or she can simply ignore a particular behavior and hope that it will diminish if it does not get the desired reaction. Alternatively, the inclusion facilitator can use humor to deflect the ineffective or inappropriate communication; can speak with the individual in private and coach him or her into improved communication; or, as a last resort, can ask an administrator to mediate with the team.

Principled Negotiation   Conflict resolution is a participatory problem-solving process in which the goal is *both/and solutions* rather than *either/or solutions* (Fisher & Ury, 1983). When there are differences of opinion on a team, two or more people may enter into negotiation with one another to advocate for their own point of view. *Negotiation* is back-and-forth communication designed to reach an agreement when two sides have some interests that are shared and others that are opposed. Although negotiation takes place every day, it is not easy to do well. Standard strategies for negotiation often leave people dissatisfied, worn out, or alienated— and frequently all three.

Table 4.6 depicts a fairly common stalemate that occurs when one person on a team wants a student included and the other disagrees. In this scenario, the special educator is arguing for inclusion, the classroom teacher is resistant, and neither side is really listen-

Table 4.6. Sample inclusion debate

Inclusion facilitator says...	Classroom teacher says...
We'd like Jason to be fully included in your fifth-grade class all day long.	I can't imagine how he could benefit from the fifth-grade curriculum.
He needs to feel a sense of belonging. We can figure out how he can participate in all of your lessons and what his priority learning objectives are.	There might be some times of the day, like when we have buddy reading, when he could come in for a little while.
I think we need to be careful about partial inclusion. What message does that give students about the value of students with differences?	I'm not so concerned about the messages that we give kids but rather what it is that they learn. I just can't see how he could benefit when I can't even understand what he says.
There are many benefits to Jason being in your class. A sense of belonging, learning to interact with classmates in an appropriate way, opportunities for Jason to practice his communication skills in real-life situations, and so forth.	Wouldn't he just be better off working on the kinds of skills he'll need once he gets to be an adult, like getting dressed in the morning, cooking, doing his laundry, and so forth?

ing to the other. From all outward appearances, they have no common interests; the chances for them to come to some mutually agreeable decision or plan seem remote. The scenario represents the most common form of negotiation: *positional bargaining*. This type of negotiation is generally ineffective because it fails to meet the three criteria of effective negotiation:

1. The process should produce a wise agreement if agreement is possible.

2. The process should be efficient in terms of time and effort.

3. The process and outcome should improve or at least not damage the relationship between the parties.

As more attention is paid to each party's position, less attention is devoted to meeting each person's underlying concern. Under these circumstances, agreement becomes less likely. Any agreement reached under these circumstances may reflect a mechanical splitting of the difference between the final positions rather than a solution carefully crafted to meet the legitimate interests of the parties.

This kind of negotiation takes a lot of time and actually creates incentives that stall settlement. People start at extreme positions, hoping that frustration or boredom will bring the other party closer to their bottom-line position. Ultimately, this type of negotiation becomes a contest of will. Anger and resentment build up. The chance for an agreeable settlement is small.

The alternative to positional bargaining is principled negotiation. *Principled negotiation* calls on teams to decide issues on their merits rather than through a haggling process focused on what each side says it will and will not do. It suggests that teams 1) separate the people from the problem; 2) focus on interests, not positions; 3) generate a variety of possibilities before deciding what to do; and 4) base the final solution on some objective standard. The steps in principled negotiation are described next.

Understand the People Involved   An effective inclusion facilitator understands that all parties to a negotiation are people first. This means that they have emotions, deeply held values, experiences, and interests that may conflict with their desire or ability to come to an agreement. Most negotiators have two interests: the substance and the relationship. Because most negotiations take place within an ongoing relationship, it is important to carry on each negotiation in a way that will help rather than hinder future relations and future negotiations.

If the primary problem between the negotiators is their relationship, then the skilled inclusion facilitator will deal directly with the people problem and not naively think that the disagreement is simply about the substance of the issue. In a situation in which the problem is mostly about the individuals' relationship, their feelings may be more important than what is said. The inclusion facilitator should acknowledge the individuals' feelings, allow them to let off steam, and refuse to overreact to emotional outbursts.

Reconcile Interests, Not Positions   By the time people are in a negotiation, they may have clearly stated their positions but perhaps not so clearly stated their interests. In the example depicted in Table 4.6, for example, the inclusion facilitator's interest may be for the student with disabilities to feel a sense of belonging with his classmates. The classroom teacher's primary interest may be knowing the academic goals of the student in her classroom and her responsibility to help the student achieve those goals. An effective inclusion facilitator should ask about each person's interests and gently guide team members to separate their interests from their positions.

Brainstorm Options for Mutual Gain   People involved in a dispute usually feel that they already know the right answer, yet a key to arriving at a mutually satisfying solution is the ability to generate and consider many possible solutions. Here is where the leadership and experience of the inclusion facilitator can help by con-

Table 4.7. Possible criteria for measuring the impact of a negoti-
ated solution to a conflict about inclusive education

Student's performance on assessment tests, reading tests, and
   observational measures
Student's acquisition of skills and knowledge
Student's increased time spent with kids without disabilities
Student's increased ability to follow classroom routines and rules
Student's improved health
Student's increased participation in class
Efficiency of time, space, staff, and effort
Cost–benefit ratio
Nondiscrimination or equal treatment
Following the requirements of federal, state, or local laws,
   policies, or regulations
Following a generally accepted moral standard
Following or supporting a school's mission statement
Following precedent
Following tradition
Following a practice supported by the professional research
Following professional standards
Following what a court would decide

vincing the opposing sides to separate brainstorming from decision making and persuading them to use techniques that expand the options under consideration. Team members may need strong leadership from the inclusion facilitator to move beyond their individual interests to make a list of common or shared interests.

When the parties are ready to articulate their proposed solutions, the role of an inclusion facilitator is to suggest that agreements other than "all or none" scenarios are possible. For example, each party may get some of his or her interests met in a particular solution. Alternatively, the parties might try a particular solution for a predetermined period of time, gather data on its impact, and return to the table to reconsider the original decision.

Determine Objective Criteria   The last step in the principled negotiation process is for the parties to establish objective criteria by which the final decision will be evaluated. They might choose from among the criteria depicted in Table 4.7.

CONCLUSION

Milton Olson wrote a short parable called "A Lesson from the Geese" that speaks to the power of teams in making a difference:

As each bird flaps its wings, it creates an uplift for the bird following. By flying in a "V" formation, the whole flock adds 71% flying range than if each bird flew alone. Lesson: People who share a common direction and sense of community can get where they are going quicker and easier because they are traveling on the thrust of one another. (1988)

Olson's parable is a powerful reminder that as a team leader, an inclusion facilitator has not only personal professional knowledge and resources to draw on but also the knowledge and resources of his or her teammates.

REFERENCES

Fisher, R., & Ury, W. (1983). *Getting to yes: Negotiating agreement without giving in.* New York: Penguin Books.

Garmston, R., & Wellman, B. (1999). *The adaptive school: A sourcebook for developing collaborative groups.* Norwood, MA: Christopher-Gordon Publishers.

Kaner, S. (1996). *Facilitator's guide to participatory decision-making.* Gabriola Island, Canada: New Society Publishers.

Nutt, P. (1992). Types of tough decisions and processes to deal with them. *The Review of Business Studies, 1*(2), 85–110.

Olson, M. (1988, November). A lesson from the geese. *Nebraska Synod (ELCCA) Update.*

Senge, P., Cambron-McCabe, N., Lucas, R.T., Smith, B., Dutton, J., & Kleiner, A. (2000). *Schools that learn: A fifth discipline fieldbook for educators, parents, and everyone who cares about education.* New York: Doubleday.

Thousand, J.S., & Villa, R.A. (2000). Collaborative teaming: A powerful tool in school restructuring. In R.A. Villa & J.S. Thousand (Eds.), *Restructuring for caring and effective education: Piecing the puzzle together* (2nd ed., pp. 73–108). Baltimore: Paul H. Brookes Publishing Co.

Facilitating
Student Relationships
Fostering Class Membership and Social Connections
Cheryl M. Jorgensen

Once the strong collaborative teams discussed in Chapter 4 are in place, an inclusion facilitator can turn his or her attention to helping the teams plan, implement, and evaluate high-quality, inclusive educational programs for students with disabilities. Many special education textbooks and curriculum guides recommend that the first step is to conduct a comprehensive assessment of students' current levels of performance, incorporating information from past evaluations. This book proposes a very different place to start, suggesting instead that the first step should be to enhance students' social relationships within the classroom, school, and community. Unless students are included and have friends, the best individualized education programs in the world will not lead to desired quality-of-life outcomes for the students.

Social relationships contribute to a good quality of life for students with disabilities in many ways. Having friends confirms a person's sense of belonging and is a necessary foundation for the achievement of self-actualization (Maslow, 1954). People with disabilities who do not have friends are lonely, isolated, and less likely to be a part of the community. To imagine that people with disabilities could have a full life surrounded only by professionals is to categorize people with disabilities as "others" rather than to understand their common humanity. We need only plot our own circle of friends

Preparation of this chapter was supported in part by a grant from the U.S. Department of Education, Office of Special Education Programs, #H324M020067.

to realize how empty our lives would be if we only interacted with our dentist, our doctor, our plumber, and our boss! For school-age students in particular, membership in a social group defines whether children are accepted or marginalized.

In her study of American high school students, Chang found that

> An individual's social status was often determined on the basis of clique affiliation, types and degrees of involvement in activities, appearance, and academic performance. . . . [P]opular cliques included . . . athletes, brains, pretty faces, and good bodies, who tended to be "high" class. Those classified as "unpopular" included smokers, [the tough kids], and special education students, who were often regarded as "low" class people. (1984, p. 169)

Supporting students to develop social relationships forces educators to go to the heart of the meaning of inclusion. Carol Tashie, a former project director with the Institute on Disability at the University of New Hampshire, used to say that a person could distinguish between a noninclusive school and an inclusive one when students with disabilities were "with" their classmates, not simply "in" a regular class (C. Tashie, personal communication).

ESSENTIAL CONSIDERATIONS FOR FRIENDSHIP

The best way to support a student's development of a wide circle of social relationships is not to announce on the first day of school, "Jamie needs friends. Who wants to volunteer?" Instead, the important thing is to ensure that the essential considerations for friendship development are solidly in place.

Martin, Jorgensen, and Klein (1998) defined seven essential conditions for friendship: 1) fully including students in a heterogeneous general education class, 2) providing students with a means to communicate all of the time, 3) providing support in a way that encourages interdependence and independence, 4) involving students in problem solving to remove barriers to social relationships, 5) giving students access to age-appropriate materials and activities, 6) forging a partnership between home and school to facilitate friendships and participation in social activities, and 7) addressing the climate of the whole school with respect to diversity. A possible eighth essential prerequisite for encouraging students with disabilities to make friendships is to treat all students as if they are competent. Unless these eight conditions are met, the facilitation of social relationships will not be addressed or will take on a low priority within the team, and there is a real risk that the relationships between students with and without disabilities will be based on benevolence rather than equity (Kunc, 1992). Each of these conditions makes a unique contribution to a student's membership; if each is not present, the chance that friendships will develop is significantly decreased.

Fully Including Students in a Heterogeneous General Education Class

Imagine that you work for the Acme Widget Company. There are 100 employees in your building, located on four floors of the company's headquarters. You, however, are not assigned to marketing widgets but rather to marketing gizmos. Your boss tells you that marketing gizmos is an honorable profession and that you are a valued employee.

When the marketing team meets on Monday morning to talk about the latest widget advertising campaigns, you are in your basement office thinking about how to get people to buy your gizmos. When you come up to the employee lounge for a coffee break, everyone is talking about the new widget marketing strategy, but you cannot really contribute because you were not part of that discussion. They have a laugh over a mistake that the team leader made when giving her report, and you laugh along just so that you will not stand out. When you strike up a conversation with a co-worker about the latest gizmo you are working on, she looks at you blankly, says, "Good job, Henry. Sounds like you are really going to town on those gizmos," but then turns to another colleague and continues the widget discussion.

At lunchtime, you go through the line to get your meal and look around for someone to sit with. The widget teams are scattered throughout the lunchroom, and you join the nearest table. During lunch, the talk is of people's home lives, families, romances, and the baseball game that the widget team went to last weekend. You jump into the conversation to share a story about the softball game in which you played as a member of the Special Gizmo Softball League, but because the widget makers were not at the game, your vivid description of the great catch you made falls flat.

At the company's annual banquet, the president shows slides of the company profits that have soared because of the hard work of the widget teams. Toward the end of the evening, you are called up to the podium and receive an award for most-improved gizmo marketer. The audience applauds, but somehow the praise is hollow.

This not-so-funny scenario parallels what happens to students with disabilities when they are only partially included in the mainstream of general education, working on different goals, pursuing different leisure activities, and not sharing in the hidden curriculum that provides students with the opportunity to learn what it really takes to become a regular kid in the school (Apple, 1979). Because students do not feel part of the class and have fewer common learning and social experiences with their classmates, they are outsiders for all intents and purposes.

Conversely, when students with disabilities are full-time members of general education classes and typical school social activities, they have a common set of experiences on which to base not only conversations but also relationships. The role of the inclusion facilitator is to teach others that students' social relationships are as valuable as their learning of math or history (Strully & Strully, 1996).

Jeff Strully (2003) illustrated how the importance of social relationships grows with each passing year when he shared his worries as a parent of a young adult with significant disabilities:

> I'm 55 years old now, and Shawntell is 31. When I wake up in the middle of the night, wondering what will happen to Shawn when I am no longer here, I don't say to myself, "If only I had taught Shawn to tie her shoes. If only she had learned to read or balance her checkbook." I worry, "What if Shawn is lonely? What if she has to live in a group home with a bunch of strangers? What if she no longer sees the friends she has made who live all over the U.S.?" Then I realize what I need to spend my energy on . . . helping Shawn become fully a part of her community and building a network of friends and acquaintances who will be there even when I am gone.

Providing Students with a Means to Communicate All of the Time

When students with disabilities have a means to communicate, they are more likely to gain a wide variety of social relationships that last over time. Although Mark's story does not have a happy ending, it is an excellent illustration of this reality. Mark was a high school student with significant disabilities who had been in self-contained classrooms throughout his school career. After attending a conference on inclusive education, his team worked hard to include him in the mainstream of the general education classroom, but without a means to communicate, his participation was limited to tasks such as setting up the science equipment, doing ready-made art projects, listening during lectures and small-group discussions, and being an observer most of the time. After the team introduced facilitated communication to him, he soon began communicating about the subject matter being taught, social topics, and his feelings.

One of Mark's friends related the change that he saw in Mark once he began communicating in a more conventional way. He said, "This year I have finally noticed a huge change in Mark's personality. He has become a lot calmer and a lot easier to talk to. Some of the best times of my life are . . . just talking to him one on one."

With Mark's expanding communication, his behavior improved radically. He stopped hurting himself and scratching others. He began participating more in his classes. He even went on a 5-day trip with several other boys and teachers to present at a national conference on inclusive education. At the conference hotel, the boys stayed up late ordering room service and watching forbidden movies on the pay-per-view channel.

Unfortunately, Mark's emergence as a communicator did not last. During the mid-1990s, some researchers in the fields of special education and augmentative communication challenged the authenticity of facilitated communication (Biklen & Cardinal, 1997). Administrators in local school districts were put in a very difficult position. On one hand, they knew that many of their students had experienced success with it; in Mark's case, for example, the improvements in his learning, behavior, and social connections were dramatic. On the other hand, they were worried about the possible legal ramifications of using an educational method that did not have the sanction of the professional organizations that licensed or certified their staff. A decision was made to explore other augmentative communication methods (that did not work out so well in Mark's situation) instead of providing Mark with the level of physical support he had been receiving. After Mark's behavior worsened, rules were put into place that kept him away from close contact with other students. Not surprisingly, his social relationships suffered.

The purpose of telling Mark's story is not to blame Mark's school, for it could have faced serious legal and even financial problems if the school's administrators had chosen to go against the recommendations of respected professional organizations. The story is meant instead to illustrate how important communication is to students with disabilities.

Providing Support in a Way that
Encourages Interdependence and Independence

Although most students with significant disabilities require specialized support from an adult at some point throughout their day,
a commitment to relying first on natural supports brings students
together. Martin et al. (1998) provided numerous examples of effective natural peer and adult supports for 10 different types of activities, including transitions, teacher-directed lessons, cooperative
group activities, individual seatwork, personal hygiene routines,
and extracurricular activities.

An inclusion facilitator must be vigilant about the balance between specialized and natural supports. An inclusion facilitator can
assess the natural opportunities for student interactions throughout
the day and then work with a student's team to plan for capitalizing
on those opportunities. Sometimes, all that needs to be done is to
instruct the paraprofessional to back away from the student to offer
him or her the chance to do the activity independently or to make
room for another student to assist.

Criteria for using natural supports in a way that is respectful of
all students include 1) honor the students' preferences about the
nature of the support, 2) ensure that students with disabilities have
opportunities for relating to other students outside of formal peer–
support relationships, 3) arrange for students with disabilities to
have opportunities to provide support to students without disabilities, and 4) judge the success of inclusion not only by academic
gains but also by an increase in the number of friends in the students' lives.

Involving Students in Problem Solving
to Remove Barriers to Social Relationships

When students themselves are empowered and supported to address
the barriers to friendship that exist for students with significant disabilities, they are more likely to own the solutions that they
develop than if the ideas come from adults. There are two different
ways that inclusion facilitators can promote this essential consideration for friendship. First, an inclusion facilitator can identify
existing groups or organizations in the school that focus on connecting students and breaking down barriers to belonging.

For example, the inclusion facilitator who supported one student, Philip, spoke to the advisor of Philip's high school Key Club

and found out that club members spent much of their weekly meeting time talking about issues of race, gender, sexual orientation, class, war, and peace in addition to discussing the group's community service activities. The inclusion facilitator encouraged Philip to join the club, and after several meetings in which the inclusion facilitator stayed to provide support, the club advisor confided that the other students had asked that Philip be allowed to attend meetings alone. During the years that Philip was a member, the club continued its volunteer activities but expanded its role in the school to include advocating for social justice issues. The club sponsored presentations by activists on a variety of topics, and Philip developed long-term friendships with several of the other club members.

The other tool that has been used to intentionally facilitate social relationships is the establishment of a "circle of friends" specifically around the student with significant disabilities (Forest, Pearpoint, & O'Brien, 1996). A *circle* is a group of people who are invited to get to know a student who is not yet connected in a meaningful way. The invitation that is extended is not, "Would you please become friends with Katherine?" but rather, "Would you like to join a group of people who are going to meet with Katherine to figure out how to get her more connected to this school?"

Marsha Forest described her own journey with her friend Judith Snow as an example of what can happen when people come together to help someone in need (Perske & Perske, 1990). Judith was a well-respected disability advocate from Canada who traveled all over the world to talk about what it would take for communities to welcome all their citizens. Through her own story, Judith delivered a powerful message about accepting all people's gifts and talents, rejecting the notion that people with disabilities are broken and need to be fixed. Ironically, Judith herself lived in a nursing home for seniors and other people with disabilities. She rarely got out in the community to socialize except when she was being paid as an expert in inclusive community living! She struggled every day to receive dignified care, and her health was in a precarious state several times because of misdiagnoses or mistreatment of a variety of health-related problems.

Under Marsha's guidance, Judith's friends came together to form a circle around her that literally saved her life. In the beginning, members of the circle took over Judith's around-the-clock care, nursing her back to physical and psychological health. Then, they worked with Judith to plan for her to leave the nursing home and live instead in the community. The group demonstrated that people who have been marginalized sometimes need others to create an intentional community around them.

This notion of a circle of support or friendship can be applied to school-age students, too. Donny was a 9-year-old boy with significant learning, physical, and behavioral disabilities. When he returned from a segregated facility to a fourth-grade class in his neighborhood school, a group of children were invited to become part of "Donny's team." Donny's team met at his house every Thursday after school to sit around and talk, snack, and play computer games together. Donny's inclusion facilitator, Sue, provided support to the kids as they tackled issues such as Donny's difficulty in participating in physical education class and his loneliness on weekends.

During one of these meetings, Sue asked the kids to talk about what they thought was standing in the way of Donny being just a regular kid in their school. Not surprisingly, none of the kids talked about Donny's disabilities. They did point out, however, that because Donny rode the special education bus, he arrived later than his whole class, he had a hard time settling into the classroom routine because he did not hear morning announcements, and he missed a 15-minute free time period at the end of the day because his bus came early. When Sue told the kids that the people who decided which bus Donny should ride were the special education director and the head of the bus company, they wrote letters to both people asking that Donny be allowed to ride a regular bus. Sue followed up to schedule a meeting with the decision makers to address this issue. When five classmates from Donny's team turned up at the meeting to discuss what supports Donny would need in order to make the switch, the attitudes of the special education director and head of the bus company softened, and they worked out a solution that addressed Donny's situation.

The role of the inclusion facilitator in facilitating a circle of support is to 1) work with the student and his or her family to issue the initial invitation to other students; 2) support the group's organizational needs such as transportation, parent permissions, and an accessible meeting location; 3) overcome any barriers that stand in the way of the student's inclusion and development of social relationships; and 4) help the group confront attitudes that stand in the way of friendship, such as peer pressure, prejudice, benevolence, and pity.

Whether the students are 3, 10, or 21 years old, the presence of an adult facilitator increases the chances that the group will stay together. An adult facilitator can also help the group to form bonds that go well beyond the students' initial motivations of wanting to help someone they perceive as less fortunate than themselves.

Giving Students Access to
Age-Appropriate Materials and Activities

Susan was a student in a self-contained program run by a regional collaborative located in a local school. Although Susan was 16 years old, she came to school wearing pigtails, ankle socks, and a sweatshirt embroidered with Minnie Mouse. The only means Susan had of demonstrating choice and control over her environment was to push a one-button switch that played "The Wheels on the Bus Go Round and Round." Is it any wonder that teachers and students alike spoke to Susan as if she were a toddler? Their voice inflections raised when they spoke to her—some even tickled her—and everyone was very resistant to including Susan in typical age-appropriate classes and social activities.

Although this description sounds like a caricature, it is all too typical of students with significant disabilities who have attended segregated schools or who have not been around typical students. In Susan's case, the inclusion facilitator, Marty, met with Susan's mom, Marla, and shared with her some of the comments that Susan's classmates were making about her clothes and accessories. Marla was very invested in Susan's successful inclusion and invited a group of girls to her house over the weekend to help redecorate Susan's room.

The Disney posters on the walls were replaced with those of the latest boy band. The Fisher-Price tape recorder was given to Goodwill, and a new boom box blasted the boy band's current number-one hit. Although Marla did not have an unlimited budget, she did ask the girls if they would be willing to go on a shopping trip with Susan to help her pick out a couple of new outfits for school. Marla purchased several bottles of brightly colored nail polish, and the girls gave each other manicures.

Beneath the surface of this seemingly innocent activity was a strong message about belonging and membership. The girls who visited Susan were not saying that they were intolerant of Susan as a person but rather that they were welcoming her into their circle that was defined in part by similar clothes and interests.

Forging a Partnership Between Home and School to
Facilitate Friendships and Participation in Social Activities

The inclusion facilitator is the link between the student's family and the school community. Although this responsibility does not supersede the general education teacher's role, the inclusion facilitator must take an active role in working with families in order to promote the participation of students with disabilities in school-sponsored extracurricular activities and social events. Furthermore, the inclusion facilitator can provide support to families to carry over school-based friendships at home. Some families of students with disabilities do not create the same opportunities at home for friendships to develop. Some families have never invited classmates to their home, helped their child call a friend on the telephone, or hosted a sleepover. Because students with significant disabilities may need assistance to extend invitations to sleepovers or birthday parties, families may need to be more directive with their children who have disabilities than with their other children who are more able to manage their own social lives.

Many parents report that when their children are young, it feels natural for them to call other parents to extend invitations to a festive event. But once typical children begin to take over those responsibilities when they are around 8 or 9 years old, families are reluctant to maintain their involvement in the negotiations that go along with friendships. An inclusion facilitator can support families during this transition by providing assistance in the form of 1) sending home a list of classmates (with their parents' permission), 2) delivering written invitations to particular classmates, 3) providing some assistance at home to help support a child's social behavior, and 4) facilitating circle discussions that solicit students' ideas for solving any barriers to friendship.

Other team members may have valuable supports to offer as well, such as 1) the speech-language pathologist might program a student's augmentative communication device with social vocabulary and messages, 2) the occupational or physical therapist might visit a student's home to make suggestions for adaptations to games or backyard play equipment, or 3) the paraprofessional may have a particular talent such as arts and crafts or playing computer games and may be willing to spend an afternoon at a student's house when other classmates are there.

Addressing the Climate of the Whole School with Respect to Diversity

Traditional disability awareness days—in which students try to read with thick glasses or spin around in borrowed wheelchairs—have frequently made people more than a little uncomfortable. Viewing disability as a different kind of diversity does not necessarily promote creating a school culture in which all differences are celebrated. Fortunately, there are a myriad of ways that respect for diversity can be taught at school. First, the school staff ought to reflect racial, cultural, linguistic, gender, and sexual orientation diversities. Because most paraprofessionals who work with students with significant disabilities are women, for example, hiring men for this role demonstrates that they, too, are capable of carrying out nurturing and supportive roles. Second, schools that truly value diversity embed social justice and diversity issues within the curriculum. Particularly at the high school level, there are many opportunities within the curriculum to do this (Fisher, Sax, & Jorgensen, 1998). Table 5.1 depicts a sample of diversity themes and opportunities that exist within the curriculum. Third, schools can establish rituals and celebrations that honor diversity, such as Black History Month, Cinco de Mayo, and Kwanzaa.

Table 5.1.   Embedding diversity topics into the curriculum

Issue	Literature	History topics	Science topics
Racial diversity	*Black Like Me* (Griffin, 1961) *The Autobiography of Malcolm X* (X, 1966) *The Color Purple: A Novel* (Walker, 1982)	Civil War Civil Rights Movement Racial profiling	Heredity IQ testing Human performance research
Cultural diversity	*A Tree Grows in Brooklyn* (Smith, 1943) *'Tis: A Memoir* (McCourt, 1999) *The Spirit Catches You and You Fall Down: A Hmong Child, Her American Doctors, and the Collision of Two Cultures* (Fadiman, 1997) *Reading Lolita in Tehran: A Memoir in Books* (Nafisi, 2003)	Immigration policies USA PATRIOT Act of 2001 (PL 107-56) Native American history	Attitudes toward the medical aspects of disability felt or expressed by different cultural groups
Disability	*Of Mice and Men* (Steinbeck, 1937) *To Kill a Mockingbird* (Lee, 1960) *Don't Worry, He Won't Get Far on Foot: The Autobiography of a Dangerous Man* (Callahan, 1989) *No Pity* (Shapiro, 1993) *The Curious Incident of the Dog in the Night-time* (Haddon, 2003)	History of deinstitutionalization Americans with Disabilities Act of 1990 (PL 101-336) Self-advocacy movement	Cloning Prenatal testing Cochlear implants Limb lengthening surgery

Treating Students as If They Are Competent

The last essential condition for friendship is for staff to treat all students as if they are competent. This means engaging students in regular conversations about gifts and talents, the social meaning of disability, and the kinds of prejudice that can get in the way of students respecting one another for their differences as well as for their similarities. When students with disabilities are talked about in their presence as if they are not even there (i.e., staff members commenting about personal hygiene issues in front of other students or directing comments such as "Didn't Antonio do a great job on his birdhouse?" to others rather than to Antonio himself), a message is communicated that the students are unable to speak for themselves and perhaps are unaware that others are talking about them. When staff members use exaggerated praise or demand standards of behavior that are not typically required of other similar-age students (i.e., prompting a high school student, "Can you say 'good morning' to the principal, Antonio?"), a lack of respect for a student's identity and self-determination is communicated. In contrast, when teachers make the least dangerous assumption about students' abilities and treat all students as if they understand, this behavior is modeled by classmates and creates an opening for students to approach one another on a more equal footing. Finally, the use of such derogatory terms such as *retarded* or *low functioning* are antithetical to the notion that all students are competent. They should never be used to refer to a student with disabilities—or to anyone else!

CONCLUSION

Inclusion facilitators are in the position to enhance students' social relationships within the classroom, school, and community. They should not take this job lightly. Students will only be able to achieve desired quality-of-life outcomes when they are included and have friends.

REFERENCES

Americans with Disabilities Act of 1990, PL 101-336, 42 U.S.C. §§ 201 *et seq.*
Apple, M. (1979). *Ideology and curriculum.* Boston: Routledge & Kegan Paul.
Biklen, D., & Cardinal, D. (Eds.). (1997). *Contested words, contested science.* New York: Teachers College Press.
Callahan, J. (1989). *Don't worry, he won't get far on foot: The autobiography of a dangerous man.* New York: Morrow.

Chang, H. (1984). *Adolescent life and ethos: An ethnography of a U.S. high school.* London: Falmer Press.

Fadiman, A. (1997). *The spirit catches you and you fall down: A Hmong child, her American doctors, and the collision of two cultures.* New York: Farrar, Straus, and Giroux.

Fisher, D., Sax, C., & Jorgensen, C.M. (1998). Philosophical foundations of inclusive, restructuring schools. In C.M. Jorgensen, *Restructuring high schools for all students: Taking inclusion to the next level* (pp. 29–47). Baltimore: Paul H. Brookes Publishing Co.

Forest, M., Pearpoint, J., & O'Brien, J. (1996). MAPS, circles of friends, and PATH: Powerful tools to help build caring communities. In S. Stainback & W. Stainback (Eds.), *Inclusion: A guide for educators* (pp. 67–86). Baltimore: Paul H. Brookes Publishing Co.

Griffin, J.H. (1961). *Black like me.* Boston: Houghton Mifflin.

Haddon, M. (2003). *The curious incident of the dog in the night-time.* New York: Doubleday.

Kunc, N. (1992). The need to belong: Rediscovering Maslow's hierarchy of needs. In R.A. Villa, J.S. Thousand, W. Stainback, & S. Stainback, *Restructuring for caring and effective education: An administrative guide to creating heterogeneous schools* (pp. 25–39). Baltimore: Paul H. Brookes Publishing Co.

Lee, H. (1960). *To kill a mockingbird.* London: Heinemann.

Martin, J., Jorgensen, C.M., & Klein, J. (1998). The promise of friendship for students with disabilities. In C.M. Jorgensen, *Restructuring high schools for all students: Taking inclusion to the next level* (pp. 145–181). Baltimore: Paul H. Brookes Publishing Co.

Maslow, A. (1954). *Motivation and personality.* New York: HarperCollins.

McCourt, F. (1999). *'Tis: A memoir.* New York: Scribner.

Nafisi, A. (2003). *Reading Lolita in Tehran: A memoir in books.* New York: Random House.

Perske, R., & Perske, M. (1990). *Circles of friends: People with disabilities and their friends enrich the lives of each other.* Nashville: Abingdon Press.

Shapiro, J. (1993). *No pity.* New York: Times Books.

Smith, B. (1943). *A tree grows in Brooklyn.* New York: HarperCollins.

Steinbeck, J. (1937). *Of mice and men.* New York: Convici-Friede.

Strully, J. (2003, October). *Friendships.* Presentation given at a workshop for the New Hampshire Leadership Series, Hampton Falls, NH.

Strully, J., & Strully, C. (1996). Friendships as an educational goal: What we have learned and where we are headed. In W. Stainback & S. Stainback (Eds.), *Inclusion: A guide for educators* (pp. 141–154). Baltimore: Paul H. Brookes Publishing Co.

USA PATRIOT Act of 2001, PL 107-56, 18 U.S.C. §§ 1 *et seq.*

Walker, A. (1982). *The color purple: A novel.* New York: Harcourt.

X, M. (with Haley, A., 1966). *The autobiography of Malcolm X.* New York: Grove Press.

Reconsidering Assessment in Inclusive Education

Identifying Capacities and Challenges within Students, Teams, and Schools

Cheryl M. Jorgensen

Assessment of students, classrooms, teams, and school environments provides a foundation to develop students' inclusive educational programs and requires that an inclusion facilitator use skills related to the role of instructional team leader discussed in Chapter 4. For many inclusion facilitators, the current types and purposes of assessment have changed since they began working. Consider Tom's story.

Tom's Story

Tom O'Reilly is an elementary inclusion facilitator in a small school district in New Hampshire, where he has worked for the last 14 years. His undergraduate background is in communication disorders, and he has a master's degree in special education. Although his original training prepared him to teach students with significant disabilities who were in self-contained classrooms, his role has evolved over the years to that of a true inclusion facilitator. Today there are eight children with significant disabilities on his caseload—two at the preschool level and six in the district's two elementary schools. All are full-time members of general education classes.

When Tom first started teaching, his understanding of assessment was that it was done primarily for three reasons: to establish a student's eligibility for special education, to assign a disability label to a student, and to

Preparation of this chapter was supported in part by a grant from the U.S. Department of Education, Office of Special Education Programs, #H324M020067.

measure a student's current level of performance across many functional categories. When Tom ran a self-contained classroom, he conducted adaptive behavior assessments. The district's psychologist administered IQ tests; the speech-language pathologist did language and communication testing; the occupational therapist measured performance in tasks related to eating, sitting, and using writing instruments; the physical therapist measured gross motor skills such as range of motion, walking, strength, and coordination; and vision and hearing consultants evaluated students' sensory systems. Most of the assessments were done right in the classroom's kitchen, the gross motor area, the bathroom, and at work tables.

The assessment reports usually described what a student could and could not do and determined a level of functioning based on typical children's development. A small number of educational program priorities were identified and written as annual goals for the individualized education program (IEP). There were goals for cognition, gross and fine motor skills, leisure, behavior, and communication. Short-term objectives leading to the achievement of these goals were written in behavioral terms, with measurable criteria as evaluation benchmarks.

Today, the educational landscape is much different. Although Tom must still coordinate assessments for the purpose of determining eligibility for special education and for assigning a disability label, the whole assessment has a much different function relative to inclusive education.

INCLUSIVE ASSESSMENT

There are three main purposes of inclusive assessment: 1) to determine students' skills in academic, social, emotional, and functional skill domains; 2) to determine the constellation of supports and accommodations that students need in order to be successful learners within the general education curriculum; and 3) to determine what support and resources teams need in order to teach these students well. At major transitions in students' educational careers, inclusion facilitators lead teams to conduct comprehensive assessments of students, their education teams, their classrooms, and the broader school environment. These major transitions occur when students first enter public school, when they move to a new building, when they make the transition from self-contained to inclusive environments, as they move into the transition to adulthood (age 18–21), and as they prepare for graduation and leaving the public education system. At the beginning of every new school year, some of the assessments might be repeated or updated. Several kinds of assessment questions and tools used by inclusion facilitators are presented next.

Assessing Students

The purpose of student assessment is to explore a student's history, personality, learning style, strengths, and needs. Perhaps the most important caveat regarding initial student assessment is that educators must not draw conclusions about the student's current skills or potential for learning unless that student has an accurate and reliable means of communication (McSheehan, Sonnenmeier, & Jorgensen, 2002). With respect to this usage, *accuracy* means that a student's communication attempts reflect just what the student intends to communicate, and *reliability* means that a student's communication is consistent over time and is interpreted in the same way by different listeners or communication partners.

For many students with significant disabilities, the application of this rule means that teams will need to withhold judgment about students' capabilities for long periods of time—perhaps years— while many different communication methods and supports are explored. During these periods of exploration and uncertainty, inclusion facilitators must be careful to avoid the use of phrases such as "We know for sure . . ." or "This student will never . . ." because such predictions are often based on scanty or inconclusive evidence (Donnellan, 2000).

Questions that will be answered as a result of an initial student-focused assessment include

- Who is this student? What is his or her history? What are the student's dreams and goals? What are the hopes of his or her parents or guardians? What are the student's likes, dislikes, preferences, and learning style?

- What is this student's educational history? What goals have been focused on in past IEPs? What supports has the student received in the past?

- What does this student know, and what can he or she do? What does the student struggle with? What methods have been used to evaluate the student's learning?

- How does this student communicate, move, and react to the surrounding world with his or her senses?

- What is a typical day like in the life of this student at school and at home?

- What are priorities for learning this year? What supports might be explored to support this student's learning?

The inclusion facilitator coordinates several information-gathering processes that will help the team develop answers to these questions.

MAPS and PATH Beginning in the early 1970s, some people in human services began to use person-centered planning processes as a foundation to develop inclusive lives in the community for people with disabilities. This practice was expanded to school-age students beginning in the early 1980s by pioneers such as Marsha Forest, Jack Pearpoint, and John O'Brien (see Forest, Pearpoint, & O'Brien, 1996). The purpose of MAPS (making action plans) and PATH (planning alternative tomorrows with hope) is for all of the people who care about a student to come together to think about dreams and wishes, to recognize the student's unique gifts and struggles, to describe an ideal day in the student's life, and to make specific action plans regarding the supports that need to be in place to make the dreams a reality. A MAP or a PATH is not an IEP, but information from a MAP or a PATH can inform the development of a student's educational plan and related supports. It is the role of an inclusion facilitator to work with the student's family and other team members to conduct a MAP or a PATH planning session.

Cara's Story

Cara was a sixth-grade student whose family and team were experiencing uncertainty about what would be the best educational program for her as she moved on to middle school. Some people on the team felt that Cara would be better served in a specialized school for students with significant disabilities, and others felt that Cara belonged in her local middle school where she would learn valuable academic and life lessons by being around her classmates who did not have disabilities.

The school district's inclusion facilitator met with Cara's parents, and together they designed the agenda for a MAP meeting that would be attended by Cara, her sister, her parents, several friends of her parents, a couple of classmates, the school principal, and members of her IEP team. The inclusion facilitator knew that it was essential to have a variety of people in Cara's life attend this meeting, not just those who knew her in school. The minutes for Cara's MAP meeting are available on-line at http://www.brookespublishing.com/inclusionfacilitator.

At the conclusion of Cara's MAP meeting, the whole group came to the consensus that what Cara needed to meet her vision for the future was best met living at home with her family; going to her local middle school; and receiving supports in the areas of literacy, augmentative communication, and a positive behavioral support plan. The action plan specified that Cara's team needed to meet on a weekly basis during the school year to plan upcoming lessons and discuss the adaptations that would be necessary in order for Cara to participate and learn. Cara's team also decided that it needed the expertise of a statewide augmentative and alternative communication (AAC) consultant to help it design a more effective communication system for her. Finally, the group decided that Cara needed to have someone take a more active role in facilitating her social relationships, so her paraprofessional volunteered to work with Cara's mom on this important task.

For some students and their families, using the PATH process is more appropriate for supporting major transitions (e.g., from preschool to elementary school, from a segregated environment back into a neighborhood school, from school to adult life; Forest et al., 1996). PATH is a person-centered planning process that helps an individual and his or her family articulate a long-term vision for the person's life and then work backward to design a year's worth of action plans that will help the person make the upcoming transition.

Review of Records   A student assessment also involves a review of the student's records. The inclusion facilitator reviews the student's records to discover the student's educational history, goals from past IEPs, the kinds of support services that the student has had in the past, results of comprehensive evaluations, and most important, consistencies and inconsistencies in information or interventions across service providers. He or she then summarizes the salient points from the review of records and presents them to the team for its consideration as it develops the student's IEP, determines the need for additional assessments, and explores how its members might work effectively together to support the student's inclusion. The following summary statements and recommendations emerged from a review of 13-year-old Alicia's records. (The inclusion facilitator's personal notes are written in italics.)

1. The report of Alicia's IQ score was accompanied by a strong caution not to take this number as an indicator of Alicia's full learning potential. It also cautioned that the results of her IQ test were undoubtedly influenced by Alicia's communication difficulties and attention. *It might be prudent to repeat this cautionary warning on Alicia's IEP so that future teachers can put Alicia's label of mental retardation into perspective.*

2. The psychoeducational evaluation did not generate any sugges-
    tions for instruction based on Alicia's learning style, strengths,
    and challenges. *It might be useful to ask the psychologist who
    did the evaluation to make some instructional suggestions
    that relate to each of the findings of her evaluation.*

3. The Child Development Clinic evaluation completed in 2000
    recommended that the team explore the use of assistive tech-
    nology to help Alicia with reading and writing, yet this has not
    yet been done. *A first step toward addressing this recommen-
    dation might be to ask the district's technology consultant to
    load the software onto Alicia's computer and for her team to
    engage in a trial of that software to enhance Alicia's reading
    and writing instruction and performance.*

4. The occupational therapist's report suggested that Alicia was
    not a candidate for direct services at this time. *It might be help-
    ful to have the occupational therapist do a functional assess-
    ment of the demands of Alicia's classes at the beginning of
    every semester and then present the team with a plan for how
    Alicia's consultative services might be delivered to other mem-
    bers of the team with regard to adaptations or modifications of
    the environment.*

Interviews   The inclusion facilitator is the one member of a
student's school team who sees the student in all environments, is
positioned to facilitate communication among team members, and
has the broad perspective required to see the big picture of the student's educational program. At the beginning of every school year,
the inclusion facilitator seeks information from all people who will
be part of the student's team and shares information with these
team members about the student's educational goals and necessary
supports. When students are in elementary school, most members
of their team might be consistent from year to year, with only the
classroom teacher changing. At the middle school level, students
are likely to have a whole new team of general education teachers
every year, but the related-services providers would probably be the
same throughout middle school. In high school, there may be new
subject area teachers every quarter or semester. Parents are also key
participants in the interview process (and the interview should be
conducted in the student's home if desired by the parents), as are the
building principal and relevant special education administrators
(either at the building or at the district levels).

The purpose of conducting formal interviews with team members shortly before or just as the school year starts is to discover 1) what they think they know about the student and the accuracy of that information; 2) their understanding of the goals of the student who is in their class, in their building, or on their caseload; 3) their past experiences with students with significant disabilities; 4) their understanding of their role on the team; 5) the level of expectations they hold for the student; and 6) any concerns they have about the student's learning, behavior, or health. Jamie's inclusion facilitator conducted formal interviews at the beginning of the school year.

Jamie's Story

Jamie was an elementary school student with significant disabilities who was making the transition to a regional middle school. The school's inclusion facilitator developed a set of interview questions to ask all team members. Some people who had just met Jamie recently were unable to answer some questions, but even these people's uninformed impressions were important to know. The inclusion facilitator assured each team member that his or her responses would be held in confidence but told everyone that a summary of the interview themes would be presented to the team for consideration at the first team meeting of the year. The interview questions are depicted in Table 6.1, and a summary of interviews concerning Jamie is available on-line at http://www.brookespublishing.com/inclusionfacilitator.

Day in the Life Observation A "day in the life" observation is done early in the school year to experience the school day from a student's perspective, to increase understanding of the factors that influence the student's educational experiences, and to provide some information about how the student's program aligns with promising educational practices. (Guidelines for completing this observation are presented in Appendix D.) The inclusion facilitator gathers the results of the student assessment into a report containing 1) MAPS or PATH notes, 2) a review of student records, 3) a synthesis of team member interviews, and 4) a "day in the life" observation.

Assessing the Classroom

Prior to planning a student's instructional programs and supports, the inclusion facilitator coordinates a comprehensive assessment of the classroom or classrooms in which the student will be a member. This assessment should answer the following questions:

Table 6.1.   Team member interview questions

Mission and philosophy questions

What is the school's mission statement?

How are decisions made about the direction of school policy and practice?

How does the mission statement apply to students with the most significant disabilities?

Is there a school policy about inclusion of students with the most significant disabilities?

What changes have you witnessed over the years with respect to how students with significant disabilities are educated?

How did those changes occur?

What information, beliefs, or other factors affect your opinion about appropriate educational programs for students with significant disabilities?

Faculty questions

How do you think the faculty feels about students with significant disabilities being in general education classes?

Do you think the faculty members feel competent to teach students with significant disabilities in their general education classes?

What professional development is available for faculty members on this topic?

Do you think there is enough time for the faculty to work collaboratively to plan, implement, and evaluate instruction for students with significant disabilities who are in general education classes?

- Is the classroom physically accessible? What are the sensory characteristics of the classroom? Lighting? Noise? Smell?

- How are the learning areas of the classroom arranged? Students' desks? Work tables? Teacher's desk? Board? Lab tables and equipment? Bookcases?

- What instructional groupings does the teacher use? Whole class? Small group? Student pairs? One-to-one direct instruction?

- What social and instructional routines are used? Choral reading? Attendance? Pledge of Allegiance? Snack time? Lecture and notetaking? Seatwork? Writing on the board? Handing in homework? Discussion and dialogue? Cooperative groups? Warm-ups? Gathering equipment and materials? Cleaning up at the end of class?

- What instructional materials does the teacher use? Books? Workbooks? Worksheets? Computer? Manipulatives? Overhead projector? Tools?

- What are the behavioral expectations and consequences in the classroom?

- How is diversity addressed in the classroom?

The inclusion facilitator answers these questions by observing in the classroom; reviewing documents such as curriculum standards, instructional materials, and classroom rules; and talking with the classroom teacher. He or she then writes a classroom profile based on these sources of information.

Assessing the School Environment

Assessment of the school environment provides essential information to the team relative to the kind of education and advocacy that might be needed to ensure that students with significant disabilities have access to the same learning environments and opportunities as students without disabilities. The inclusion facilitator's role as a schoolwide leader and advocate is thoroughly addressed in Chapter 7, but the inclusion facilitator must also promote an understanding of school culture by members of individual students' teams. The questions that need to be answered as part of the student-related assessment of the school environment include

- What is the school's mission statement? How is diversity addressed within the school's mission? Where does special education fit relative to general education?

- What are the governance structures within the school? When policies or structures need to be modified to promote access or learning for students with significant disabilities, how are those changes made?

- What professional development opportunities and resources are available for staff?

- What role do families and the community play in the school?

- Is the school safe?

To gather this information, the inclusion facilitator reviews school documents and conducts administrative interviews. Public documents are reviewed, such as the school's mission statement, handbook, yearly improvement and professional development plans, and discipline policies and local curriculum manuals. Administrative interviews (e.g., using the questions presented in Table

6.1) reveal the building leaders' attitudes about students with disabilities as well as their leadership styles.

Asssessing the Team's Capacity to Implement Best Practices

Following this comprehensive assessment of the student, classroom, and school, the inclusion facilitator then suggests to the team the issues that surfaced as needing work in order for the whole team to work most effectively to support the student's education. These issues might include 1) reaching consensus about the student's pursuit of general education curriculum content and the role that functional skills instruction should have in the student's educational program, 2) expanding the student's communication system, 3) gaining clarity about team member roles and responsibilities, 4) using more effective collaborative teaming processes and structures, 5) improving assessment of student learning by examining samples of student work on a regular basis, 6) providing intentional facilitation of social relationships, and 7) exploring what resources will be available to support the student when he or she leaves school and beginning to plan for that eventuality. From among a list of possible team priorities for improvement, members are asked to rank these issues according to their importance, and the issues that receive the highest rank become the priorities for the team's work over the course of the academic year.

DEVELOPING STANDARDS-BASED INDIVIDUALIZED EDUCATION PROGRAMS

In the 1970s, the educational programs of students with significant disabilities focused on their acquisition of developmental milestones similar to those of students without disabilities. Students were grouped together with classmates who were at a similar developmental level, and classrooms sometimes had students ranging in age from 3 to 21. Students worked on prerequisite skills such as stacking, matching, object permanence, color identification, and cause and effect, and a significant portion of their school day was spent in various therapy activities or personal care routines (Calculator & Jorgensen, 1994). IEPs during that era were similar to Jill's, which is depicted in Figure 6.1. Students leaving school in the early 1970s went on to day habilitation programs, or, if they were "higher functioning," sheltered workshops.

Then, in the late 1970s, Brown, Branson, Hamre-Nietupski, Pumpian, Certo, and Gruenewald (1979) postulated that students with significant disabilities needed to learn functional skills and

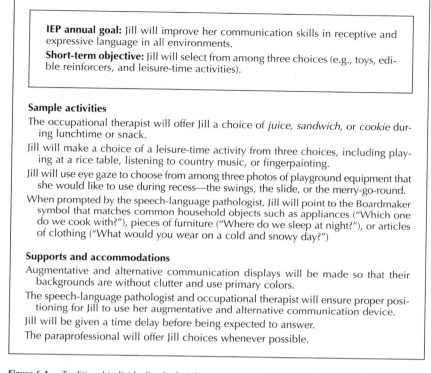

IEP annual goal: Jill will improve her communication skills in receptive and expressive language in all environments.

Short-term objective: Jill will select from among three choices (e.g., toys, edible reinforcers, and leisure-time activities).

Sample activities

The occupational therapist will offer Jill a choice of *juice, sandwich,* or *cookie* during lunchtime or snack.

Jill will make a choice of a leisure-time activity from three choices, including playing at a rice table, listening to country music, or fingerpainting.

Jill will use eye gaze to choose from among three photos of playground equipment that she would like to use during recess—the swings, the slide, or the merry-go-round.

When prompted by the speech-language pathologist, Jill will point to the Boardmaker symbol that matches common household objects such as appliances ("Which one do we cook with?"), pieces of furniture ("Where do we sleep at night?"), or articles of clothing ("What would you wear on a cold and snowy day?")

Supports and accommodations

Augmentative and alternative communication displays will be made so that their backgrounds are without clutter and use primary colors.

The speech-language pathologist and occupational therapist will ensure proper positioning for Jill to use her augmentative and alternative communication device.

Jill will be given a time delay before being expected to answer.

The paraprofessional will offer Jill choices whenever possible.

Figure 6.1. Traditional individualized education program (IEP) goal and objective for Jill.

that despite the students' perceived developmental levels, they ought to be engaged in age-appropriate functional activities across many domains during their school day. A student's IEP was written to reflect learning goals in the areas of domestic and self-help skills, community, leisure and recreation, and vocational skills. Related-services goals regarding communication, social skills, movement, and behavior were embedded within each of the major domain areas (Rainforth & York-Barr, 1997).

Today, however, this educational model is outdated because of its lack of attention to the academic content of the general education curriculum. The Individuals with Disabilities Education Improvement Act of 2004 (IDEA 2004, PL 108-446) and research findings in the areas of literacy and AAC both point to the need for all students to work toward the achievement of academic content goals that reflect general education learning standards. Consequently, the manner in which IEPs are written must change dramatically. High-quality IEPs contain learning goals from the general education curriculum, core skills (i.e., reading, writing, computer, mathematics), career skills, and functional life skills. These IEPs specify the individualized supports and accommodations necessary for students to achieve their IEP goals within a typical, age-appropriate general education classroom, other school environments, at home, and in typical community settings.

Many excellent resources are available to help inclusion facilitators and teams develop IEPs and supports related to functional and core academic skills (e.g., Giangreco, Cloninger, & Iverson, 1998), but this chapter focuses on the part of the IEP that relates to the broader general education curriculum.

Standards Terminology

Several terms are used in writing a high-quality standards-based IEP. In educational parlance, a *standard* is an acknowledged measure of comparison for quantitative or qualitative value or a degree or level of requirement, excellence, or attainment. Some students with significant disabilities can learn general educational curriculum standards "as is," demonstrating their learning in the same way as students without disabilities. Some students with significant disabilities pursue the standard "as is" but demonstrate their learning through alternate means. A good example of this situation is a student who does not use his voice to communicate but can give a presentation in social studies using an augmentative communication device.

When general education standards are not achievable by students with significant disabilities, even with assistive technology or other accommodations, the students might pursue the *critical function* of the standards. The critical function of the standards maintains the intent of the standards but expresses it in more generic terms that allow greater flexibility in how the standards are measured. For example, a language arts standard from the New Hampshire Curriculum Frameworks states, "Students will demonstrate the interest and ability to read age-appropriate materials fluently, with understanding and appreciation," whereas the critical function states, "Students will use words, pictures, objects, gestures, or symbols to read for the purposes of learning new information, getting instructions, and enjoyment" (New Hampshire Department of Education, 2001). To meet the assessment and accountability requirements of IDEA 2004 and the No Child Left Behind Act of 2001 (PL 107-110), most states have developed curriculum standards and their critical functions for core academic areas such as language arts, mathematics, social studies, science, fine arts, and career development.

Individualized Education Programs Terminology

Annual goals are broad general statements that help focus on the general areas in which individualized services will be provided (Giangreco et al., 1998). Short-term objectives focus on the specific things that a student will learn during the time the IEP is in effect and indicate a behavior that will be learned, the condition under which the behavior will occur, and a criterion that will be used to judge success. Instructional activities provide the context in which students will be taught the skills specified on their IEP. Figure 6.2 illustrates the relationship among educational standards, instructional activities, and IEP skills.

Model for Writing Standards-Based Individualized Education Programs

Kleinert and Kearns (2001) provided a model for writing standards-based IEPs that begins with identifying a skill that a student needs to acquire and then linking it to general education curriculum standards. It includes the following steps:

1. Identify a skill that a student needs to master. This becomes the IEP objective.

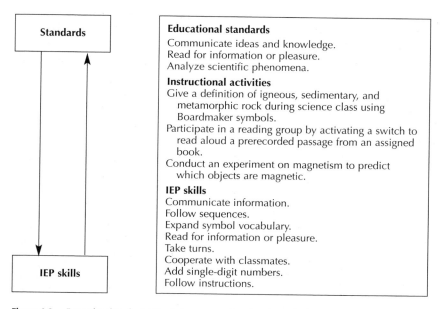

Figure 6.2. Examples that depict the links among educational standards, instructional activities, and individualized education program (IEP) skills. *Source:* Kleinert and Kearns (2001).

2. Identify typical activities and settings (reading in a small group, baking cookies in the culinary arts class, recycling cans as part of a service learning project, using a computer at a job site) in which this skill will be taught. These become the conditions in which the skill will be learned.

3. Identify the general education standards (or critical function) that relate to the IEP skill in these settings and activities. These standards become the student's IEP annual goals.

4. Determine the supports the student will need to achieve the standard. These supports are reflected both in the short-term objectives as part of the condition under which learning will take place and on the IEP's accommodations or modifications page.

5. Specify the criterion-based evidence that will be used to judge whether the student has learned the standard. This becomes the standard against which student progress (and instructional effectiveness) is measured throughout the year.

Another method for writing standards-based IEPs is to start the process by identifying a few standards from each core curriculum area (annual goals) and specifying what skills the student will learn in each area (short-term objectives) and the conditions or context (instructional activities).

Both methods have advantages and disadvantages. With the first method—beginning the process with skills—a shorter, more manageable IEP might be written that describes only the priority learning objectives that the student needs to learn this academic year. The risk in using this method is that the student's IEP might then be viewed as his or her whole educational program, and the student's learning across all of the other general education content areas would not be addressed. If no skill is identified in a particular general education content area, the team might be tempted to pull the student out of the general education class because the team is not targeting a priority IEP objective in that environment.

With the second method—beginning the process with the general education curriculum standards—students' educational programs are more likely to represent the breadth of the general education curriculum, and teams then identify important skills to teach in a greater variety of classes and instructional activities. The downside of using this method is that a student's IEP can be very long, and the team might be unsure about what are the most important learning goals for the student to achieve in the current year.

Examples of the Goals, Objectives, and Supports
of Standards-Based Individualized Education Programs

The characteristics of high-quality IEPs are presented in Table 6.2, and the example of Jill's IEP is presented in Figure 6.3, which illustrates how curriculum standards, annual goals, short-term objectives, classroom activities, and supports and accommodations are linked. Four examples (for Arthur, Jill, Ryan, and Crystal) that illustrate the relationship between general education standards, critical function of the standards, and classroom activities in which the standards will be addressed are available on-line at http://www.brookespublishing.com/inclusionfacilitator.

Arthur is representative of students who are able to master some but not all of the standards in the state curriculum frameworks. He is 2 years older than most of the other students in the class because he attended readiness class and was retained early in his school career. He comes from an impoverished background and has experienced much family instability throughout his life. He loves cars—looking at pictures of cars, playing with cars, talking about cars, going to car racing events, and so forth. His knowledge of the world beyond his school and home is very limited. He is unable to grasp complex concepts in science, social studies, math, or language arts. He has emerging literacy and math skills and is a

Table 6.2.   Characteristics of high-quality standards-based individualized education programs (IEPs)

Goals reflect high expectations for learning.

Family input is considered.

Activities and environments in which skills will be taught are inclusive.

Age-appropriate goals, skills, and learning activities are taught.

Communication, movement, and behavior skills are embedded within typical instructional activities.

Activities represent opportunities for interactions with classmates without disabilities.

Objectives are measurable.

Students have the opportunity to make choices and learn self-determination skills.

Objectives represent real-life skills.

Targeted skills can be addressed in multiple settings.

Natural supports are used before specialized supports.

Assistive technology, including augmentative communication, and other supports and accommodations are provided to enable students to gain access to instruction and demonstrate learning.

General education standard: Students will demonstrate competence in using the interactive language processes of reading, writing, speaking, listening, and viewing to communicate effectively.
Critical function of the standard: Communicate effectively.

IEP annual goal: Jill will improve her communication skills in the receptive and expressive language areas in all environments.
Short-term objective: When involved in the following activities and given a choice between three objects, symbols, activities, or people, Jill will communicate information by using Speaking Dynamically programmed on her laptop computer.

Classroom activities

During reading group, Jill will read a prerecorded passage from a book, sequencing the first part of the story, the second part, and the conclusion.

Jill will give her part of a group book report on the contrasting styles of Flannery O'Connor and Emily Dickinson by making selections that are programmed with each author's story.

Jill will choose which elective physical education class she wants to register for during the spring semester when offered a choice of aerobics, yoga, or swimming.

Jill will choose which store she wants to visit to pick out a dress for the semiformal dance.

Supports and accommodations

Jill will always be given access to her augmentative and alternative communication device, with the premade symbols with print corresponding to the messages she needs to communicate in a variety of environments, classes, and situations (Speaking Dynamically via Boardmaker symbols on a laptop computer).

Jill will be given physical support by her classmates, teaching assistant, or occupational therapist to improve her accuracy in pointing.

Jill will be given emotional support by being a full-time member of her class and any cooperative group activities.

Augmentative and alternative communication displays will be made so that their backgrounds are without clutter and use primary colors.

The speech-language pathologist and occupational therapist will ensure proper positioning for Jill to use her augmentative and alternative communication device.

Jill will be given a time delay before being expected to answer.

Figure 6.3. Standards-based (from New Hampshire Curriculum Frameworks) individualized education program (IEP) goal and objective for Jill.

candidate for his state's alternate assessment per the new requirements of IDEA 2004.

Ryan is a student who needs a great deal of support and assistive technology in order to be a full participant in the general education classroom. His classmates or a teaching assistant push him in his wheelchair. He communicates using the EZKeys software on a portable computer activated by a head switch. It takes Ryan much longer than other students to do his schoolwork because of the time it takes for his technology to work. In addition, the curriculum has to be adapted somewhat because Ryan has missed large portions of learning throughout his educational career due to illness, problems with the communication technology, and a general lack of coordination. Ryan also is a candidate for his state's alternate assessment per the IDEA 2004 requirements.

Crystal is representative of students who have many splinter skills and bits and pieces of knowledge in the various academic subject areas. Because of the vast differences in her present skills across subject areas and her need for significant supports for communication and movement, she will be a candidate for her state's alternate assessment test. Crystal has excellent decoding skills but poor abstract reasoning skills. She does best when she is given visual supports along with the written vocabulary during class lectures and as a part of any assessment of her learning. The greatest challenge for Crystal is to understand those academic areas in which the performance expectations can be close to or at grade level and those areas in which significant modifications must be made in order to support her performance.

INSTRUCTIONAL PLANNING AND EVALUATION OF LEARNING

A student's IEP is a roadmap that specifies the most important things for the student to learn during the year and the evidence that will inform evaluation of instructional effectiveness. Without a way to plan day-to-day instruction and supports, however, the IEP is a lifeless document that resides in a manila folder in the school's central office. The team must meet on a regular basis to plan instruction, supports, and assessment. This section describes strategies and tools for answering the following questions:

- How is the student currently participating in the general education class and other school and community routines? What are the discrepancies between his or her participation and performance and that of typical students?

- What are the demands of the general education classroom? What is expected in terms of student performance? What are the behavioral norms of the classroom?

- What supports does the student need in order to participate fully, learn some of the general education curriculum, and achieve his or her IEP goals?

- What evaluation methods will be used to measure student learning?
- How will the quality of instruction and supports be measured?

Activity and Participation Assessment

The first step in designing student supports is to assess the demands of a specific activity within a typical classroom, school, or community environment. Table 6.3 shows a classroom assessment for Ashton. The first column is the time of day, the second column depicts the steps of the lesson or activity, the third column depicts how Ashton is participating, the fourth column depicts how Ashton is demonstrating his learning, and the fifth column depicts the support that Ashton is receiving.

Discrepancy Analysis

With this information, the inclusion facilitator can then guide the team to ask the following questions that analyze the discrepancy between the demands of the classroom and the student's current level of participation:

1. In what activities can the student participate just like students without disabilities without any individualized supports?

2. What activities can the student participate in with natural supports?

3 What activities require specialized supports?

The activity observation in Table 6.3 demonstrates that Ashton is not currently participating in the classroom activities but rather in parallel activities with the exclusive support of his paraprofessional. After reviewing the activity observation, Ashton's team answered the three questions, which will ultimately evolve into a lesson support plan.

Student Support Plans

A support plan should consider a student's needs in the learning, movement, communication, behavior, and sensory areas. A catalog of possible supports, found in Appendix B, is grouped into the following four categories: 1) physical, emotional, and sensory supports; 2) modified materials and/or technology; 3) individualized demonstration of learning; and 4) personalized instruction (Jorgensen & McSheehan,

Table 6.3. Classroom activity observation for 8-year-old Ashton

Time	Activity	Student participation	Demonstration of learning	Support
7:30 A.M.	Students arrive. Students receive class folders. The teacher reviews the agenda on the board.	Ashton's wheelchair is pushed into the room by his paraprofessional, and they go to his desk in the back of the room. Other students greet Ashton, and he smiles at each one.	Maintaining eye contact and smiling at his classmates	Paraprofessional
7:45	The teacher reviews last week's quiz.	Ashton sits quietly and waits.	Sitting quietly and waiting during quiz review	Paraprofessional
8:00	The teacher introduces the theme of habitat.	Ashton listens.	Sitting quietly and looking at the teacher	Paraprofessional
8:30	Students get into small groups and begin to assemble their frog habitats.	Ashton joins a group and is supported to reach for various materials that will go into the habitat.	Reaching and grasping	Paraprofessional
8:45	The teacher reviews new vocabulary for the habitat unit.	Ashton's paraprofessional directs his attention to his schedule board, and Ashton places the science icon in his folder and takes out the math icon.	Identifying symbols on the schedule board Reaching, grasping, and placing the icon in folder pocket	Paraprofessional

2005). The support plan for Ashton's science lesson is available online at http://www. brookespublishing.com/inclusionfacilitator.

Chapter and Unit Plans

Curriculum—defined by coherent lessons or other learning experiences based on a set of learning standards—is typically organized into blocks by chapters or by unit themes. Inclusion facilitators can help teams plan ahead by developing chapter or unit support plans if the basic skeleton of the teacher's instructional plan is available. The information necessary for developing a chapter or unit support plan includes

- General education learning standards (e.g., knowledge, skills, dispositions) that will be addressed in the chapter or unit

- Student's IEP objectives that will be targeted during the chapter or unit

- Instructional materials that will be used by the teacher

- Core vocabulary of the chapter or unit

- Kinds of assessments that will be given

Even if a classroom teacher does not have all of this information far ahead of time (which is usually the case), newer textbooks are a rich resource for this information as a typical chapter in both the students' and teacher's copies outlines learning standards, key vocabulary, suggested activities, and assessment options. The unit plan template can be started with the information that is known and then fleshed out as the time draws closer to when the unit will be taught. A sample unit plan for a high school student (Alicia) is available online at http://www.brookespublishing.com/inclusionfacilitator.

Evaluating Student Learning

There are a variety of assessment methods and sources of evidence to evaluate student learning, including

- Observations of students in structured and unstructured settings

- Surveys of parents or teachers regarding their assessment of whether skills are generalized at home

- Collections of student work, including written models, audiotapes, videotapes, performance events, and tasks

- Self-evaluations or peer-evaluations performed by classmates

- Review of written records

- Report cards or progress reports

Strategies for designing individualized grading plans might include

- Developing a grading contract with points assigned for various academic tasks such as homework, classwork, projects, and tests
- Writing a rubric that specifies levels of performance from novice to mastery and linking the rubric score to the grade
- Counting participation, behavior, and effort as part of a grade
- Grading based on improvement over time
- Including performance on IEP objectives as part of a course grade

A sample rubric for evaluation of attendance, class participation, and readings from a high school can be found on-line at http://www.brookespublishing.com/inclusionfacilitator.

Evaluating the Quality of Instruction and Supports

Teams should refrain from making judgments about a student's performance without carefully evaluating the quality of the instruction and support provided to that student (McSheehan et al., 2001). If teams can say that they are confident that quality instruction and support were provided, then their judgments about student performance are on more solid ground. But if a student fails a vocabulary test when necessary and planned supports were not provided, then that *F* is probably not valid and should not be counted. If the student earns a *B* or a *C* (average performance) and the supports delivered were accurate and reliable, then the team can be fairly confident that the student's performance is a true representation of his or her learning.

The team faces a dilemma, however, when the student performs poorly when supports were delivered just as planned. A team that is committed to the least dangerous assumption (discussed in Chapter 2) would conclude that it just has not found the right constellation of supports that work for that student in that type of assessment situation. Team members might make a commitment to try other supports, assess again, and then come back to the table for another conversation about student performance and team accountability.

FUNCTIONAL BEHAVIOR ASSESSMENT AND POSITIVE BEHAVIORAL SUPPORT PLANS

Historically, behavioral interventions have had a narrow focus on identifying a person's challenging behaviors and then using rewards or punishment to make those behaviors stop. There is a growing body of research, however, that shows that the use of positive behavior approaches is more likely to result in students learning new skills, generalizing those skills to novel situations, and maintaining a good relationship with their teachers (Koegel, Koegel, & Dunlap, 1996). This approach is based on a number of values and beliefs about people with disabilities, including the following: 1) All individuals have the right to a self-determined life free of coercive control by others; 2) all individuals have the right to be fully included in their schools and communities; 3) from every person's perspective, all behavior serves a function and has meaning; and 4) one can change certain elements in a person's environment and teach the person new skills so that his or her behavior becomes more effective and typical (TASH, 2000).

Functional Behavior Assessment

Planning positive behavioral approaches begins with a functional behavior assessment. This assessment process identifies learner-related and environmental factors that contribute to and/or influence a student's behavior (Koegel et al., 1996). All behavior occurs within a context that includes a person's biological state, health status, relationships with others, past experiences, current life situation, emotions, and skills, so a functional behavior assessment must identify the relationships between the person and all of these factors and the occurrence or nonoccurrence of identified behaviors. It is not a one-time event that can be conducted effectively by an outside expert. A good functional behavior assessment leads to hypotheses about a student's behavior. Based on these hypotheses, the team then develops a support plan that helps the student get his or her needs met in more effective and efficient ways.

The following sources of information are used during a functional behavior assessment.

- Review of medical and school records
- Student interview and time spent with the student
- Family interview and time spent with the family
- School staff interviews
- "Who is this student?" description that includes likes and dislikes, interests, communication and learning style, talents, and challenges
- Classroom, school, home, and community observations and data collection

Cathy Pratt, director of the Indiana Resource Center for Autism, suggested that school teams (that include the parent or guardian) rather than clinical experts are qualified to conduct high-quality functional behavior assessments. These teams must be committed to work collaboratively over time. Team members must be knowledgeable about the principles and methods of behavior analysis, know the student well and be familiar with the school environment, and be experienced in using a variety of social, communication, sensory, movement, and instructional strategies to support the student (Pratt, 2004). Furthermore, team members must acknowledge that their behavior or program might need to change in order to affect the student's behavior problems.

The steps of a functional behavior assessment include the following: 1) Spend time with the student in a variety of situations and become familiar with the student's communication system; 2) evaluate the student's current quality of life to determine if he or she is a valued member of a general education classroom, has fulfilling social relationships, and has choice and control in his or her life; 3) conduct formal observations in a variety of situations that result in a clear description of the problem behavior and its frequency, duration, intensity, and overall impact; 4) identify the antecedents and consequences of the behavior; and 5) develop a single hypothesis (or several hypotheses) for why the student is exhibiting the behavior. An example of a functional behavior assessment for Jake, a 16-year-old high school student, is depicted in Appendix E.

Positive Behavioral Support Plans

A high-quality behavioral support plan 1) addresses the foundations of the student's inclusion and social relationships; 2) is socially acceptable, as judged by whether it would be appropriate if the student did not have a disability; 3) is feasible and supported by enough resources and team expertise; and 4) includes a plan to monitor its effectiveness over time (Koegel et al., 1996). The greatest emphasis in a respectful behavioral support plan is on enhancing the person's overall quality of life, expanding social relationships, increasing choice and control, and providing the person with the means to communicate (Lovett, 1996). Because all of us respond positively to various types of reinforcement in our lives (e.g., our paychecks, being taken out to dinner as a reward for a job well done, praise from people we respect and care about), creatively providing these kinds of reinforcement to people with disabilities is appropriate and much more effective in the long run than artificial reinforcers. Jake's behavioral support/intervention plan is depicted in Appendix F.

PLANNING FOR GRADUATION AND LEAVING SCHOOL

IDEA 2004 requires that older students with disabilities have a formal plan within their IEPs to support their transitions from school to adult life. An inclusion facilitator can help teams develop plans that go beyond simply shifting the responsibility for the student's life from one agency (the school) to another (the developmental service agency).

Planning for graduation and adult life ought not to be dependent on a service system based on labels, segregated options, dead-end employment, and long waiting lists. A quality high school graduation plan is characterized by 1) the same options and choices as for students without disabilities, 2) a plan based on the least dangerous assumption of competence, 3) use of a person-centered planning approach that respects student and family preferences, 4) involvement of young adults in choosing who provides supports to them, 5) utilization of both generic community and specialized resources and funds, and 6) built-in accountability for the accomplishment of tasks (Cotton & Sowers, 1996).

There are two complementary approaches that inclusion facilitators can use to support a student to plan for graduation and adult life. The first is to work with faculty or guidance departments to embed graduation planning into the general high school curriculum or guidance program for all students. This approach provides a naturally occurring opportunity for students with disabilities to focus on their future plans alongside their classmates who do not have disabilities. The second strategy is for inclusion facilitators to use a focused futures planning process to help students develop an individualized graduation plan.

Graduation Planning for All Students

Most high schools have a variety of life, career, and college planning services for students. These services include course planning, internships or community service, courses in consumer and family studies, guidance with planning for college, tutoring for college entrance exams, assessments to help students identify their interests and talents, and a variety of clubs and activities geared to adult roles, such as the National FFA Organization, Future Teacher's Association, and

Mock Trial. When these activities are open to all students and students with disabilities have the supports necessary to fully participate, specialized planning for individual students can be targeted to fill in the gaps. Malloy, Frejie, Tashie, and Nisbet (1996) designed a curriculum for career and life planning that is meant to be used in high school advisory groups, guidance programs, or a for-credit class that focuses on planning for adult life. Table 6.4 depicts the topics addressed in each of the curriculum's chapters.

Focused Planning for Students with Disabilities

The second strategy for planning enviable futures for students with disabilities is to use a specialized planning process (Merritt, n.d.; Mount, 2000). Cotton and Sowers (1996), for example, described an eight-stage process of consumer and family-directed planning (see Table 6.5) based on the principles of quality graduation planning. The inclusion facilitator's role in the specialized planning process can be as the leader of the plan's development or as a participant who is led by someone designated by the family as the resource broker or futures planning facilitator. It is often useful to have someone outside the school system collaborate closely with the inclusion facilitator because most students experience several years

Table 6.4. Planning for the future: themes, topics, and activities contained in a career- and life-planning curriculum

Themes	Topics/activities
Getting to know you	Survival game
	Learning styles
	My bag of skills
	My work, play, and learning history
	My typical day in my dreams
	My strengths and weaknesses
The world around me	Where people work
	Interviewing a worker
	Profiling a job
	Choosing a job
	Applying for a job
Career and educational planning	Developing a personal template
	Dreams: my job, home, community
	Turning dreams into plans
	Linking school to my dreams
	Developing job or internship goals

Source: Malloy, Frejie, Tashie, and Nisbet (1996).

Table 6.5.   The eight stages of futures planning

1. Deciding to take control
2. Building understanding of the person's values, preferences, and beliefs
3. Making goals, identifying support roles, and clarifying expectations
4. Considering different options for support
5. Deciding how to spend support funds
6. Trying choices on for fit
7. Figuring out ways to stay on course
8. Growing and refining the plan

From Cotton, P., & Sowers, J. (1996). *Choice through knowledge. Knowledge = power.* Durham: Institute on Disability at the University of New Hampshire; reprinted by permission.

between the ages of 18 and 21 when they are still connected to the school system but are in the process of making the transition to adult life.

CONCLUSION

Comprehensive assessments of students, their educational teams, their classrooms, and the broader school environment are necessary for the development of appropriate IEPs. Educators should be careful not to draw conclusions about a student's current skills or potential based on outdated evaluations. All students need to work toward learning goals from the general education curriculum, core skills, career skills, and functional life skills. Therefore, team members should meet on a regular basis to plan relevant instruction, supports, and assessment.

REFERENCES

Brown, L., Branson, M., Hamre-Nietupski, S., Pumpian, I., Certo, N., & Gruenewald, L. (1979). A strategy for developing chronological age-appropriate and functional curriculum content for severely handicapped adolescents and young adults. *Journal of Special Education, 13*(1), 71–90.

Calculator, S., & Jorgensen, C. (1994). *Including students with severe disabilities in schools: Fostering communication, interaction, and participation.* San Diego: Singular Publishing Group.

Cotton, P., & Sowers, J. (1996). *Choice through knowledge. Knowledge = power.* Durham: Institute on Disability at the University of New Hampshire.

Donnellan, A. (2000, May). Absence of evidence: Myths about autism and mental retardation. *TASH Connections,* 26–32.

Forest, M., Pearpoint, J., & O'Brien, J. (1996). MAPS, circles of friends, and PATH: Powerful tools to help build caring communities. In S. Stainback & W. Stainback (Eds.), *Inclusion: A guide for educators* (pp. 67–86). Baltimore: Paul H. Brookes Publishing Co.

Giangreco, M.F., Cloninger, C.J., & Iverson, V.S. (1998). *Choosing outcomes and accommodations for children (COACH): A guide to educational planning for students with disabilities* (2nd ed.). Baltimore: Paul H. Brookes Publishing Co.

Individuals with Disabilities Education Improvement Act of 2004, PL 108-446, 20 U.S.C. §§ 1400 *et. seq.*

Jorgensen, C., & McSheehan, M. (2005). *Supports for students with significant disabilities.* Durham, NH: Institute on Disability at the University of New Hampshire.

Kleinert, H.L., & Kearns, J.F. (2001). *Alternate assessment: Measuring outcomes and supports for students with disabilities.* Baltimore: Paul H. Brookes Publishing Co.

Koegel, L.K., Koegel, R.L., & Dunlap, G. (1996). *Positive behavioral support: Including people with difficult behavior in the community.* Baltimore: Paul H. Brookes Publishing Co.

Lovett, H. (1996). *Learning to listen: Positive approaches and people with difficult behavior.* Baltimore: Paul H. Brookes Publishing Co.

Malloy, J., Frejie, G., Tashie, C., & Nisbet, J. (1996). *Planning for the future: A manual of career and life planning.* Durham: Institute on Disability at the University of New Hampshire.

McSheehan, M., Sonnenmeier, R., & Jorgensen, C. (2002). Communication and learning: Creating systems of support for students with significant disabilities. *TASH Connections, 28*(5), 8–14.

Merritt, D. (n.d.). *Future planning guide: Life planning for a person with a disability.* Durham: Institute on Disability at the University of New Hampshire.

Mount, B. (2000). *Life building: Opening windows to change.* New York: Graphic Futures.

New Hampshire Department of Education. (2001). *New Hampshire Educational Improvement Assessment Program: Alternate assessment educator's guide.* Concord, NH: Author.

No Child Left Behind Act of 2001, PL 107-110, 115 Stat. 1425, 20 U.S.C. §§ 6301 *et seq.*

Pratt, C. (2004, August). *Positive behavioral approaches for children with autism spectrum disorders.* Presentation at the Sixth Annual Summer Institute on Educating Children with Autism in General Education Classrooms, Durham, NH.

Rainforth, B., & York-Barr, J. (1997). *Collaborative teams for students with severe disabilities: Integrating therapy and educational services* (2nd ed.). Baltimore: Paul H. Brookes Publishing Co.

TASH. (2000). *Resolution on positive behavioral support.* Baltimore: Author.

Identifying
Nontraditional Supports
The Inclusion Facilitator's Role as an Information
and Resource Broker

Mary C. Schuh

The average personnel preparation experiences afforded to most special educators provide only limited opportunities to prepare for their new role as inclusion facilitators. According to Ryndak, Clark, Conroy, and Stuart (2001), the research base offers little guidance when considering the expertise required to serve students with significant disabilities. A course in special education law, an elective in the social work department, and student teaching in a self-contained classroom do not offer a special education teacher the background, knowledge, and skills necessary to tackle the ongoing challenges of being an inclusion facilitator. Most special educators were trained to be teachers, not grant writers, case managers, legal advisors, or experts in the multitude of systems involved in the lives of the students and families whom they serve. Yet inclusion facilitators must take on a myriad of responsibilities many never have imagined. This chapter presents the inclusion facilitator's responsibilities as an information and resource broker who provides students with disabilities with the supports necessary to succeed in the community within and beyond the school walls.

The inclusion facilitator's role as collaborative team leader includes assessing; writing individualized education programs (IEPs); planning, implementing, and evaluating student supports; evaluating student learning; conducting functional assessments and developing positive behavior support plans; facilitating social relationships; and planning for students' graduations and transitions to adult life. Yet, there are other activities that are equally important in order to successfully achieve positive outcomes for students with significant disabilities, including

- Knowing the first steps to take when planning for students' inclusion
- Scheduling related-services providers and outside consultants
- Participating in wrap-around services and comprehensive systems of care with agencies and systems outside of the school system and educational community
- Budgeting for support needs and communicating about expenses in a manner that is respectful and promotes greater understanding of overall student and community benefit
- Grant writing to secure additional resources
- Knowing the law in order to advocate for supports and appropriate placement

AN INCLUSIVE EDUCATION SCENARIO

Jackson, a 12-year-old boy with a love for computer games, science, and movies, recently entered middle school. Until now, he was successfully included in the bulk of elementary school life. A one-to-one assistant accompanied him everywhere and was familiar with the myriad of strategies to address his ever-present behavioral support needs. His previous school team attended many workshops on autism (Jackson's primary label) and appreciated the support from an expert in autism who consulted with the team. His mother drove him to and from school and supported him and a friend during the late afternoons. Jackson enjoyed his academic classes—particularly when his teachers were familiar with his communication style, which included pointing to choices and using body language and some sign language. He was a master at computer games and particularly enjoyed reading magazines about electronics and video games.

As Jackson entered middle school, many things in his life changed. His mother began a job that made her unable to drive him to school. The one-to-one assistant who had been with Jackson for 5 years chose to stay at the elementary school. Jackson's behavior escalated to a point of hospitalization over the summer, and new communication, behavioral, nutritional, and medical interventions needed to be explored.

In the beginning of August, the middle school hired a new inclusion facilitator, Samantha (Sam), for Jackson and other students with significant disabilities in the school. Sam had not met any of the students on her caseload and was hired because of her unwavering belief and commitment to educating all students in the typical school community. This scenario is the reality for many new inclusion facilitators. The organizational and administrative skills needed to successfully include students are vast but manageable if an inclusion facilitator believes in the values of inclusive education.

Sam held these beliefs and was determined to use them to guide the process of developing inclusive educational experiences for all five of the students assigned to her caseload. She quickly learned that the reality and challenges of the educational system required her to develop new skills. Moreover, she learned that her beliefs and attitudes about the capacity of all students to learn and grow in a general education setting would not magically result in supports and services or a widespread understanding of why Jackson and the other students with disabilities were in general education classes.

To achieve success in her role as an inclusion facilitator, Sam needed skills that allowed her to perform positive outcomes activities. These skills included coordination and facilitation skills, such as the ability to schedule and organize meetings with people who have limited availability; a knowledge of budgeting, grant writing, and law; and IEP development and monitoring. Each of these skills required expertise in creative problem solving and group facilitation, as discussed elsewhere in this book.

Sam's Early Strategies

Sam's first task was to identify the teams associated with each of her five students and schedule meetings to identify the long- and short-term goals of enrolling and supporting the students in general education. She visited each of the students in their homes and learned from their families their expectations for the school year. Three of the families were expecting their sons or daughters to enter a self-contained classroom while the remaining two (including Jackson's parents) expected that their children would be fully included in the mainstream of general education. In short, three families preferred to move slowly, or not at all, toward full inclusion, whereas the other two families were impatient for a typical school year to begin. One of the parents explicitly stated, "I don't want my son to step foot in any special education environment because of the potential for stigma and lower expectations among peers and teachers." Sam's efforts were split between educating families about the natural benefits of an inclusive experience and trying to move quickly enough so that Jackson and the other student would enter middle school as fully included middle school students. Creating the balance between these efforts was a continual challenge for Sam.

Sam determined that the natural solution was for all students to be placed in homerooms and classes, and she made sure that her students were assigned to appropriate teachers. She secured lockers and regular transportation schedules and arranged for the students to tour the school with their families prior to orientation. In addition to playing the role of team leader for her students, Sam needed to attend to various administrative responsibilities that were not covered in her teacher-preparation experiences.

Sam scheduled a team meeting for the second week of school, and the team members decided to meet on a weekly basis for the first 2 months of school during the teachers' common planning period. Team members always included Sam, the paraprofessional supporting Jackson, and a minimum of two of Jackson's general education teachers. Additional members—who were always welcome and often specifically invited—included Jackson himself and his mother, occupational and physical therapists, school administrators, the behavior consultant, classmates, and general education classroom teachers. Once the school schedule was underway, weekly meetings moved to every other week.

Coordinating Related Services

For Sam, the most challenging aspect of including Jackson in general education was the issue of behavior. A predictable schedule was a known way to decrease Jackson's anxiety and challenging behaviors, but the middle school appeared to offer little in the way of consistency. Sam knew that relying on Jackson's behavior consultant was going to be critical for success. She secured his participation prior to and during the beginning of the school year to observe Jackson, revise the positive behavior support plan to be appropriate for a middle school student, and offer professional development and technical assistance to Jackson's IEP team.

Educational teams typically rely on the inclusion facilitator to coordinate services and supports. Once necessary services and supports are identified through the team meeting process, it is usually up to the inclusion facilitator to locate the most appropriate supports and schedule the most appropriate time for these supports to be available. Supports can include occupational, speech-language, and physical therapy; literacy services; medical services; positive behavior support intervention; and futures planning services. Giangreco, Prelock, Reid, Dennis, and Edelman (2000) found that educators most appreciate specialist or related-services providers who 1) function as collaborative team members rather than in isolation as experts, 2) help teachers and parents work on the child's education goals, 3) provide assistance at times and in ways that consider the classroom's structure in order to avoid disruption, and 4) use approaches that are not overly technical and specialized so that students may avoid being unnecessarily stigmatized.

Creative Use of Supports   For many students with disabilities, the provision of supports is concomitant with reduced time in the general education classroom. More often than not, supports and services are delivered in isolated, separate settings (e.g., resource rooms, speech therapist cubbies, nurse's office), and generalization of the skills learned is impossible or difficult at best. Although isolated related-services delivery may be the norm in many schools, these services can be delivered in a direct or collaborative consultation model. Before deciding on a method of service delivery, it is important to first decide on the optimal outcomes for students.

Collaborative Consultation   For many students and teachers, a *collaborative consultation model* is an ideal approach to achieve desired outcomes. In this model, service delivery personnel work directly in the general education environment (i.e., classroom, gym class, cafeteria, school bus) and support the transfer of skills and knowledge to the natural supports in the environment. For example, the positive behavior support consultant for Jackson has mentored the bus driver, classroom teachers, cafeteria personnel, and others to understand Jackson's emotions and how to support him to relax (e.g., through the use of headphones and music) in order to prevent a behavioral outburst. The behavior consultant's time may be more intensely needed during certain times of the school year, such as the beginning of the year and after holidays. Collaboration is dynamic, and the possibilities for improving and expanding positive outcomes are identified as an ongoing process in the collaborative consultation model (Thousand, Villa, Paolucci-Whitcomb, & Nevin, 1992).

Bank of Services   A *bank of services model* should be encouraged by the inclusion facilitator. In this model, a team estimates the amount of services that may be needed over the course of the year and creates a "bank account" of hours to draw from. This model moves away from the traditional weekly or half-hour block scheduling of services toward a model of service delivery that uses outside supports as needed in the most natural location possible.

Direct Service Delivery   *Direct service delivery* may be the optimal strategy to achieve favorable outcomes, and this service delivery should occur during the natural routines of a student's day. These routines should include both the traditional hours within a school day as well as before school and during extracurricular activities. Examples include a speech therapist who delivers services during drama club to support communication goals, an occupational therapist who provides services during art or writing class to improve fine motor skills, and a physical therapist who delivers range-of-motion exercises during the stretching portion of physical education classes.

Providing direct services during creative times such as after school, before school, weekends, and summers is also possible by promoting a flexible view of the scheduling issues of related-services providers. For example, related-services providers often work on a contractual basis and can negotiate their schedules to provide support during times that make sense for the student's schedule. Students who learn skills during natural experiences while involved in typical routines are more likely to retain and generalize these skills than students who are taught in isolated settings. An inclusion facilitator can work with school administrators on the contracting and hiring process to encourage developing contracts that provide services based on needs rather than on the traditional school schedule.

For example, Jackson is working on improving his fine motor skills to be able to get himself dressed on his own before school. The occupational therapist provides services in Jackson's home two mornings per week. In addition, the therapist provides collaborative consultation to the natural supports in Jackson's life (i.e., mother, teacher, paraprofessional) on strategies to encourage Jackson to become more independent in dressing.

Participating in Wrap-Around Comprehensive Systems of Care

The *wrap-around process* is a collaborative approach to help children and youth with complex needs and their families meet their needs and improve their lives (Goldman, 1999). In 1982, Jane Knitzer wrote her groundbreaking monograph, *Unclaimed Children*, based on a study conducted for the Children's Defense Fund. Knitzer's report described the lack of positive outcomes for children and youth with emotional and/or behavioral disabilities. These poor outcomes have been directly tied to the quality and fragmentation of the services delivered by public agencies charged with the care and support of these young people, including education, mental health, child protective services, juvenile justice, public health and welfare, and substance abuse agencies. Knitzer described gaps in the service delivery systems for children and youth—particularly for those with labels of emotional and/or behavioral disabilities.

Since Knitzer's report was released in 1982, major changes have taken place in both federal and state service delivery systems. These changes promote a comprehensive system of care and a wrap-around planning approach centered around children and families. This means that the needs of the child and family dictate the types and mix of services provided and also that these services are community based and culturally competent because the agencies, programs, and services are responsive to the cultural, racial, and ethnic differences of the populations they serve. Alcohol, Drug Abuse, and Mental Health Administration (ADAMHA) Reorganization Act (PL 102-321) authorized the new Child Mental Health Services Initiative, which is a program that provides grants to develop a broad array of community-based services for children with a range of emotional and behavioral disabilities (Stroul, 1996). Since this initiative took effect, the majority of states have adopted the *comprehensive systems of care* approach that brings together the primary community-based agencies to meet the needs of children and families. Essential philosophical elements of the wrap-around process are listed in Table 7.1.

Because schools are important partners in the wrap-around approach, it is necessary for inclusion facilitators to be knowledgeable about the variety of agencies that affect the lives of a student and his or her family. A primary value of the wrap-around approach is that of unconditional care (Stroul, 1996). This value results in policies that seek to create an inclusive entrance into services and prevent discharge or exclusion. Although the wrap-around process and comprehensive systems of care approach were initiated to respond to the needs of children and youth with emotional and behavioral disabilities, there is widespread agreement that this process benefits children and their families with complex needs regardless of the disability label. Participation in a wrap-around system of care approach involves the acknowledgment that there

Table 7.1.   Essential philosophical elements of the wrap-around process

Philosophical element	Description
Voice and choice	Children, youth, and their families must be active partners at every level of the wrap-around process.
Children, youth, and family teams	The approach must be a team-driven process involving families, children, youth, and agencies as well as natural supports and community services working together to develop, implement, and evaluate the individualized plan.
Community-based services	Services must be based in the community with all efforts toward supporting children and their families in their homes and local school communities.
Cultural competence	The process must be culturally competent, building on the unique values, preferences, and strengths of children and families and their communities.
Individualized and strengths-based services	Services and supports must be individualized and build on strengths, meeting the needs of children and families across life domains to promote success, safety, and permanence in home, school, and the community.
Natural supports	Plans must include a balance of formal services and informal community and family supports.
Continuation of care	There must be an unconditional commitment to serve children, youth, and their families.
Collaboration	Plans of care should be developed and implemented based on interagency, community-based collaborative processes.
Flexible resources	Teams must have flexible approaches and adequate and flexible funding.
Outcome-based services	Outcomes must be determined and measured for the child or youth, family, program, and system.

Adapted from a wrap-around meeting at Duke University in 1998, as discussed in Burns and Goldman (1999).

are many service providers in the lives of some families; therefore, all service providers need to work collaboratively to address the family's needs at home, at the neighborhood school, and in the local community. Some of the inclusion facilitator's responsibilities on a wrap-around team may be to

- Coordinate the delivery of counseling services outside of classroom instruction periods

- Participate in creative problem solving around earning course credits for experiential-based learning

- Coordinate behavior consultation services in a student's home with family members

- Contact other community-based agencies to procure services such as transportation for a student and family

- Develop a transition plan for a student returning from a court-ordered out-of-district placement

- Coordinate community health care services with in-school health services to create a broad understanding and appropriate medical supports for students with complex medical issues

- Represent the school in efforts to contribute pooled financial resources to solve complex problems, such as a need for an alternative family placement or improved physical accessibility in a family's home

- Coordinate training for family members and after-school programs on topics such as positive behavior intervention and supports and/or the use of augmentative and alternative communication

- Collaborate with other agencies in grant writing to secure additional resources for students and families

- Research agencies that might also provide support to students and families, such as after-school and mentoring programs

The summer after he entered middle school, Jackson experienced a medical and behavioral crisis that resulted in law enforcement involvement with the family and a brief hospitalization in a psychiatric unit of the local hospital. Following this incident, Jackson's mother became concerned that she would no longer be able to care for her son at home. Sam contacted the local mental health center, and a therapist was assigned to develop a wrap-around team to coordinate a comprehensive system of care for the family. Members of the wrap-around team included Sam, Jackson's mother, Jackson's therapist, Jackson's behavior consultant, the district's special education administrator, and a family support worker from the local developmental services agency. The team's primary goal was to provide the family with supports and services to enable Jackson to be safe and to thrive in his own home. In addition to supporting Jackson in a neighborhood after-school program, the team increased the respite hours available to the family and provided training in communication and positive behavior support to all staff. The team meets monthly and shares in the decision-making process as well as the financial responsibilities that affect positive outcomes in Jackson's life. The school covers expenses that occur during the typical school day, and the developmental service agency covers expenses related to the student's social activities that occur before or after school and on weekends.

Budgeting

An inclusion facilitator must have an understanding of the school's policies and practices related to special education funding. This knowledge can often change the course of events during dialogues about the merits of educating students with and without disabilities in general education classrooms. Although data on the fiscal consequences of inclusive education over time are limited, most school districts report that the overall cost of inclusive education is no greater than that of educating students in two separate systems and may even produce cost savings as the program is implemented over time (Lipsky & Gartner, 1997).

The National Council on Disability summarized the costs issue as follows, "The costs associated with integration can be modest, with possible savings because of fewer due process hearings, fewer mediations, fewer referrals to special education, fewer non-public school placements, and lower transportation costs" (1995, p. 80). The pattern reported most frequently by school districts that are implementing inclusive education programs is that they support the restructuring by using the same financial resources previously used in separate special education, but they use them in a manner to support all students in general education classes and school communities (Lipsky & Gartner, 1997; Roach, 1995). Savings gained by eliminating dual administrative and physical systems of special education are put back into personnel and programming in the general education community. Resources can be used for additional paraprofessionals to support all students and professional development to increase competence in areas such as positive behavior support, cooperative learning, or multiple intelligences.

It is also important for inclusion facilitators to know about federal and state funding practices. Medicaid reimbursement funds can be recouped for some instructional and related services. Federal funds from the Individuals with Disabilities Education Improvement Act (IDEA) of 2004 (PL 108-446) should be utilized to support students in their neighborhood school, supplemented with state funds for catastrophic costs.

When Sam first began meeting with educators in the middle school, there were many misconceptions about the costs of educating Jackson in his home school that created early barriers to including Jackson. Some team members and administrators focused on the high costs of special education and were unwilling to engage in a discussion of Jackson's supports. With her knowledge of special education funding research and federal and state resources, Sam dispelled the myth that it would be more expensive for Jackson to attend his neighborhood school than it would be for him to be educated outside of the district. The team was then able to focus on how to include Jackson rather than why.

Grant Writing

During times of shrinking resources and rising educational expenses, school districts with great wealth, as well as those with limited resources, can benefit from discretionary grants to bring in new sources of funding. Grant funding can be used to procure new technology to benefit all students, to enhance professional development opportunities beyond those funded by the school district, and to hire outside professionals to augment the skills of in-district professionals. School districts in New Hampshire, for example, have applied for state, federal, and private grants for a variety of innovative projects, including 1) providing specialized training to school teams on the topic of strategies to welcome and include students with autism, 2) purchasing state-of-the-art assistive listening devices for students with hearing disabilities attending their neighborhood high schools, 3) hiring an inspirational speaker to present to students and faculty on the topic of social justice and students with disabilities, and 4) creating a community study circle of parents, educators, and general community members to discuss issues of diversity, inclusion, and social justice.

Sam had never written a grant proposal and was reluctant to consider such an endeavor until she heard about the availability of minigrants from the state's education department. These minigrants were made available through the federally funded School Improvement Grant. Although the purpose of the minigrants was to improve transition practices for youth with disabilities, Sam knew that planning for transition should begin as early as middle school. She assembled a grant-writing team that included the assistant principal, financial management personnel, and a parent with grant-writing experience. The team completed the application and was awarded funding to hire a paraprofessional who worked after school during extracurricular activities. Now, students with disabilities are able to fully explore career options in the same way as students without disabilities through participation in the drama club, Future Business Leaders of America, sports, and other opportunities available to encourage the exploration of knowledge and interests.

Knowing the Law

The Civil Rights movement and Supreme Court's landmark decision in *Brown v. Board of Education* (1954), which led to the Civil Rights Acts of 1964 (PL 88-352) and 1968 (PL 90-284), are the underpinnings of the legal and constitutional rights held by children with disabilities (Yell, Drasgow, Bradley, & Justeen, 2004). Litigation and legislative efforts from 1964 to 1974 produced strong legal and federal support to educate children with disabilities. Significant cases included *Pennsylvania Association for Retarded Children (PARC) v. Commonwealth of Pennsylvania,* (1971), *Mills v. Board of Education of the District of Columbia,* (1972), and more recently *Sacramento City Unified School District v. Rachel H.,* (1994) (Villa, 2000). Prior to 1975, education for children with disabilities was seen as a privilege, not a right, and access to supports and services through typical school systems was unthinkable. Many students were completely excluded from public education, and the only options available to families were programs in church basements or segregated facilities far from many families' homes.

In 1975, Congress enacted the Education for All Handicapped Children Act (PL 94-142) as the most expansive piece of legislation related to educating children with disabilities. This act was reauthorized several times and is divided into four parts.

- Part A contains the general provisions that include the purpose and definitions.

- Part B is particularly important to an inclusion facilitator because it outlines the services that states are required to provide to children with disabilities ages 3–21, along with procedural safeguards.

- Part C authorizes federal grants to states to provide early intervention services to infants and toddlers from birth to 3 years.

- Part D outlines the national activities in which states can partake to improve the education of children with disabilities in areas such as research, teacher training, technical assistance, technology, information dissemination, parent training, and evaluation.

Since IDEA 2004, inclusive education, individually and systemically, has been taken to new levels. It is critical for inclusion facilitators to understand the ramifications of this law in order to best support the placement of students with disabilities in general education. Inclusion facilitators should be familiar with all aspects of IDEA 2004 so that they can understand and articulate the legal underpinnings of inclusive education as well as seek out resources that are available through the law. Specifically, subsection 5 of IDEA 2004 states

Over 30 years of research and experience have demonstrated that the education of children with disabilities can be made more effective by—

(a) having high expectations for such children and ensuring their assessment in the general curriculum to the maximum extent possible;

(b) strengthening the role and responsibility of parents and ensuring that families of such children have meaningful opportunities to participate in the education of their children at school and at home;

(c) coordinating this Act with other local educational service agency, State, and Federal school improvement efforts, including improvement efforts under the Elementary and Secondary Education Act of 1965, in order to ensure that such children benefit from such efforts and that special education can become a service for such children rather than a place where they are sent;

(d) providing appropriate special education and related services and aids and supports in the regular classroom to such children whenever appropriate;

(e) supporting high-quality, intensive preservice preparation and professional development of all personnel who work with such children with disabilities in order to ensure that such personnel have the skills and knowledge necessary to improve the academic achievement and functional performance of children with disabilities, including the use of scientifically based instructional practices, to the maximum extent possible;

(f) providing incentives for whole-school approaches, scientifically based early reading programs, positive behavioral interventions and supports, and early intervening services to reduce the need to label children as disabled in order to address the learning and behavioral needs of such children;

(g) focusing resources on teaching and learning while reducing paperwork and requirements that do not assist in improving educational results.

(h) supporting the development and use of technology, including assistive technology devices and assistive technology services, to maximize accessibility for children with disabilities.

In summary, the law requires that students with disabilities be educated in general education classrooms to the maximum extent appropriate with supports necessary to be successful, that students with disabilities be held to the same high expectations as students without disabilities, and that all student learning be measured. With this knowledge about the law, an inclusion facilitator may be able to prevent unnecessary due process challenges. When school districts are reluctant to follow the intention of the law, parents and guardians may need to be referred to their state's protection and advocacy agency to gain support for the high-quality inclusive educational practices required under the law. The protection and advocacy agencies that exist in every state are mandated to provide information, referral, and legal advocacy services to individuals with disabilities and their family members. In addition, parent advocacy organizations exist locally and nationally to support parents who disagree with school districts regarding legal issues.

When Jackson's mother initially requested that Jackson register for general education classes in his neighborhood middle school, the school administrators were reluctant to support this placement. Their response was that they had never had a student with such significant needs before, and their teachers were not trained. They recommended that Jackson would be better off enrolled in a functional skills special education classroom. Jackson's mother contacted the local protection and advocacy agency and requested legal advice and representation to support her request. Sam supported the parent's request by educating others about the law and investigating resources available to the school district through Part D. Because of Sam's successful intervention, costly mediation and due process proceedings were avoided, and members of Jackson's team were able to focus on identifying and supporting his needs in middle school instead of reasons and strategies for exclusion.

CONCLUSION

Some people wonder if being a good inclusion facilitator is more a matter of possessing a set of skills related to promising practices or whether it is more important to possess an attitude and set of philosophical values. It is both. The skill set is easy to learn once one has the philosophy that all students can learn in general education classes when high academic expectations and the right supports are in place. Inclusion facilitators who work in separate classrooms where students with disabilities spend more than 50% of the day may possess 80% of the skills outlined in this book, but without a belief in the value of inclusive education, students will still be in that self-contained classroom years from now.

REFERENCES

ADAMHA Reorganization Act, PL 102-321, 42 U.S.C. §§ 201 *et seq.*
Brown v. Board of Education, 347 U.S. 483 (1954).
Burns, B., & Goldman, S. (Eds.). (1999). *Systems of care: IV. Promising practices in children's mental health.* Washington, DC: American Institutes for Research, Center for Effective Collaboration and Practice.
Civil Rights Act of 1964, PL 88-352, 20 U.S.C. §§ 241 *et seq.*
Civil Rights Act of 1968, PL 90-448, 42 U.S.C. §§ 3601 *et seq.*
Education for All Handicapped Children Act of 1975, PL 94-142, 20 U.S.C. §§ 1400 *et seq.*
Giangreco, M.F., Prelock, P.A., Reid, R.R., Dennis, R.E., & Edelman, S.W. (2000). Roles of related services personnel in inclusive schools. In R.A. Villa & J.S. Thousand (Eds.), *Restructuring for caring and effective education: Piecing the puzzle together* (2nd ed., pp. 360–388). Baltimore: Paul H. Brookes Publishing Co.
Goldman, S. (1999). The conceptual framework for wraparound. In B. Burns & S. Goldman (Eds.), *Systems of care: IV. Promising practices in children's mental health* (pp. 27–34). Washington, DC: American Institutes for Research, Center for Effective Collaboration and Practice.
Individuals with Disabilities Education Improvement Act of 2004, PL 108-446, 20 U.S.C. §§ 1400 *et. seq.*
Knitzer, J. (1982). *Unclaimed children: The failure of public responsibility to children and adolescents in need of mental health services.* Washington, DC: Children's Defense Fund.
Lipsky, D.K., & Gartner, A. (1997). *Inclusion and school reform: Transforming America's classrooms.* Baltimore: Paul H. Brookes Publishing Co.
Mills v. Board of Education of the District of Columbia, 348 F. Supp. 866 (D.D.C. 1972).
National Council on Disability. (1995). *Improving the implementation of the Individuals with Disabilities Education Act: Making schools work for all of America's children.* Washington, DC: Author.
Pennsylvania Association for Retarded Children v. Commonwealth of Pennsylvania, 334 F. Supp. 1257 (E.D. Pa. 1971).
Roach, V. (1995). *Winning ways: Creating inclusive schools, classrooms, and communities.* Alexandria, VA: National Association of State Boards of Education.
Ryndak, D.L., Clark, D., Conroy, M., & Stuart, C.H. (2001). Preparing teachers to meet the needs of students with severe disabilities: Program configuration and expertise. *Journal for The Association for Persons with Severe Handicaps, 26*(2), 96–105.
Sacramento City Unified School District v. Rachel H., 14 F.3d 1398 (9th Cir. 1994).

Stroul, B.A. (1996). Service coordination in systems of care. In B.A. Stroul (Ed.), *Children's mental health* (pp. 265–280). Baltimore: Paul H. Brookes Publishing Co.

Thousand, J., Villa, R., Paolucci-Whitcomb, P., & Nevin, A. (1992). A rationale for collaborative consultation. In W. Stainback & S. Stainback (Eds.), *Divergent perspectives in special education* (pp. 223–232). Boston: Allyn & Bacon.

Villa, R.A. (with Holland, R., & Connor, K.). (2000). A conversation with Rachel Holland's parents. In R.A Villa & J.S. Thousand (Eds.), *Restructuring for caring and effective education* (pp. 493–502). Baltimore: Paul H. Brookes Publishing Co.

Yell, M., Drasgow, E., Bradley, R., & Justeen, T. (2004). Contemporary legal issues in special education. In A. Sorrells, H. Reith, & P. Sindelar (Eds.), *Critical issues in special education* (pp. 16–37). Boston: Pearson Education.

Restructuring to Support Inclusive Education
Organizational Structures that Enable Inclusion Facilitators to Succeed

Cheryl M. Jorgensen

When people say, "Inclusion doesn't work," a major contributing factor is almost always the lack of supportive school policies and structures rather than a student's particular challenge or characteristic. Many organizational changes must be made to support a school that is moving from including one or two students with significant disabilities in general education classes toward having a capacity to include all students. This chapter discusses the need for changing a variety of organizational structures or policies with respect to teachers' roles and responsibilities, instructional planning time, accessible technology, configuration of services for students age 18–21, and professional development for staff. Examples are shared from elementary, middle, and high schools, and suggestions are offered for what an inclusion facilitator can do to manage the change process.

CHANGING ROLES

In a school where students with significant disabilities are educated in separate classes, the roles of general and special education staff perpetuate segregation, not inclusion. For example, special education teachers are responsible for assessment, instructional planning, teaching, and grading for students with disabilities who are in their

Preparation of this chapter was supported in part by a grant from the U.S. Department of Education, Office of Special Education Programs, #H324M020067.

classes. All of their energies are devoted to those tasks, and they have little time left over to work toward inclusion. Likewise, general education teachers in such a school are responsible only for students without disabilities. Their knowledge of students with significant disabilities is limited to occasional contact in the hallways or playground, and there is no incentive for general educators to initiate discussions with special educators about inclusion. Related-services professionals deliver services within the special education classroom and rarely have the opportunity to seek out opportunities for students to learn communication or movement skills within the general education environment. The special education administrator oversees policies and procedures that govern students with disabilities and their staff, whereas principals are responsible for general education policies, procedures, and staff.

When the first student with a disability in a traditional school is included in general education classes, a tension is created between teachers' primary roles and teachers' new responsibility of supporting that one student to be successful in general education. The special education teacher usually finds that he or she does not have time to consult with the general education teacher who has the student with significant disabilities because the special education teacher is in the self-contained classroom teaching other students. Likewise, the general education teacher may have one planning period every day and may not want to give up that time to plan for just one student with disabilities.

Related-services providers are accustomed to providing direct services to students in the special education classroom and often have difficulty finding time to go to the general education classes and support the one student with significant disabilities. They are used to providing more medically based therapies that may not be linked to the curriculum and may be unsure how to meet a student's needs within the context of a math, biology, or history class.

When schools shift to including all students, it is essential to reconfigure staff roles. In Chapters 4–6, new roles are described for each team member, emphasizing collaborative responsibility for many aspects of educational planning, instruction, and evaluation. Additional detail is provided in the remainder of this section regarding these necessary role changes.

Role of the Special Education Teacher

When some students with significant disabilities are included and others are still being taught partially or fully within a self-contained classroom, a special education teacher is not positioned to do the inclusion facilitator's job well. Perhaps the greatest challenge for the special education teacher is managing the diverse educational programs and placements of a large group of students.

Carol's Story

Carol Maneros is a high school special education teacher. For years, she taught a self-contained class of 12 students with moderate and significant disabilities while the other special education teachers in her building provided resource room support to students with mild disabilities. Some of Carol's students attended one general education class in physical education or the arts, but most were with her all day. Two years ago, the school examined the outcomes for these students. The administrators discovered that there was little contact between these students and their classmates without disabilities, most of these students were not participating in any extracurricular activities other than Special Olympics, none graduated with a high school diploma, most were unemployed after high school because they were on waiting lists for the state's developmental services, and all lived at home.

A decision was made to begin to include students with significant disabilities in more general education classes, making Carol's job nearly impossible to do well. Carol is now the case manager for eight students, but the students' programs are so diverse that she must continue to provide direct instruction to students throughout the day as well as support those who are in general education classes. Three of her students are in general education classes for most of the school day, two have a half-and-half schedule, two are in her room for three of four blocks during the day, and one 20-year-old spends the whole day learning in the community in preparation for transition to adult life. The building's special education coordinator has worked hard to give Carol two planning blocks every day, but this time is not nearly enough to do the job of an inclusion facilitator well. Carol is constantly faced with the challenges of preparing lessons for the students in her classroom and trying to find time to meet with general education teachers or other team members, and she almost never finds time to go out into the community with the older student who is supported by a skilled paraprofessional.

A better solution would be for the school to restructure all of the special educator roles and for Carol to be the school's inclusion facilitator, responsible just for students with significant disabilities who are included in general education classes. In this model, teachers who work with students with less significant disabilities might be assigned to grade levels or departments (and support the students placed there), and Carol would be the case manager for students with significant disabilities in ninth through twelfth grades. A learning center would provide the services previously offered in a resource room, and students with and without disabilities could receive academic support and tutoring there. Students provided with special education services between the ages of 18 and 21 might be served by a transition coordinator whose expertise is employment, housing, community inclusion, creative budgeting, guardianship, and postsecondary education.

Carol would then have the whole day free to perform the tasks needed to support inclusion well, including 1) meeting with general education teachers to find out about upcoming lessons, materials, assessments, and instructional routines; 2) meeting with each student's core instructional planning team to develop supports for the student's participation and learning; 3) observing, modeling for, and supervising paraprofessionals; 4) working within the general education classroom to provide occasional direct instruction to students; 5) meeting with other special education staff who work in the school's learning center (i.e., resource room); and 6) maintaining contact with students' families.

In reality, schools do not usually move from a self-contained model of education to a fully inclusive one overnight, and they usually continue to do pull-out instruction for some students some of the time. In Carol's school, they might manage this intermediate step by having students attend a learning center for direct instruction that is provided by a teacher whose expertise is with students with less significant disabilities, supported by consultation from Carol.

Table 8.1 illustrates how an inclusion facilitator's school day is significantly different from that of an elementary school special educator in a self-contained classroom. It is critically important that principals and special education administrators understand that the inclusion facilitator's role requires an expert level of skills in facilitation, observation, problem solving, instructional planning and evaluation, and mentoring, and that even when an inclusion facilitator is not spending time teaching individual students, he or she is supporting all members of students' teams to provide quality inclusive education. Even when it appears that an inclusion facilitator is just standing in the back of the general education classroom, he or she is not daydreaming but rather thinking about a myriad of questions concerning a student's inclusion that will become the focus for discussion, planning, and action at an upcoming team meeting.

Table 8.1. Comparison between the schedules of an elementary school special educator in a self-contained classroom and an inclusion facilitator

Time	Elementary school special educator's schedule	Inclusion facilitator's schedule
7:30 A.M.	Assist students in exiting the special education bus	Meet with the first-grade team to plan a Halloween play
8:00	Lead a circle time activity	Teach a reading group in a third-grade classroom to determine how one student's augmentative and alternative communication system is working
8:45	Teach language arts	Meet with the third-grade team to discuss the student's alternate assessment portfolio
9:30	Supervise toileting	Meet with two paraprofessionals to teach them how to use Boardmaker and Writing with Symbols
10:00	Observe the occupational therapist working with students during an art activity	Meet with the sixth-grade team to discuss an upcoming trip to an environmental camp
10:45	Observe and participate in physical therapy sessions	Review the state curriculum frameworks in preparation for developing students' individualized education programs
11:30	Teach students to make sandwiches for lunch	Eat lunch in a teacher's room
12:00 P.M.	Eat lunch with students and paraprofessionals in the classroom	Meet with a sixth-grade teacher to preview an upcoming unit on Native Americans
12:30	Supervise teeth brushing and toileting	Observe the playground to assess accessibility to all equipment and to support students' social relationships
1:00	Teach math	Meet with the preschool team and parents to discuss the transition of a 5-year-old child into kindergarten
1:30	Teach science	Use individual planning time to adapt worksheets for fourth-grade social studies
2:00	Escort students to the special education bus	Perform hall duty as school dismisses

Role of the General Education Teacher

As a student's primary teacher, the general educator becomes a part of a team of professionals who assess, instruct, and evaluate all students, including those with significant disabilities. The student with significant disabilities is not a visitor to the classroom but rather one of the general educator's students. Lesson plans (i.e., what to teach, how to teach it, the materials and assessments to use) now include consideration of a student with significant disabilities. The teacher devotes a regular preparation period to meeting with the inclusion facilitator or other members of the student's team to discuss upcoming lessons, review student progress, and design supports and accommodations that promote student learning.

Role of the Related-Services Provider

The related-services provider's role also changes significantly when students with disabilities are enrolled in general education classes (Rainforth & York-Barr, 1997). When students with significant disabilities are educated in self-contained classes, their related-services goals tend to focus on discrete skills in the areas of communication, movement, or behavior. Hunt and Farron-Davis (1992) found that IEP goals of self-contained students focused on isolated skills (e.g., maintaining eye contact, making choices, reaching and grasping objects), but when the students were included in general education activities and classes, their IEP goals emphasized the use of skills in functional contexts (e.g., maintaining eye contact in order to get information from the blackboard, making choices from among several books in the library, using fine motor skills to gain access to a keyboard).

Related-services providers also must change where they deliver supports and services. Communication skills can be supported within reading groups or on the playground. Gross motor skills can be supported as students move from class to class or participate in physical education. Fine motor skills can be supported as students use computers, participate in art activities, or complete vocational tasks. The question that focuses the activities of related-services professionals in an inclusive school is "What support does the student need in order to fully participate in the general education class and other inclusive environments?"

In a self-contained model, the speech-language pathologist might be accustomed to seeing a student three times per week for 30 minutes per session. In an inclusive model, communication supports and services might be better provided through longer blocks of time, for example, 45 minutes of support with the student in his science lab group and 45 minutes meeting with the student's core instructional planning team discussing needed messages for the student's communication device.

PLANNING TIME

All teams supporting students with significant disabilities need regular, uninterrupted, and effectively used planning time. Although the amount of time and its frequency vary greatly from school to school, many teams report that a core instructional planning group needs to meet at least once a week at the beginning and end of the school year and once every other week if things are going smoothly. Scheduling regular instructional planning meetings depends largely on how the whole school schedule is organized, but there are archetypal models in elementary, middle, and high schools. In most elementary schools, general education teachers identify themselves as members of grade-level teams. They usually meet once a month or so to talk about curriculum, standards, assessment, and grade-level instructional themes. Within this grade-level team model, an inclusion facilitator might meet with individual teachers once a week during a planning period to talk about specific students and attend the monthly grade-level meetings to participate in discussion of broader grade-level issues. For example, an inclusion facilitator might meet with first-grade teachers on Mondays, second-grade teachers on Tuesdays, and so forth.

In most middle schools, general education teachers also identify themselves as members of grade-level teams or clusters, but they meet nearly every day during a common planning period to plan instructional themes, discuss social issues of adolescence, and meet with other school staff such as guidance counselors or social workers. Just as in the typical elementary school, an inclusion facilitator can meet with individual teachers once a week during a planning period and meet with the whole grade-level team on a regular basis.

High schools present a host of challenges for an inclusion facilitator who wants to collaborate with general education teachers. A student who is fully included might be enrolled in five or six general education classes. Maximizing student participation and learning requires that comprehensive support plans be developed for all subject areas.

Gail Larson is a high school inclusion facilitator who is the case manager for the educational programs of several students with significant disabilities in Grades 10–12. She has developed a schedule to meet with each general education teacher (for 30 minutes) and each student's core instructional planning team (for 1 hour) every other week to find out about upcoming units and lessons and to plan student supports for those classes. Her weekly routine consists of general education teacher meetings on Tuesdays, core instructional planning team meetings on Wednesdays, meetings with related-services providers on Fridays, and meetings with students' paraprofessionals on Mondays and Thursdays. She reserves one block each day for making adapted materials or doing case management paperwork, two blocks for meetings, and one block for classroom observations and supervision of paraprofessionals.

ACCESSIBLE TECHNOLOGY

Although it is not strictly an organizational or policy change per se, ensuring that the school's technology is accessible is an essential component of ensuring full student participation and learning. There are two areas in which technology must be adapted for students with significant disabilities. First, computers and other information technology must be physically accessible for students. Computer desks must accommodate wheelchairs or other seating adaptations. All students must have physical access to the computer with adaptive keyboards, switches, or screen readers. Students who do not write with pencils need to have access to computers or AlphaSmart keyboards (AlphaSmart) in every class so they can take notes or do in-class writing.

Second, all print resources in a school must be available in digitized format to facilitate accessibility and personalized adaptations (Rose & Meyer, 2002). During the 2003 school year, Carol Maneros' students were enrolled in classes in which they had to have access to texts as diverse as *Romeo and Juliet,* soldiers' first-hand accounts of the Vietnam War, math worksheets, cookbook recipes, the student handbook, and the Internet! None of her students were fluent readers or writers, so they needed access to a variety of learning technologies, including text-to-speech and speech-to-text software, adaptive keyboards, Co-Writer (Don Johnston), Writing with Symbols (Widgit Software), and Boardmaker (Mayer-Johnson). Carol and the other team members also needed to have access to the digitized text to manipulate font size and style, color, background, and white space and to create adapted versions of readings, worksheets, and tests. Until all educational materials are available in accessible formats, inclusion facilitators will need to work with the school's technology staff and other outside resources to customize both software and hardware for students.

EDUCATION FOR STUDENTS AGES 18–21

When students with significant disabilities are included in general education classes and their teams determine that they need special education services after their senior year, a new component to the school program must be created that is not based within the high school building. This component is educational services that help a student make the transition from high school to adult life.

The core principle in inclusive education is that the educational programs of students with significant disabilities should parallel the educational opportunities of students without disabilities of the same age. Thus, from the ages of 18 to 21, students with significant disabilities should be pursuing some combination of postsecondary education, community living, and employment outside of the high school building. The natural environments for these students' educational programs would include 2- and 4-year colleges or technical schools; adult education programs; home or apartment; integrated workplaces; and the broader community, including restaurants, libraries, and fitness facilities (Shapiro-Barnard et al., 1996).

Supporting this new educational program component requires restructuring job roles, schedules, transportation services, and financing. Many larger schools designate a teacher to work exclusively with students in this age group. This transition coordinator— a community-based inclusion facilitator of sorts—is responsible for working with each student and family to develop a futures plan and then to establish relationships with supports in the community that will help the student make progress toward his or her life goals. Rather than creating a transition program in which all students are automatically enrolled, creating individualized learning opportunities is essential. For example, Nate may want to enroll in several community college courses and still live at home. Alicia may want to sample several jobs and move from living at home to living in an apartment with roommates. Julia may want to gain experience volunteering. Each of these students' transition programs would be different and require different levels of support from friends, co-workers, or paid staff from the community. A transition coordinator's job must be structured to give him or her the same level of flexibility as an inclusion facilitator as he or she no longer has a classroom of students to teach but rather a group of students to connect to the community.

PROFESSIONAL DEVELOPMENT

In an inclusive school, general and special educators participate in professional development activities related to the promising practices described in Chapter 2. In the past, professional development has consisted primarily of 1-day workshops or the occasional graduate course. Since the mid-1990s, however, the definition of high-quality professional development for all teachers has changed dramatically. Today, there is a greater emphasis on job-embedded professional development grounded in the principles of reflective practice (Hole & McEntee, 1999).

Reflective practice is defined as "a cognitive process and open perspective that involves a deliberate pause to examine beliefs, goals, or practices in order to gain new or deeper understanding that leads to actions improving the lives of students" (Montie, York-Barr, Kronberg, Stevenson, Vallejo, & Lunders, n.d., p. 2). Reflective practice is being used across the United States in teacher education programs (Weir, Jorgensen, & Dowd, 2002a). It is a cornerstone of national school reform organizations such as the Coalition of Essential Schools and the Annenberg Institute for School Reform (McEntee et al., 2003). The principles of reflective practice inform national standards for professional development such as those of the National Staff Development Council (Sparks & Hirsh, 1997).

Reflective practice is characterized by teachers' participation in small learning communities that meet on a regular basis to talk about school culture, teaching, and student learning. Although the names of these groups vary from school to school (e.g., study groups, action research groups, critical friends groups, lesson study groups, reflective practice groups), they all have in common a focus on collaborative, nonjudgmental conversations about improving student performance.

Reflective practice groups can be a powerful tool for teams trying to solve challenges relating to inclusive education, such as

- Reorganizing staff assignments and caseloads so that all students are well supported

- Solving problems related to a student's challenging behavior

- Determining why a student is having difficulty using an augmentative and alternative communication (AAC) device

- Gaining insight into what supports best facilitate a student's learning of the general education curriculum

- Developing strategies for promoting acceptance of diversity within a school

- Finding ways to improve a student's social connections and friendships

Reflective practice groups often use structured protocols in their group meetings rather than simply having open discussions that seldom result in consensus around a plan of action. The term *protocol* has taken on a specific meaning in education in recent years. In the context of educators working to improve their practice, a protocol is a structured set of process guidelines to promote meaningful and efficient communication and learning (Hole & McEntee, 1999).

There are many different types of reflective practice protocols, but all have common elements, including

- One or a few people presenting problems, ideas, syllabi, lesson plans, support ideas, communication boards, positive behavior support plans, descriptions of a critical incident (Tripp, 1993), or samples of student work for reflection by their colleagues

- Small group of colleagues who will serve as consultants to the presenter/s

- Structure for engaging in conversation, reflection, or problem solving

- Facilitator of the process who guides group norms, protocol steps, roles, and time

An inclusion facilitator is in a good position to lead a reflective practice protocol. His or her role would be

- Providing logistical support for the group and arranging locations and times for meetings

- Supporting and monitoring the group's use of protocols and other reflective practice tools to constantly move its work forward

- Supporting the group to establish and maintain group norms

- Keeping the group focused on the problem identified by the presenters in a protocol

- Bringing problems in communication to the surface and providing support to group members to improve their skills

- Teaching the group about new problem-solving protocols and strategies

- Monitoring the group's adherence to time guidelines during protocols

- Assisting in resolving conflicts

The Consultancy Protocol, depicted in Figure 8.1, is an example of job-embedded professional development that is focused on improving student learning results.

Description
A consultancy is a structured process for helping an individual (or a small group of people) think more expansively about a particular concrete problem or dilemma. Outside perspective is critical to this protocol working effectively; therefore, some of the participants in the group must be people who do not share the presenter's specific problem at that time.

Sample introduction
"During our session, we will engage in a small group process called a *consultancy*. So, as you prepare for our work together, please do some thinking and writing ahead of time about a dilemma or problem related to our student. Please bring copies of a 1-page description of your dilemma ending with a specific question or issue with which you would like our help. Dilemmas deal with issues with which you are struggling, a nagging hunch that you should be doing things differently, a recently hatched plan for what to do next, or something that is problematic or not as effective as you would like it to be—anything related to our work with the student that you would like to examine with two to three other participants in our Reflective Practice group. If our past experience offers any indication, you will be able to rely on the people in your consultancy to provide respectful, thoughtful experience."

Time
45–55 minutes

Process
1. Presentation of issue (5–10 minutes)

   The presenter gives an overview of the dilemma or problem, highlighting the major issues with which he or she is struggling, and names a question for the consultancy group to consider. The framing of this question, as well as the quality of the presenter's reflection on the dilemma being discussed, are key features of this protocol. At some point in Step 1, the group reads or listens to the dilemma.

2. Clarifying questions (5 minutes)

   The consultancy group asks clarifying questions of the presenter. These questions have brief, factual answers.

3. Probing questions (10 minutes)

   The group then asks probing questions of the presenter. The goal here is for the presenter to learn more about the question he or she framed or to analyze the dilemma being presented. The presenter responds to the group members' questions, but there is no discussion by the group about the presenter's responses.

4. Discussion (15 minutes)

   The group members then talk with one another about the dilemma presented (e.g., "What did you hear?" "What didn't you hear that might be relevant?" "What do you think about the problem?"). Members of the group occasionally suggest solutions to the dilemma; most often, however, the group works to define the issues more thoroughly and objectively. The presenters are not allowed to speak during the discussion but instead listen and take notes.

5. Presenter response (5–10 minutes)

   The presenter then responds to the discussion (if there is more than one presenter and if the presenters prefer to proceed that way, a small group of participants can gather in the middle of the room [i.e., the fishbowl] while the others observe), followed by a whole-group discussion.

6. Debriefing (5 minutes)

   The facilitator leads a conversation about the group's observations of the process (e.g., "What worked?" "What didn't work?" "What was learned?").

Figure 8.1. Consultancy protocol. (From Weir, C., Jorgensen, C., & Dowd, J. [2002b]. The consultancy protocol. In C. Weir, C. Jorgensen, & J. Dowd, *Promoting excellence in college teaching: A reflective practice toolkit for coaches* [pp. 63–65]. Durham: Institute on Disability at the University of New Hampshire; adapted by permission.)

CONCLUSION

The organizational changes described in this chapter all serve to advance inclusion from an experimental program with one or a few students to a broad-based school reform effort that affects the entire school's culture, curriculum, professional practice, and relationships.

REFERENCES

Hole, S., & McEntee, G. (1999). Reflection is at the heart of practice. *Educational Leadership, 56*(8), 34–37.

Hunt, P., & Farron-Davis, F. (1992). A preliminary investigation of IEP quality and content associated with placement in general education versus special education classes. *Journal of The Association for Persons with Severe Handicaps, 17*(4), 247–253.

McEntee, G., Appleby, J., Dowd, J., Grant, J., Hole, S., Silva, P., et al. (2003). *At the heart of teaching: A guide to reflective practice.* New York: Teachers College Press.

Montie, J., York-Barr, J., Kronberg, R., Stevenson, J., Vallejo, B., & Lunders, C. (n.d.). *Reflective practice: Creating capacities for school improvement.* Minneapolis: University of Minnesota, Institute on Community Integration.

Rainforth, B., & York-Barr, C. (1997). *Collaborative teams for students with severe disabilities: Integrating therapy and educational services* (2nd ed.). Baltimore: Paul H. Brookes Publishing Co.

Rose, D., & Meyer, A. (2002). *Teaching every student in the digital age. Universal design for learning.* Alexandria, VA: Association for Supervision and Curriculum Development.

Shapiro-Barnard, S., Tashie, C., Martin, J., Malloy, J., Schuh, M., Piet, J., et al. (1996). *Petroglyphs: The writing on the wall.* Durham: Institute on Disability at the University of New Hampshire.

Sparks, D., & Hirsh, S. (1997). *A new vision for staff development.* Alexandria, VA: Association for Supervision and Curriculum Development and National Staff Development Council.

Tripp, D. (1993). *Critical incidents in teaching: Developing professional judgment.* New York: Routledge Press.

Weir, C., Jorgensen, C., & Dowd, J. (2002a). *Promoting excellence in college teaching: A reflective practice toolkit for coaches.* Durham: Institute on Disability at the University of New Hampshire.

Weir, C., Jorgensen, C., & Dowd, J. (2002b). The consultancy protocol. In C. Weir, C. Jorgensen, & J. Dowd, *Promoting excellence in college teaching: A reflective practice toolkit for coaches* (pp. 63–65). Durham: Institute on Disability at the University of New Hampshire.

Preservice Education
of Inclusion Facilitators

One University's Program

Cheryl M. Jorgensen

Rebecca (Becka) Kaas grew up in southern New Hampshire with her brother, Ben, who experiences significant disabilities, including Tourette syndrome. Becka is a few years older than Ben and has been an active part of his educational team since he entered high school, advocating for Ben's inclusion in a regular schedule of courses and extracurricular activities. Due in large part to Becka's experiences as Ben's advocate, she decided that becoming an inclusion facilitator was one way she could make a positive difference in the lives of other students with significant disabilities and their families.

> *I have always wanted to be a teacher but didn't really think about special education until I began attending Ben's IEP [individualized education program] meetings while I was still in high school. Although Ben had a few really great teachers throughout his schooling, there were many times when I felt that his special education teachers were not very well prepared with the necessary advocacy skills or the knowledge about the technical aspects of inclusion. So when I looked around at graduate schools, I was immediately attracted to the UNH [University of New Hampshire] Inclusion Facilitator Option. It had the mix of philosophy*

Preparation of this chapter was supported in part by a grant from the U.S. Department of Education, Office of Special Education Programs, #H324M020067.

and skills that I was looking for. I know that I will face lots of struggles when I try to promote inclusion out in the "real world," but I think that the UNH program has given me a great foundation for that challenge.

This chapter begins with a brief description of the national context that underlies UNH's Inclusion Facilitator Option that prepares teachers for students with significant disabilities. It then describes the program's philosophical and pedagogical foundations, program competencies, required courses, and other learning experiences. Although the UNH program was designed specifically to fit within the broader teacher education program at UNH and to be responsive to New Hampshire's teacher certification system, many of its features can be generalized to other states and institutions of higher education.

NATIONAL CONTEXT

Many universities face a major dilemma. They believe that one of the best ways to promote the inclusion of students with disabilities is to prepare all teachers to teach all students (TASH, 2002). Thus, many teacher education programs have been restructured to infuse relevant special education content into general education courses or to combine relevant special education content with general education content in a unified program (Blanton, Griffin, Winn, & Pugach, 1998; Keefe, Rossi, De Valenzuela, & Howarth, 2000). Others believe that some professionals on a student's team need specialized knowledge and skills related to the complex needs of students with significant disabilities. This belief has led to the maintenance of specialized teacher education programs in severe disabilities at the undergraduate and graduate level (Eichinger & Downing, 2000). Programs designed to prepare teachers for this population of students are varied, however, due to several factors, such as 1) differing philosophies regarding what constitutes promising practices for students with significant disabilities; 2) the lack of a universally accepted set of beliefs, knowledge, and skills necessary to teach students with significant disabilities; 3) the great variety of state certification standards governing teacher education programs; and 4) the lack of a clear description of the experiences required to acquire competence (e.g., the combination of courses, field experiences, research experiences, and experiences with families or individuals with disabilities).

For example, the Council for Exceptional Children (CEC; 2004) has defined two different competency sets for teachers of students with significant disabilities. One set is for teachers of students who are pursuing the general education curriculum content, and another set is for teachers of students who are pursuing an individualized independence curriculum. In other words, the CEC believes that some students with significant disabilities will not be pursuing the general education curriculum content.

Jackson, Ryndak, and Billingsley (2000) conducted a study to collect information on the configuration of nationally recognized master's programs and the areas of expertise that they considered essential for teachers of students with significant disabilities. Twenty university programs across the country were asked to provide information about the types of graduate students enrolled, the population of students for whom teachers were being prepared, the program's structure, and the specific competencies being taught. Although there were some differences across programs, all required students to have field experiences with students with significant disabilities of different ages. Most considered that an inclusive school was the ideal setting for students' internships, although not all required such a placement. There was strong agreement across all programs regarding the areas of expertise needed by teachers, including collaboration and technical assistance, inclusion, advocacy and self-determination, knowledge of the curriculum content, effective instruction, functional behavioral assessment, transition to adulthood, physical and sensory disabilities, and research methods.

NEW HAMPSHIRE CONTEXT

Against this backdrop of an emerging consensus regarding what constitutes an appropriate education for teachers of students with significant disabilities (if not consensus regarding the job title), the Inclusion Facilitator Option at UNH was born.

Teacher Certification and the Teacher Education System in New Hampshire

The special education teacher certification system in New Hampshire includes a beginning teacher's license, called *General Special Education*, and endorsements in the areas of learning disabilities, emotional disabilities, sensory disabilities, and mental retardation (which serves as the state's severe disabilities or intensive special needs certification). For many years, one of New Hampshire's state colleges had a master's level program leading to certification in mental retardation. But beginning in 1990, it gradually decreased the number of students admitted into the program, and by the mid-1990s, few teachers were being prepared in this category at all. Thus, there was a significant shortage of teachers certified in mental retardation and no higher education capacity to remedy the shortage.

To respond to this need, the Institute on Disability (IOD) at the UNH received funding from the U.S. Department of Education, Office of Special Education Programs, to create a series of courses and other learning experiences leading to state certification in mental retardation. The program operated from 1998 through 2001 and was designed for two primary trainee groups: teachers already working full time in schools but not certified in mental retardation and graduate students at UNH who would work toward their General Special Education and mental retardation certifications concurrently. The program was highly successful, graduating 19 of 22 students who enrolled, and as the grant-funding period approached its conclusion, plans were developed to make the program a permanent part of UNH's special education teacher education program. In the spring of 2002, faculty approved the new coursework associated with the Inclusion Facilitator Option.

THE INCLUSION FACILITATOR OPTION

There are many dimensions of the Inclusion Facilitator Option that are exemplary, including the program's philosophical and pedagogical foundations and underlying competencies. Coursework, participation of individuals with disabilities and their families, evaluation of student work, and other learning experiences are also provided to enrolled students.

Philosophical Foundations

The philosophical foundations of the Option are based on a number of beliefs, including 1) disability is primarily a social construct; 2) students with disabilities have gifts and talents that make a positive contribution to our schools and communities; 3) all people are competent, given the right supports; 4) in the absence of definitive information about an individual's abilities, an assumption of competence should apply; and 5) inclusive education provides the best learning model for all students, including those with the most significant disabilities. Several resolutions adopted by TASH (formerly known as The Association for Persons with Severe Handicaps) were particularly instrumental in providing direction to the development of the Option's competency statements that relate to philosophy, including the TASH Resolutions on Inclusive Quality Education and Teacher Education (TASH, 2000, 2002).

Pedagogical Foundations

Quality teacher education consists of more than book learning in the college classroom. It must include opportunities to explore values, develop professional dispositions, learn about promising practices, practice the skills required of future job roles, and develop the habits associated with being a reflective practitioner. The Inclusion Facilitator Option was designed to reflect these elements of high-quality teacher education.

A variety of learning experiences and teaching strategies are used in every course that is part of the Option, including

- Listening to the personal stories of and having conversations with people who experience a label of developmental disability and/or their family members who represent diverse cultures and backgrounds

- Listening to experts discuss current promising practices from the professional literature and practice

- Reading professional literature in the field

- Viewing videotapes that depict critical issues or promising practices

- Visiting schools and classrooms where students with significant disabilities are included

- Working with families and school teams to complete assignments

- Participating in facilitated whole-class discussions

- Participating in small classroom groups that use systematic problem solving and reflective practice groups

- Engaging in personal reflection about topics, learning experiences, and related writing assignments

Although some states have established certification-only options to quickly respond to teacher shortages, UNH is committed to a

5-year teacher education program, built on the foundation of a strong undergraduate major in liberal arts. All students in the Inclusion Facilitator Option who do not already have a master's degree must be enrolled at least part time in UNH's master of education program, although individual courses in the Option may be taken for professional development hours by any practicing teacher. The Inclusion Facilitator Option was designed based on the belief that students must demonstrate their growing knowledge and skills by learning and doing the same kinds of things that are done by teachers in the field. Therefore, within every course, students go out into schools to perform the work typically done by inclusion facilitators with support from their course instructors, cooperating teachers, and teams.

Competencies

The competencies associated with the Inclusion Facilitator Option, depicted in Appendix A, are derived from many sources, including TASH, CEC, the American Association on Mental Retardation, and the New Hampshire Teacher Certification Standards in Mental Retardation. The competencies are written to reflect four teacher attributes (i.e., values, dispositions, knowledge, skills) across seven broad skill/role areas. Although the competencies are written to reflect attributes that teachers need to support students who are already in inclusive educational programs, the competencies also reflect the skills needed to advocate for and develop a quality inclusive program for students who are not currently educated in a general education classroom in their neighborhood school.

All of the competency standards discussed next imply collaboration even if collaboration is not stated explicitly.

Cultural Competence   Culture comprises all aspects of children's familial and community backgrounds and often has significant impact on their educational experience (Webb-Johnson, Artiles, Trent, Jackson, & Velox, 1998). Although New Hampshire is not one of the most heterogeneous states in the United States, it does have strong Franco-American, Lao, and Hispanic neighborhoods in several small and large communities. Students in the Inclusion Facilitator Option are taught to consider the influence of their own culture and background on the ways they view disability and to learn about the educational community in which they work, including the role of families in their children's education. They are also taught to consider the role of their students' cultures and family backgrounds with respect to the determination of disability, behavioral expectations in school, language development, and how families view issues such as self-determination and going to college. Coursework contains specific readings and assignments designed to teach these awarenesses and related skills.

Performance-Based Evaluation   Assignments within four of the program's courses are rated by both the student and instructor using a 5-point rubric evaluation system: *0* = did not hand in/attempt the assignment, *1* = novice, *2* = basic, *3* = proficient, and *4* = advanced mastery. If a student is not satisfied with an instructor's evaluation of an assignment, the assignment may be done over and the better grade counted toward the final course grade. At the end of the course, the student's self-evaluation scores and the instructor's scores are computed. If the instructor's grade is lower than the student's self-evaluation, the instructor and student try to resolve the discrepancy through discussion. In the event that complete agreement cannot be reached, the instructor's grade stands. UNH still uses a traditional letter grading system, and Table 9.1 shows how the rubric scores are converted to a grade at the end of the course.

Students at UNH are not allowed to apply toward degree courses in which they earned a grade of C or lower. Furthermore, in order to be recommended for state certification, students in the Inclusion Facilitator Option must earn a 3.0 average on all assignments (although they will pass any individual assignment with a score of greater than 2.0). All courses have expectations regarding attendance, class participation, and completion of assigned readings; this information can be found on-line at http://www.brookes publishing.com/inclusionfacilitator.

Individuals with Disabilities and Their Families as Course Instructors   A cornerstone of the Inclusion Facilitator Option is to involve individuals with disabilities and family members as guest

Table 9.1.   Conversion of rubric scores to grades

Rubric score	Grade
0.0 up to but not including 1.0	F
1.0 up to but not including 2.0	D
2.0 up to but not including 2.5	C
2.5 up to but not including 3.0	B
3.0 up to but not including 3.5	A–
3.5 up to 4.0	A

lecturers and instructors. The introductory course—Contemporary
Issues in Developmental Disabilities—is co-taught by a full-time
faculty member and Jocelyn Curtin, who experiences Rett syndrome and was included in general education classes during her
public school career. Other individuals with disabilities of various
ages and life experiences provide guest presentations in various
courses on topics such as deinstitutionalization, self-determination,
inclusive education, augmentative and alternative communication,
and social relationships. Family members also present their experiences to students in several of the Option's courses. Class sessions
that are taught by individuals with disabilities or family members
are among the most highly rated of the semester.

Inclusive Settings for Preinternship and Internship Experiences
All preinternship and internship opportunities are located in inclusive classrooms at the preschool, elementary, middle school, and
high school levels. Because the Inclusion Facilitator Option is an
integral part of UNH's master's program in special education, students in the Option must fulfill two different certification requirements during their internship—those associated with General Special Education certification and those associated with the Inclusion
Facilitator Option. Although every student's internship is slightly
different, the usual arrangement is that interns work 3 days per
week serving in the role of a general special educator, supporting
students with a variety of mild disabilities in numerous classrooms.
The other 2 weekdays the intern works with a few students with
significant disabilities who are also included in general education
classes. Although this arrangement makes the internship experience very intense and rigorous, interns remark that they benefit
from working in both roles and with a diverse array of students.

Mentoring from Institute on Disability Faculty and Staff
Every student who enrolls in the Inclusion Facilitator Option has
other learning experiences besides coursework and internships.
Mentorships with IOD faculty and staff also provide valuable learning opportunities. Some students receive graduate assistantships to
work on funded research or model demonstration projects. Some
attend professional conferences to co-present workshops or the results of student research projects. Others assist IOD staff with
workshops in New Hampshire schools or conferences. Students
report that one of their most valuable experiences is their participation in the IOD's New Hampshire Leadership Series. Two days per

month, individuals with disabilities, their family members, and graduate students come together to learn from national experts and self-advocates about promising practices, how to articulate and plan for current and future hopes and dreams, and community organizing and advocacy skills. These outside-of-the-classroom experiences provide practice-based opportunities for students to apply the lessons they are learning in coursework.

Course Sequence and Faculty   The courses in the Inclusion Facilitator Option are designed to be taken over a 2-year period, usually one course per academic semester.

Fall, Year 1:	Contemporary Issues in Developmental Disabilities (4 credits)
Spring, Year 1:	Positive Behavior Approaches (4 credits)
Summer, Year 1:	Augmentative and Alternative Communication (3 credits)
Fall, Year 2:	Inclusive Assessment, Curriculum, Instruction, and Communication Supports (4 credits); Facilitating Social Relationships, Part I (1 credit)
Spring, Year 2:	Facilitating Social Relationships, Part II (1 credit); Teaching Reading to Students with Disabilities (4 credits)
Summer, Year 2:	Leadership and Systems Change in Inclusive Education (2 credits)
Total:	23 credits

Course Descriptions   Five courses in the Inclusion Facilitator Option were designed specifically for this Option, and two are existing Education and Communication Sciences and Disorders departmental offerings. Descriptions of each course, course requirements and assignments, and examples of readings or other source materials are available on-line at http://www.brookespublishing. com/inclusionfacilitator.

CONCLUSION

Establishing the Inclusion Facilitator Option has taught the authors of this book many lessons. First, the program must have a strong philosophical base and provide intensive learning opportunities for students to debate, articulate, and defend the philosophy of inclusion in both supportive and challenging situations. Second, it is better to have a mix of students in the class that represent those who have never taught in schools as well as new and veteran teachers. Each group brings valuable perspectives to class discussions. Third, it is essential to involve people with disabilities and family members in teaching. Although they may not be able to cite chapter and verse from the latest professional journal articles, their experiences are essential and keep the Option's focus on making a difference in the lives of real people.

Fourth, faculty must be prepared for students being disillusioned with the reality of day-to-day public school life that they experience during their preinternship or internship assignments. Within the college classroom they are exposed to ideals and ideal situations. Coursework must include time to share in-school experiences and use problem-solving and reflective practice techniques to help students reconcile the discrepancy between the ideal and the real. Time should also be allowed for students to work through practical strategies as well as acquire noble philosophies.

Fifth, it would be difficult for an Option such as this to be financially self-sustaining, particularly in small population areas. Teacher educators must be creative in leveraging a variety of funding resources to support a program focused on the preparation of teachers for students with low-incidence disabilities. Personnel preparation grants, student-initiated research grants, model demonstration grants, and other external funding sources will likely be required to supplement university contributions to faculty salaries.

Sixth, students need a faculty or internship mentor who can support them to negotiate the Option's requirements and deadlines and who can provide a sounding board when their emerging ideals are challenged from outside the university. Finally, although distance- and technology-based instruction have their place in a teacher education option, there is no effective substitute for face-to-face interactions among students, individuals with disabilities, family members, faculty, and school staff.

REFERENCES

Blanton, L., Griffin, D., Winn, J., & Pugach, M. (1998). *Teacher education in transition: Collaborative programs to prepare general and special educators.* Denver, CO: Love Publishing.

Council for Exceptional Children. (2004). *Professional standards: Knowledge and skill base.* Retrieved May 21, 2005, from http://www.cec.sped.org/ps/perf_based_stds/knowledge_standards.html

Eichinger, J., & Downing, J. (2000). Reconceptualizing special education certification: What should be done? *Journal of The Association for Persons with Severe Handicaps, 25,* 109–112.

Jackson, L., Ryndak, D.L., & Billingsley, F. (2000). Useful practices in inclusive education: A preliminary view of what experts in moderate to severe disabilities are saying. *Journal of The Association for Persons with Severe Handicaps, 25*(3), 129–141.

Keefe, E.B., Rossi, P.J., De Valenzuela, J.S., & Howarth, S. (2000). Reconceptualizing teacher preparation for inclusive classrooms: A description of the dual licensure program at the University of New Mexico. *Journal of The Association for Persons with Severe Handicaps, 25*(2), 72–82.

TASH. (2000). *TASH resolution on inclusive quality education.* Baltimore: Author.

TASH. (2002). *TASH resolution on teacher education.* Baltimore: Author.

Webb-Johnson, G., Artiles, A., Trent, S., Jackson, C., & Velox, A. (1998). The status of research on multicultural education in teacher education and special education: Problems, pitfalls, promises. *Remedial and Special Education, 19,* 7–15.

Competencies that Form the Foundation of the University of New Hampshire's Inclusion Facilitator Teacher Education Option

Philosophy and values

Demonstrates through language and practice a belief in the inherent value of students with disabilities and the philosophy that disability is a natural part of the human experience

Presumes competence in students with disabilities by having high expectations for their learning and the development of their literacy skills

Demonstrates a belief in the value of diversity by including students in age-appropriate, typical classrooms in local schools

Promotes the development of students' self-determination and their graduation to typical adult lives in inclusive community settings

Assessment of the student and the learning environment

Identifies opportunities for learning and communication in a variety of inclusive environments, including general education classrooms, typical school routines and activities, extracurricular activities, the community, and the home

Assesses students' learning and communication styles, strengths, and needs using a variety of authentic assessment strategies such as criterion-based assessments, ecological inventories, futures planning assessments, and other classroom or typical activity-based strategies

Assesses factors that affect learning and communication, such as the physical and sensory environments, the curriculum, instructional methods, and classmates' and teachers' attitudes

Design of educational programs and supports

Collaborates with others to develop students' educational programs that reflect individualized goals based on the content of the general education curriculum, including 1) subject matter knowledge, 2) literacy, 3) social skills, 4) career skills, 5) community service learning, 6) skills for independent living, and 7) general learning habits and behaviors

Designs and coordinates individualized natural and specialized supports in the classroom, school, and community in the areas of curriculum, instruction, communication, assistive technology, and medical and related services

Supports graduation planning that leads to students' participation in a variety of typical adult roles and inclusive environments such as postsecondary education, work, and community living

Promotes the use of a variety of augmentative communication symbols, modes, aids, and techniques (e.g., letters, words, graphic language symbols, sign/gesture symbols, posture and gaze, communication boards and books, electronic and nonelectronic communication devices) that support students' active participation, learning, and communication in the general education curriculum, during typical school routines, and in the community

Understands the unique nature of communication by students who use augmentative and alternative communication and uses advanced assessment and problem-solving skills to enhance their interactions with others

Demonstrates awareness of appropriate seating, positioning, personal care, eating, and mobility principles, strategies, and equipment and collaborates with others to provide these supports to students

Collaborates with others to secure funding for augmentative communication and other learning aids and assures their optimum functioning through regular maintenance and service

Social relationships

Identifies barriers (e.g., attitudes, educational practices, communication supports, transportation) to the development of students' social relationships and develops strategies for avoiding and/or overcoming them

Facilitates interactions between students with disabilities and their age-appropriate classmates in order to develop, maintain, and enhance social and communicative relationships

Identifies opportunities and facilitates support for students' participation in typical extra- and co-curricular activities, based on students' interest and desires

Positive approaches to behavioral support

Understands the complex interrelationships among behavior, communication, and sensory and movement differences

Conducts comprehensive functional behavior assessments

Designs positive approaches to challenging behavior and supports teams in their implementation of individualized student support plans

Evaluation of learning and communication outcomes

Develops meaningful documentation procedures to evaluate students' learning and communication skills and provides this information for general education and alternate assessment purposes

Evaluates educational programs in order to improve team collaboration, enhance the effectiveness of supports, and maximize student achievement

Leadership and systems change

Uses leadership skills to promote quality inclusive education, students' access to augmentative and alternative communication and assistive technology, and general school reform and systems change

Provides intensive and sustained support to teams as they make decisions regarding students' educational programs

Coordinates and provides professional development for professionals, administrators, paraprofessionals, family members, and the general community in the areas of inclusive education and communication supports for students with disabilities

Promotes the development of students' self-determination and the
leadership skills of their families by connecting them with self-
advocacy and community resources

Supports for Students with Significant Disabilities

PHYSICAL, EMOTIONAL, AND SENSORY SUPPORTS

For many students with significant disabilities, assistance with moving, managing their emotions, and perceiving their world is a prerequisite to learning. Thus, the provision of physical, emotional, and sensory supports facilitates access required for participation. Some examples include

1. Provide physical supports.

   - Ensure access to all learning environments.
   - Push the student's wheelchair.
   - Provide support to the student's arm as he or she types.
   - Take notes for the student.

2. Provide emotional supports.

   - Express confidence in the student's capabilities.
   - Acknowledge the student's feelings.
   - Teach stress or anger management strategies.

3. Provide sensory supports.

   - Turn down the lights.
   - Provide soothing music through headphones.
   - Provide a different type of seat.
   - Adjust the student's schedule to provide for activity breaks.

MODIFICATION OF MATERIALS
OR PROVISION OF TECHNOLOGY

In order for students to learn, they must have access to the same information and ideas as their classmates. Because of their unique learning styles and needs, instructional materials may need to be modified in some way to ensure that access. Some examples include

1. Change the format of materials.

    • Convert an assignment from essay to short answer format.

2. Supplement the classroom materials.

    • Add audiovisual media, models, or manipulatives.

3. Substitute different materials.

    • Create a synopsis of a book.

    • Provide content-related material at a different reading level.

4. Provide technology.

    • Use an augmentative communication device.

    • Use a computer for notetaking.

    • Use a switch to turn on a blender.

5. Enhance materials.

    • Digitize text to change size, color, and spacing.

    • Add graphics.

    • Add scaffolding.

COMMUNICATION MATERIALS AND SUPPORTS

Students with significant disabilities may not communicate—through speech or writing—all of the things their classmates without disabilities communicate. This situation may not be due to students' disabilities but rather to the design of and support for students' communication systems (e.g., communication boards, voice output communication aids). Communication materials and supports are provided to enhance the engagement of students with disabilities in the academic and social interactions of the classroom. Some examples include

1. Enhance materials for understanding.

    •   Incorporate the student's symbol set (DynaSyms, Picture Communication Symbols) into the teacher's presentations.

    •   Use vocabulary and messages that are already programmed into the student's communication device during the teacher's presentations.

    •   Add pictures to the teacher's visual aids to convey key concepts.

    •   Enhance directions on worksheets with symbols.

2. Enhance materials for expression/demonstration of participation and learning.

    •   Use communication displays that have preprogrammed messages with academic answers.

    •   Teach the student to use a communication device for spoken, written, and physical communication tasks (e.g., program the device with vocabulary for brainstorming activities).

3. Support the use of communication materials.

    •   Model and value multiple means of expression within the classroom.

    •   Use the student's communication displays during classroom instruction.

    •   Give classmates copies of the student's communication displays at their desks, and use the displays during large- and small-group instruction and during partner activities.

    •   Provide pause time to give the student (extra) time to generate responses.

    •   Select and program vocabulary on communication displays to enhance participation, not to show that the student "knows" the right answer (e.g., for a brainstorming activity, an array of acceptable answers are available—not two choices of one correct answer and one incorrect answer).

PERSONALIZED INSTRUCTION

Like their classmates without disabilities, students with significant disabilities need to have teaching personalized for their learning style, level of knowledge, interests, and goals. Personalized instruction can take many forms. Some examples include

1. Ask different questions based on Bloom's taxonomy or multiple intelligences.

2. Provide instructional scaffolding.

   - Provide background information.

   - Use graphic organizers.

   - Teach metacognitive strategies.

3. Provide systematic instruction.

4. Define vocabulary.

   - Place a speech-language pathologist in a small cooperative group to help with vocabulary definitions.

5. Break down tasks into manageable units.

   - Have the student do problems 1, 2, and 3 first, check the answers, and then do problems 4, 5, and 6.

POSITIVE APPROACHES AND POSITIVE BEHAVIORAL SUPPORTS

Challenging behavior is one of the biggest reasons students with disabilities are excluded from the general education classroom. The best way to deal with challenging behavior is to prevent it from happening in the first place. Positive approaches to behavior focus on this as well as on teaching alternative behaviors and creating supportive learning environments. Some examples include

1. Conduct a comprehensive functional behavior assessment, and examine possible quality-of-life changes.

   - Collect information about the student, the problem behavior, and the environment in order to make hypotheses about potential reasons for the behavior.

   - Consider enhancing supports for inclusive education.

2. Develop a prevention plan for setting events and triggers/antecedents.

- If the student is more likely to have challenging behavior following a poor night's sleep, then provide supports around sleep.

- If challenging behavior occurs when the student is given paper and pencil tasks, then enhance instructional materials or change the task demand in another way.

- If the challenging behavior is a result of communication breakdowns, improve the communication supports and learn new ways of interacting with the student.

3. Develop an intervention plan for teaching new skills to the student.

- Teach the student a new routine around preparing for and waking up from sleep.

- Teach the student how to use a computer for writing.

- Teach the student how to use augmentative communication to ask for assistance.

4. Develop a postintervention plan for the student's individualized education program (IEP) team.

- Following an occurrence of significantly challenging behavior, convene with other IEP team members to debrief the event—looking for things they could have done differently to prevent it and to make a plan for supporting the student, team members, classmates, and others in the building.

5. Develop a crisis management plan (if needed for *crisis* situations).

- Design the crisis plan to interrupt or diffuse a situation.

- Focus the crisis plan on short-term intervention with safety and protection as the goals.

- Along with other team members, learn to recognize the crisis and how to intervene.

PERSONALIZED LEARNING STANDARDS, DEMONSTRATION, AND ASSESSMENT

Personalized standards, demonstration of learning, and assessment go together. Some students may be working on lower than grade-level standards or the "critical function" (essential element) of a standard. Furthermore, the ways that most students in a class demonstrate learning—by speaking or writing—may not accurately assess what a student with disabilities knows or can do. Finally, assessment and grading must be based on the unique expectations identified for each student. Some examples include

1. Allow the student to do less work to demonstrate the same standard.

   - Assign fewer math problems.

   - Assign a shorter essay.

2. Allow the student to create a different product to demonstrate the same standard.

   - Have the student produce a hands-on demonstration instead of a written essay if writing is not the primary learning objective.

3. Adjust the standard within the same content area.

   - Within a science unit focusing on deoxyribonucleic acid, use a synonym for the vocabulary word *heredity*.

   - Adjust the expectations in physical education so that the student is expected to run 50 yards in 2 minutes instead of 30 seconds.

4. Develop a personalized grading rubric or contract.

   - Evaluate effort and progress.

   - Evaluate achievement of IEP objectives.

Agenda Template
for a Team Meeting

Facilitator _____   Date _____

Timekeeper _____   Notetaker _____

_____ Set agenda, times, and roles.

_____ Share personal updates.

_____ Make school announcements.

_____ Report on past to-do tasks.

_____ Cover any instructional planning issues:

    1.   Report on past lessons.

    2.   Discuss upcoming lessons.

    3.   Discuss student supports needed.

_____ Discuss behavior supports.

_____ Discuss social relationship issues.

_____ Discuss collaborative teaming issues.

_____ Cover any other agenda items.

_____ Confirm to-do assignments and due dates with those responsible:

	Task	Person responsible	Date to be completed
1.			
2.			
3.			

_____ Schedule next meeting date and note items on the coming agenda.

Next meeting date: _____

Agenda items:

1. _____

2. _____

3. _____

_____ Evaluate meeting.

1. What worked?

2. What did not work?

3. What should we do differently next time?

4. Were there any "ah-ha" moments?

Guidelines for a
"Day in the Life" Observation

This observation involves accompanying a student with significant disabilities through his or her day strictly as an observer. The purpose of the task is to experience the school day from the perspective of the student, to increase your understanding of the factors that influence the student's educational experiences, and to provide some information about how the student's program aligns with promising educational practices.

ETIQUETTE

Make arrangements to observe when it is convenient for the teacher and other staff. If you are told that the student is experiencing a particularly difficult day and your presence might interfere, reschedule the observation. If classmates ask why you are there, explain the purpose of the observation.

Introduce yourself to the teacher you are observing. Tell the teacher that you are doing a "day in the life" observation as part of the planning process for supporting the student to be a successful member of the classroom. Reconfirm that it is still a good day and time to observe.

FOCUS QUESTIONS

Use the following questions to focus the observation. (The *you* in the following questions refers to the student you are shadowing.)

How do you get to school?

How similar or dissimilar is your day to that of students without disabilities?

Is your schedule just like other students who are your age or in your grade?

In class, are you treated the same as or different from other students?

Do you receive pull-out instruction outside of the general education classroom?

What is this instruction like?

What do you miss by being out of the general education classroom?

Is your seat with the other students in the general education classroom?

Do you have the same materials?

Do you have the same access to the classroom, the learning materials, and the teacher's instruction as the other students do?

Does the teacher call on you?

Are you assigned to groups like the other students?

How are the class expectations personalized for your learning needs?

How are your relationships with other students? Adults?

How do people communicate with you?

What kinds of conversations are you involved in? Academic? Social?

Do you have a way to communicate every minute of the day?

How do people talk about you?

Do they speak directly to you?

When people are talking about you, do they include you in the conversation, or do they talk about you as if you aren't there (or aren't listening or understanding)?

Do people treat you as if you are smart and valuable?

How is support provided to you?

Do you have opportunities to be helpful to other students?

If you didn't have a disability, would you be happy at this school?

CONCLUSION

After your observation is complete, write a summary about whether this student's educational program aligns with promising educational practices that you have studied. The following four-column chart may assist you in taking notes during the observation.

Time	Activity	Student's participation and support	Comments about promising practices

Sample Functional
Behavior Assessment

WHO IS THIS STUDENT?

Strengths, Interests, and Learning Style

Jake is a 16-year-old young man who lives in a group home due to his having been removed from his home by the Department of Human Services. He moved to Seaport in September 2000 and began school at the Middle School of Seaport in November 2000. Jake experiences a variety of typical adolescent feelings and behaviors as well as some serious emotional and behavioral challenges that have been associated with his difficult childhood. Jake wishes that he could live with his father and his family and looks forward to visits with them. He visits his father on regularly scheduled weekends and participates in family counseling sessions. Jake can be quite thoughtful, considerate, and giving. He expresses certain feelings and wants quite clearly, such as when he is ill, is tired, or is just not interested in working.

Jake is very interested in and is developing more knowledge of automotive mechanics. He enjoys working on the computer, and in his spare time, he hangs out at his uncle's garage and watches wrestling on television.

When Jake is frustrated and starts to show his anger verbally or physically, he does not demonstrate the ability to interrupt his escalating reaction by thinking about the consequences of his behavior,

---

Note that a positive behavior support/intervention plan for Jake is provided in Appendix F.

generating possible alternatives, and avoiding a confrontation. Jake does not hold grudges and can be seen interacting peacefully with a peer shortly after an angry outburst. Jake desperately wants to fit in and be liked by both adults and peers. He desperately tries to fit in with both boys and girls at the high school and appears to be most comfortable working with male adults at school. At home, Jake works well with both male and female staff.

Jake responds well to empathy, engagement, attention, being given choices, and engaging in activities that match his interests. He does not appreciate being compared with more competent students and does not deal well with failure or losing in competitive situations. He can be easily swayed by peers into behavior that gets him in trouble. He does not respond well to authoritative commands (e.g.,"You must do this," "You need to do this," "Stop doing that immediately") and meets this kind of show of power with his own. Jake enjoys humor and bantering with adults and peers.

Jake appears to experience sensory and/or emotional overstimulation (sources and situations not yet entirely clear) and copes by putting his head down on the table, refusing to continue with schoolwork, pulling his jacket over his head, turning or walking away, or striking out verbally.

Jake is a visual and hands-on learner. He likes to draw and has some artistic skill, particularly in mechanical/architectural drawing. His reading skills are improving and are at about the third-grade level. In relative terms, his academic interests are in the areas of science (especially the physical sciences relating to how things work) and math.

Description of Challenging Behaviors

Verbal threats, such as "I'm going to punch you"

Physical aggression, such as pushing

Use of profane language

Leaving assigned area and school building

Refusal to participate in instruction or to complete tasks

Inability to identify and follow through on alternatives to aggression in frustrating situations

Poor social skills and social understanding

Settings in Which Challenging Behaviors Occur

Jake's problem behaviors occur across all settings at home and at school.

Intensity

When Jake becomes verbally assaultive, he is disruptive to all individuals in the area. Concerns have been expressed regarding the safety of Jake and others.

Duration

Incidents generally last 10–30 minutes. After a moderately disruptive incident, Jake returns to his classwork. After a seriously disruptive incident, he is taken home.

Procedure Followed During Previous Interventions

Jake is taken to a safe room for a break (deescalation). Staff members attempt to calm Jake by not talking to him during the outburst and then talking to him in soft, calming tones. If staff members are unable to calm Jake and the physical safety of staff or students (including Jake) is a concern, the group home is called, and they take Jake there for 30–45 minutes. If he calms in that time, he returns to school. If not, he stays home for the rest of the day. There does not appear to be a plan in place to intervene when Jake's behavior starts to escalate, only when he has become out of control.

Educational Impact

Jakes's challenging behaviors reduce the time he is able to be academically engaged, disrupt the learning of others, and limit his socialization and his development of both peer and adult relationships. There are also concerns regarding the safety of Jake and others.

FUNCTION OF BEHAVIOR

Affective Regulation/Emotional Reactivity

Jake has suffered serious developmental traumas in his life unrelated to his educational disability per se. These experiences have left an indelible mark on his personality, neurology, and behavior. He has longstanding difficulties with mood and emotional regulation. Once his emotional response has reached the anger stage, he has difficulty listening to verbal input that asks him to consider consequences, plan, and follow through with more adaptive and socially acceptable behaviors. If he is exposed, made vulnerable, or embarrassed in any way, he is likely to shut down emotionally or escalate to an unacceptable behavior as a way of coping with the emotional or sensory stress that he feels. Jake is unable at this time to screen out some internal and extraneous stimuli (his own feelings, environmental noise, the influence of nearby peers) in such a way that he can divert his attention to problem-solving alternative responses to frustrating situations. He does not yet recognize his own bodily responses to stress and frustration. Jake does show the ability to empathize with others' feelings and misfortunes.

Cognitive Distortion

Even when Jake is calm, he has not yet internalized the connection among events, his emotional response to them, and his subsequent behavior. He needs to be taught these understandings. At this time, Jake tends to perceive some consequences as capricious, unfair, or making little sense to him. While not experiencing distortion, per se, Jake does not have good social perception skills. He may not recognize when he is acting in a way that makes peers feel uncomfortable or not want to be around him.

Triggers

A *trigger* can be any event that occurs directly before difficult behavior and influences the likelihood that the behavior will occur.

Authoritative requests or demands from adults

Use of directives such as *no, don't, stop,* or *you need to*

Being asked to complete work that is too difficult or uninteresting

Requests to do something that Jake does not want to do

Confusing, noisy, overstimulating environments

Being in loosely structured environments with other students who are misbehaving

Losing in a competitive activity or feeling incompetent after a particular performance

Perceiving that adults are disappointed or frustrated with him

Activities or environments that provide little structure or boundaries

MOTIVATING FACTORS AND REINFORCEMENTS

Jake is eager to fit into school and community settings, to experience genuine affection from adults and peers, and to feel as if he is competent. This will not happen if he is separated from the mainstream of school life with other students who are marginalized and also experience similar difficulties. Jake's motivations seem to arise not so much from the promise or receipt of tangible rewards but out of a desire to socialize successfully, feel accepted, and focus on what interests him. In this respect, Jake is just like every other typical high school student.

Jake's motivation to do academic work is tied to whether he is interested in the subject matter. Jake responds well to attention, empathy, understanding, and situations that he views are fair to him. He responds negatively to reinforcement or punishment in the form of criticism, lack of choices, teasing, and comments about his own poor performance in comparison to other students. Jake understands that being disruptive occasionally earns him a ticket out of an unwanted situation and judges the consequence as worth the price he has to pay for that ticket.

Modeling

Jake can model other peers' appropriate and inappropriate behaviors.

Family Issues

Jake enjoys family visits, and having planned visits cancelled or rescheduled serves as a setting event for problem behavior.

Setting Events

Setting events are conditions that occur concurrently with problem behaviors or at some point distant in time.

Returning from a visit home over the weekend

Being tired

During the last half of an academic period

After lunch

Being told that he will not be going home for a visit

Physiological-Constitutional

Jake may be experiencing sensory and emotional stimuli in a different way than students who do not exhibit challenging behaviors. This difference probably reflects a long-standing and complex interplay between his neurological functioning—including the characteristics that go along with the attention-deficit/hyperactivity disorder (ADHD) label—his past experiences, learning style, past emotional traumas, and current environment. Staff members need to remember that most of Jake's emotional and behavioral difficulties are not the result of his willful intention to be difficult but reflect this more complex interplay of past and current factors. Jake's apparent fatigue may also be caused by other factors rather than the simple explanations of not getting enough sleep, avoiding a task, or laziness.

Communicative Function of Behavior

Disruptive behavior is often the only way a student knows how to communicate. Based on the information gleaned from a review of records and the functional behavior assessment observations, the following first-person statements may reflect what Jake is trying to communicate through his problematic behaviors.

"I want to have friends—to have people like me—and it makes me sad, angry, and frustrated when it seems like I'm not a part of the school or when adults and other students don't want to be around me."

"I feel stupid and incompetent, and that makes me feel sad and frustrated. Sometimes I just want to give up."

"I want my family and my friends to genuinely like me. I feel an emptiness inside when they don't. This makes me feel sad."

"People don't seem to understand that my life is very hard. They criticize me, tease me, and make me feel even worse."

"Most everything I do at school makes me feel dumb. I'm not as smart and athletic as other kids, and I feel embarrassed by that."

"It's really frustrating not to have the words to communicate my feelings. When I swear, yell, and run away, this makes me feel better temporarily because it reduces my frustration and stress. Getting away from confusing and noisy situations makes me feel calmer."

"Sometimes I have no idea what my schoolwork has to do with my life, so it seems pointless for me to do some of the work. It makes much more sense for me not to do things that seem so stupid."

"When people criticize me, tell me 'no,' or tell me that I only have one or two choices, I feel all boxed in and start to get anxious. The only thing that seems to help in this situation is for me to get out of that situation as fast as I can."

"Sometimes when things get too hard in school or when I am feeling frustrated, I act out because then people will make me leave the school. That makes me feel better for the moment and is easier than staying."

"When I joke around with other students, even if it gets me in trouble, it's great to be one of the guys and feel like I fit in with them."

"Sometimes when the work is so hard or I am feeling frustrated, burying my head in the desk or pulling my coat over my head blocks out all the noise and makes me feel calmer."

Curriculum and Instruction

Jake exhibits problem behavior when 1) he thinks the work he is being asked to do is pointless or does not interest him, 2) the concepts being taught are way too difficult for him, 3) he has not been given a choice of tasks to do that are within his ability and interest range, and/or 4) when the instruction or the instructional environment make him feel different from the other kids and not a part of the school. When the number of modalities that Jake is being asked to use is too great, he refuses to do the work. For example, when he is asked to listen to instructions, read difficult or uninteresting text, pay attention in a noisy environment, and write longhand, he finds this combination of tasks to be too taxing on his neurological and emotional systems, and he shuts down.

HYPOTHESES

On the basis of the functional behavior assessment, the following hypotheses have been generated that should serve as the foundation of Jake's positive behavior support plan.

1. Some of Jake's problem behaviors are related to the typical struggles of adolescence.

2. Some of Jake's problem behaviors are related to past and current emotional and physical traumas.

3. Some of Jake's problem behaviors are related to how his sensory system reacts to the environment.

4. Some of Jake's problem behaviors represent the only way that he can effectively communicate difficult feelings.

5. Some of Jake's problem behaviors are related to his schoolwork being too hard, not interesting, or stigmatizing as compared with the work of typical students.

Sample Positive Behavior Support/Intervention Plan

SUPPORTS AND ACCOMMODATIONS TO BE PROVIDED TO JAKE

As Jake is learning more appropriate responses to challenging internal and external stimuli, the team will need to arrange his learning environment and provide supports that minimize the factors that lead up to his problem behaviors and maximize Jake's chances for using appropriate behaviors, including

1. Plan and share with Jake what his day will look like so that there are as few surprises as possible. Consider using a visual aid that represents his schedule.

2. Make sure that Jake knows what is expected of him within a particular activity.

3. Within an instructional activity or period of time, let Jake know when his break is scheduled, and what he should do if he needs another one. When Jake needs to be redirected, use nonverbal gestures or cues whenever possible, which tend to be less confrontational and negative, and avoid verbal sparring or arguing.

4. Interact with Jake when he is doing well—ask questions, stand nearby, elicit his opinion, and ask for his help.

5. Include Jake in a group with positive role models during class activities.

Note that a functional behavior assessment for Jake is provided in Appendix E.

6. Within an instructional activity, reduce the number of modalities or demands on Jake's neurological system by providing a laptop computer with such programs as AlphaSmart, speech-to-text software, and word prediction software for written work.

7. Analyze Jake's day for the proportion of time spent on favored versus nonfavored activities, and use creative instructional ideas to engage Jake in academic work around topics of interest to him.

8. Reduce the focus on competition, and measure progress by how far Jake has come from previous assessments.

9. Give Jake classroom responsibilities, including helping other students.

10. Minimize Jake's contact with other students who act out or misbehave.

11. Do not get into a verbal power struggle with Jake.

12. Schedule regular breaks in Jake's routine so that he can do acceptable alternative activities such as working on a computer or a favorite project, listening to calming music, drawing, making a delivery, shooting baskets, checking out a book or video, or chatting with a teacher or a friend.

13. Use humor to diffuse tense situations with Jake.

14. Empathize with Jake when he is doing a tough assignment or having a bad day.

15. Use low-level frustrating situations as opportunities to teach Jake and/or have him practice different coping or problem solving strategies.

16. Assess at several points throughout the day whether the triggers or setting events are present for Jake. If they are, be prepared to help Jake recognize them. Rehearse "what if" plans.

17. Don't use phrases such as "No, you can't do that"; "Don't do that"; "You must do this"; or "You have no choice here." Instead, use phrases such as "Here's another way to do that, Jake." "Take a deep breath, Jake, and tell me what you are feeling right now." "You've been at this for about 20 minutes, Jake. After you take a break, you'll be raring to go again."

SKILLS TO TEACH JAKE

Jake needs to learn to recognize the situations that are potentially difficult for him to deal with. He needs to learn alternate behaviors for dealing with both internal stressors (e.g., anxiety, frustration, sadness, anger) and external demands (e.g., being asked to do a task that is too difficult or uninteresting, being asked by other kids to do something dangerous or inappropriate). He needs to learn new words/scripts to express challenging feelings or to problem-solve challenging situations *and* new motor responses to deal with stressors (e.g., exercising, relaxation techniques, painting, hammering out a dented car body).

Jake would probably learn these new responses best through writing social stories (e.g., through dictation into the computer) and being a part of a peer group that utilizes cooperative learning strategies and in which Jake has a valued and meaningful role. Jake will need immediate feedback and support to use these skills in natural contexts with peers and adults.

RESPONSES TO POSITIVE BEHAVIORS

It is important for everyone in Jake's life to remember that he is motivated by most of the same things that motivate everyone: attention, affection, money, leisure time, smiles, empathy, understanding, having choices, enjoying the sense of satisfaction about a job well done, and feeling good about being of service to others. For a change in Jake's behavior to occur, the number of positive reinforcers such as these must be much greater than the negative ones in his life over an extended period of time. When Jake exhibits a positive behavior, he needs someone to direct his attention to it, in an age-appropriate and typical way. For example, if Jake allows someone to go through a door before he does, a teacher could say, "You are a real gentleman, Jake. Thanks." If Jake does a good job on an assignment, a teacher could tell him, "This stuff isn't easy for you, and it took a lot of concentration for you to finish this. Nice going."

Jake needs to be involved in more than one activity or situation in which he contributes to the lives of others or the school community. Putting Jake in counseling or a social skills class to build his self-esteem will not work. Getting Jake involved in Habitat for Humanity or recycling old cars for the Lung Association are opportunities for him to contribute and receive legitimate accolades for his service.

RESPONSES TO CHALLENGING BEHAVIORS

The team needs to remember that it will take Jake a long time to learn more effective strategies to deal with his anger, anxiety, frustration, sadness, and feelings of incompetence and that he will be dependent on peers and adults for support. Jake will make many, many mistakes as he is learning new ways of coping with his frustrations and feelings.

The following plan will be used by all staff to help Jake choose appropriate behaviors and avoid problematic ones and to support him and others when his behavior escalates to the point of being dangerous.

Plan A: Disruptive Behavior But Not Dangerous to Self or Others

Apply coaching and teaching strategies, but do not remove Jake from the situation if the behavior has not escalated beyond the point of Jake's being able to redirect it. Talk to Jake calmly and quietly while monitoring his behavior.

Plan B: Dangerous Behavior Where There Is a Concern for the Safety of Jake or Others But His Behaviors Are Not in Violation of the School District's Violence Policy

Isolate Jake to a safe, quiet place. Minimize stimuli. Talk to him calmly and quietly about matters unrelated to the incident while monitoring his behavior. When Jake is able to return to the classroom and is calm enough to talk, be sure to listen and do the following:

- Empathize with Jake's loss of control and his feelings of embarrassment about the incident. Emphasize that staff members are not disappointed with him.

- Help Jake analyze the situation and think of alternatives for the next time a similar situation occurs.

- Encourage him to make amends and apologize to any people he may have offended or hurt.

- Call a meeting of the team to review the behavioral support plan, and determine where the breakdown occurred.

- Revise the plan as necessary.

Plan C: Dangerous Behavior in Violation of the School District's Violence Policy

Isolate Jake in a safe, quiet place. Minimize stimuli. Talk to him calmly and quietly about matters unrelated to the incident while monitoring his behavior. Send him home, with his return to school pending an investigation and review by team and school authorities. When Jake returns to school and is calm enough to talk and listen, do the following:

- Empathize with Jake about his loss of control and his feelings of embarrassment about the incident.

- Emphasize that staff members are not disappointed with him.

- Help him analyze the situation and think of alternatives for the next time a similar situation occurs.

- Encourage him to make amends and apologize to any people he may have offended or hurt.

- Call a meeting of the team to review the positive behavior support plan, and determine where the breakdown occurred.

- Revise the plan as necessary.

TEAM FUNCTIONING AND PROFESSIONAL DEVELOPMENT

The success of this support plan is contingent on several factors related to how well the team implements it. The following recommendations are related to team functioning and professional development.

1. All team members need training in a problem behavior deescalation strategy. Provide this training to Jake and selected peers as well. Team members must know what to do to support Jake at every point along the continuum of escalation and not just when he is past the point of no return.

2. Team members need to discuss and understand why the behavioral expectations for Jake are different from those for other students in the district. This is especially true for classroom teachers. This might include reading parts of the Individuals with Disabilities Education Improvement Act of 2004 (PL 108-446, 20 U.S.C. §§ 1400 *et seq.*), or hearing from the district special education director.

3. Team members who have difficulty managing their own anger and/or stress when dealing with Jake should have access to a resource to help them develop more effective ways of handling their own responses.

4. Team members should read articles or chapters dealing with students with challenging behavior and effective support strategies, such as Herbert Lovett's book, *Learning to Listen: Positive Approaches and People with Difficult Behavior* (available from Paul H. Brookes Publishing Co., http://www.brookespublishing.com), which is a great resource that is written in nontechnical language.

5. Jake's educational team, including his classroom teachers and paraprofessionals, should meet at least every other week to discuss how well this support plan is being implemented. A checklist should be developed to monitor the various supports and strategies listed, and the team should monitor its own accuracy and consistency.

6. When the team identifies a need to learn more information, the school district should provide it with professional development, a consultant, and/or the necessary release time so that they can build their own capacity to better support Jake.

Index

Page references followed by *t* or *f* indicate tables or figures, respectively.

AAC, *see* Augmentative and alternative communication
AAMR, *see* American Association on Mental Retardation
Academic curriculum content, 32
Accessible technology, 190
Accommodations
  standards-based IEP supports and accommodations, 154*f*
  traditional IEP supports and accommodations, 149*f*
Accountability structures, 111
Achiever (personality type), 85
  case study, 91*t*
Activities
  age-appropriate, 133
  classroom activity observation, 156, 157*t*
  instructional, 151, 151*f*
  social, 133–134
  standards-based IEP classroom activities, 154*f*
  traditional IEP activities, 149*f*
Activity and participation assessment, 156
ADAMHA Reorganization Act, *see* Alcohol, Drug Abuse, and Mental Health Administration Reorganization Act (PL 102-321)
Adaptations, curriculum, 75*t*
Advocacy, 11–13
  balancing with inquiry, 71–73
  improved, 73
Affective regulation, 227–228
Agendas
  standardized, 110–111
  template for, 219–220
Agreements
  sustainable, 115–119

  among team members, 118, 118*t*
Alcohol, Drug Abuse, and Mental Health Administration (ADAMHA) Reorganization Act (PL 102-321), 173
AlphaSmart keyboards (AlphaSmart), 190
Altruism, 78*t*, 79–81
American Association on Mental Retardation (AAMR), 8, 202
Americans with Disabilities Act of 1990 (PL 101-336), 98
Analysis, discrepancy, 156
Assessment, 139–165
  activity, 156
  classroom, 145–147
  classroom activity observation, 156, 157*t*
  of concerns, case study, 89
  functional behavior, 159–162, 160–161
    sample, 225–232
  inclusive, 140–148
  of learning environments, 104*t*
  methods for evaluating student learning, 158–159
  participation, 156
  personalized, 217–218
  of school environment, 147–148
    student-related, 147
  of staff identities, case study, 88–89
  student, 104*t*, 141–145
    competencies associated with, 209–210
    reports, 145
  student-focused, 141
  student-related, of school environment, 147

Assessment—*continued*
team member identity, case
study, 89–90, 91*t*–92*t*
of team members, 106–108
of values, case study, 88–89
The Association for Persons with
Severe Handicaps, *see*
TASH
Augmentative and alternative
communication, 8
appropriate, 47–50
How to Know It When You See
It, 48–50
opportunities for teaching, 75*t*

Bank of services model, 171–172
Behavior(s)
appropriate, 233–234
challenging
sample, 226, 227
sample responses to, 236–237
communicative function of,
230–231
dangerous, sample responses to,
236, 237
disruptive, sample responses to,
236
functional assessment of,
159–162, 160–161
sample, 225–232, 227–229
positive, sample responses to,
235
Behavioral support
high-quality plans, 161
opportunities for teaching
strategies, 75*t*
positive, 216–217
approaches, 104*t*–105*t*
competencies associated with,
211
examples, 216–217
plans, 159–162, 233–238
see also Positive behavioral
support plans; Positive
behavioral supports
Beliefs
about students with disabilities,
160
of successful inclusion facilitators, 20, 21*t*

Brainstorming, 122–123
Brown v. Board of Education, 178
Budgeting, 176–177

CBAM, *see* Concerns-Based
Adoption Model
CEC, *see* Council for Exceptional
Children
Celebrating success, 16–21
Celebrations that honor diversity,
135
Certification, teacher, 199–200
Challenger (personality type), 85
case study, 89, 91*t*
Challenging behaviors
sample, 226, 227
sample responses to, 236–237
Change agents, 68–77
case study, 85–99
effective
characteristics of, 69–77
principles of, 69–70
skills of, 70–77
inclusion facilitators as, 65–101
suggested phrases for, 73
teachers as, 68–69
Chapter and unit plans, 157–158
Child Mental Health Services
Initiative, 173
Circles of friends, 131, 132
Civil Rights Act of 1964 (PL 88-
352), 178
Civil Rights Act of 1968 (PL 90-
284), 178
Class membership, 125–137
Classroom activities
observation of, 156, 157*t*
standards-based IEP example, 154*f*
Classroom assessment, 145–147
classroom activity observation,
156, 157*t*
questions for, 145–157
Classroom materials, 214
Classroom support strategies, 75*t*
Coalition of Essential Schools, 52,
192
Cognitive distortion, 228
Collaboration
characteristics of, 83*t*
concerns for, 83

case study, 91t
description of, 174t
team, 10–11
Collaborative consultation model,
    171
Collaborative team leaders,
    103–124
  inclusion facilitators as, 106–123
  role competencies, 103,
    104t–105t
Collaborative teams, 41–43,
    105–106
  activities associated with devel-
    opmental stages, 106, 107t
  characteristics of, 42–43, 106
  definition of, 41, 105
  fermenting, 106, 107t
  forming, 106, 107t
  formulating, 106, 107t
  functioning, 106, 107t
  members of
    assessment of, 106–108
    levels of agreement among,
    118, 118t
  power in making a difference,
    123–124
  specialized roles in, 108–109,
    109t
Commitment to inclusion, 37–39
Communication
  augmentative and alternative, 8,
    47–50
    How to Know It When You See
    It, 48–50
  opportunities for teaching, 75t
  effective skills of, 119–120, 120t
  effective supports for, 48–50
  evaluation of outcomes, 105t, 211
  facilitated, 128–129
  function of behavior, 230–231
  materials for, 214–215
  means for students, 128–129
  supports for, 48–50, 214–215
Community
  diversity as value-added contri-
    bution to, 35
  enhancement by diversity, 34–35
  liaison between school, home,
    and community, 13–15
  school, 35
Community-based services, 174t

Comprehensive systems of care, 173
  wrap-around, 172–176
Concerns About Inclusive
    Education Questionnaire,
    90f
Concerns-Based Adoption Model
    (CBAM), 67, 82
  limitations of, 67–68
Conflict resolution, 119–123
Connections, social, 125–137
Consultancy Protocol, 193, 194f
Consultation, collaborative, 171
Coordinating related services,
    170–172
Costs, of inclusive education,
    176–177
Council for Exceptional Children
    (CEC), 8, 32, 199, 202
Crisis management plans, 217
Cultural competence
  description of, 174t
  Inclusion Facilitator Option
    (UNH), 202–203
Cultural diversity, 44, 135t
Curriculum
  adaptations and modifications, 75t
  creation based on universal
    design for instruction prin-
    ciples, 75t
  embedding diversity topics into,
    135, 135t
  functional behavior assessment
    sample, 231
  life-planning, 163, 163t

Dangerous behavior, sample
    responses to, 236, 237
"Day in the life" observations, 145
  guidelines for, 221–223
Decision making
  "out of the box" solutions,
    117–118
  participatory, 103–124, 111–119
Demonstration of learning, person-
    alized, 217–218
Direct service delivery, 172
Disabilities
  embedding into curriculum, 135t
  individuals with, as course
    instructors, 203–204

Disabilities—*continued*
  significant, students with
    benefits of inclusive class-
      rooms for, 31–32
    negative effects of separation
      from peers for, 36–37
    supports for, 213–218
    teacher of students with, case
      study, 87
    societal perceptions about and
      response to, 80
  students with
    and education of classmates, 34
    focused planning for, 163–164
    self-determination of, 58
    teaching of, 35
    values and beliefs about, 160
Disability Awareness Day, 98
Discrepancy analysis, 156
Disruptive behavior, sample
  responses to, 236
Disruptive team dynamics, 119
Diversity, 34–35
  celebrations that honor, 135
  cultural, 135t
  embedding topics into curricu-
    lum, 135, 135t
  opportunities for teaching value
    of, 75t
  in points of view, 116
  racial, 135t
  rituals that honor, 135
  school climate with respect to,
    134–135
  school culture that celebrates, 44
  value of, 75t
  as value-added contribution, 35

Early strategies, scenario, 169–170
Education
  of classmates, 34
  inclusive
    concerns about, 82–83
    Concerns About Inclusive
      Education Questionnaire,
      90f
    models that support, 75t
    opportunities to teach others
      about, 74, 75t
    restructuring to support,
      183–195

  scenarios, 168–170
  practices committed to inclusion,
    37
  preservice, 197–207
  for students ages 18–21, 190–191
  teacher, 199–200
Education for All Handicapped
    Children Act of 1975
    (PL 94-142), 25, 178
Emotional reactivity, sample,
    227–228
Emotional supports for students
    with significant disabili-
    ties, 213
Enneagrams, 84–85
Enthusiast (personality type), 85
  case study, 91t, 94
Environments, learning or school
    assessment of, 104t, 147–148
    inclusive, 15–16
Evaluation
  of communication outcomes,
    105t, 211
  of learning, 155–159
  of learning outcomes, 105t, 211
  performance-based, 203
  of quality of instruction and
    supports, 159
  of student learning, 158–159
  of supports, 46
Evidence-based rationale for
    inclusion, 75t

Facilitated communication,
    128–129
Facilitation
  of circles of support or friend-
    ship, 132
  of friendship, 50–52
  fundamental skills of, 113
  of open discussion, 114–115
  of student relationships, 125–137
Facilitators, 10–11
  see also Inclusion facilitators
Families, 229
  as course instructors, 203–204
  school partnerships, 39–41
  support for, 134
Flexible resources, 174t
Focus questions, 221–222
Focused planning, 163–164

Fostering class membership,
    125–137
Fostering social connections,
    125–137
Framework of understanding,
    shared, 116–117
Friendship(s)
    circles of support or friends, 131,
        132
    essential considerations for,
        126–136
    facilitation of, 50–52,
        133–134
    How to Know It When You See
        It, 51–52
Functional behavior assessment,
    159–162, 160–161
    sample, 225–232
    sources of information used
        during, 160
    steps, 161
Futures planning
    person-centered, 59–60
    stages of, 164t

General education classes
    heterogeneous, 127–128
    membership and full participa-
        tion in, 30–39
General education reform, 52–56
General education teachers
    role of, 187–188
    specialized roles in collaborative
        teams, 108–109, 109t
General Special Education license,
    199–200
Grading plans, individualized,
    158–159
Graduation planning, 162–164
    for all students, 162–163
    high school graduation plans, 162
    themes, topics, and activities in,
        163t
Grant writing, 177–178
Guide for action, 25–65

Helper (personality type), 85
    case study, 91t, 92, 96
Heterogeneous general education
    classes, 127–128

High school graduation plans, 162
Home partnerships
    to facilitate friendships and
        participation in social
        activities, 133–134
    liaison between school, home,
        and community, 13–15

IDEA 1997, see Individuals with
    Disabilities Education Act
    Amendments of 1997
IDEA 2004, see Individuals with
    Disabilities Education
    Improvement Act of 2004
IEPs, see Individualized education
    programs
Inclusion, 31
    commitment to, 37–39
    concerns about
        assessing, case study, 89
        SoC (Stages of Concern)
            Questionnaire, 89
        stages of, 82–83
    definition of, 2, 30
    evidence-based rationale for, 75t
    full, 127–128
    misunderstandings about, 36
    presumptive value of, 35–36
    requirements for settings, 15–16
    sample debate, 120–121, 121t
    social, 52
    as special education initiative,
        55–56
    see also Inclusive education
Inclusion Facilitator Option
    (UNH), 200–205
    competencies associated with,
        202–205, 209–212
    course descriptions, 205
    course instructors, 203–204
    course sequence and faculty, 205
    inclusive settings for preintern-
        ship and internship experi-
        ences, 204
    learning experiences used in, 201
    pedagogical foundations, 201–202
    philosophical foundations,
        200–201
    teaching strategies used in, 201
Inclusion facilitators, 10–11
    beliefs of, 20, 21t

Inclusion facilitators—*continued*
  biographical information, 4–6
  case study, 86, 89
  as change agents, 65–101
  as collaborative team leaders,
    103–124, 106–123
  early strategies, scenario, 169–170
  effective
    characteristics of, 69–77
    principles of, 69–70
    skills of, 70–77
  guide for action, 25–65
  as information and resource
    brokers, 167–182
  job titles, 3, 8–10
  knowledge of, 7–8
  opportunities to teach others
    about inclusive education,
    74, 75t
  organizational structures that
    enable, 183–195
  participatory decision making
    fundamentals for, 113–115
  personality traits, 20, 21t
  planning strategies, case study,
    92–97
  preservice education of, 197–207
  as reflective practice protocol
    leaders, 193
  as resource brokers, 167–182
  responsibilities of, 174–175
  roles of, 1–23, 183–195
  schedules of, 186, 187t
  skills of, 7–8
Inclusive assessment, 140–148
Inclusive education
  benefits of, 31–32
  concerns about, 82–83
  Concerns About Inclusive
    Education Questionnaire,
    90f
  development of solutions, 117
  How to Know It When You See
    It, 55–56
  models that support, 75t
  opportunities to teach others
    about, 74, 75t
  promising practices, 25–65
  restructuring to support, 183–195
  scenarios, 168–170
  see also Inclusion
Inclusive placement

  misunderstandings about, 36
  presumptive value of, 35–36
Inclusive settings
  for preinternship and internship
    experiences, 204
  requirements for, 15–16
Individualized education programs
    (IEPs)
  standards-based
    characteristics of, 153t
    development of, 148–155
    links with skills, 151, 151f
    model for writing, 151–152
    sample goals, objectives, and
      supports of, 153–155, 154f
    terminology, 151
    traditional goals and objectives,
      148, 149f
Individualized grading plans,
    158–159
Individuals with Disabilities
    Education Act (IDEA) of
    1990 (PL 101-476), 32,
    35–36
Individuals with Disabilities
    Education Act
    Amendments of 1997
    (IDEA 1997) (PL 105-17), 1,
    25–26, 36
Individuals with Disabilities
    Education Improvement
    Act of 2004 (IDEA 2004)
    (PL 108-446), 25, 77, 149,
    150, 176, 179, 237
Inquiry
  balancing with advocacy, 71–73
  improved, 73
Institute on Disability (IOD)
    (UNH), 6, 200
  Beyond Access Model
    Demonstration Project,
    47
  Equity & Excellence conference,
    57
  mentoring from faculty and staff,
    204–205
  New Hampshire Leadership
    Series, 204
Instruction
  curriculum creation based on
    universal design principles,
    75t

evaluating quality of, 159
personalized, 216
sample functional behavior
assessment, 231
Internship experiences, 204
Intervention plans, 217
Intervention strategies, 77–85
Interviews, 144–145
team member, 145, 146t
Investigator (personality type), 85
case study, 91t
IOD, see Institute on Disability

Job titles, 3, 8–10
evolution of, 4–10

Laws, 35–36, 178–180
Leadership
collaborative team leaders,
103–124
inclusion facilitators as,
106–123
role competencies, 103,
104t–105t
competencies associated with,
211–212
distributed roles, 111
reflective practice protocol, 193
schoolwide, 11–13
Learning
evaluation of, 155–159, 158–159
evaluation of outcomes, 105t, 211
expression/demonstration of,
215
personalized demonstration of,
217–218
Learning environments
assessment of, 104t
inclusive, 15–16
Learning specialists, 52
Learning standards, personalized,
217–218
Learning style, 225–226
Least dangerous assumption
How to Know It When You See
It, 30
policies and practices based on,
26–30
principle of, 28
Legislation, 35–36, 178–180

Liaison between school, home, and
community, 13–15
Life skills teachers, 5
case study, 88, 89–90, 97
Life-planning curriculum, 163, 163t
Loyalist (personality type), 85
case study, 91t, 93–94

Making action plans (MAPs), 142
Management concerns, 83
case study, 91t
characteristics of, 83t
MAPS (making action plans), 142
Materials
age-appropriate, 133
communication, 214–215
enhancement of, 214, 215
modification of, 214
Mediating, 74–76
Meetings, team
purposes of, 110
standardized agendas for, 110–111
structures and processes,
110–111
Membership, 37–39
class, 125–137
in general education classes,
30–39
Mentoring, 204–205
Mills v. Board of Education of the
District of Columbia, 178
Motivating factors, sample,
229–231

Natural supports, 130, 174t
Negotiation, 76–77, 120
effective, 76, 121
principled, 76–77, 120–123,
122
New Hampshire Leadership Series
(IOD), 204
No Child Left Behind Act of 2001
(PL 107-110), 150

Observations
classroom activity observation,
156, 157t
"day in the life," 145, 221–223
Open discussion, 114–115

"Out of the box" solutions, 117–118
Outcome-based services, 174t

Paraprofessionals
   case study, 87, 96–97
   specialized roles in collaborative teams, 108–109, 109t
Parent Information Center, 98
Participation
   expression/demonstration of, 215
   full, 37–39
      benefits of, 31–37
      in general education classes, 30–39
   in social activities, 133–134
Participation assessment, 156
Participatory decision making, 111–119
   fundamentals for inclusion facilitators, 113–115
   principles of, 112
Participatory problem solving, 111–119
Partnerships
   family and school, 39–41
   home and school, 133–134
PATH, 142, 143
Peacemaker (personality type), 85
   case study, 90, 91t, 92t
Pennsylvania Association for Retarded Children (PARC) v. Commonwealth of Pennsylvania, 178
Performance-based evaluation, 203
Person-centered planning
   characteristics of, 59
   How to Know It When You See It, 59–60
   strategies for, 59
Person-first language, 30
Personal futures planning, 59
Personality types, 84–85
Personalized assessment, 217–218
Personalized instruction, 216
Personalized learning standards, 217–218
Planning
   behavioral support plans, 161
      positive, 159–162
   chapter plans, 157–158

focused, 163–164
futures, 164t
graduation, 162–164
   for all students, 162–163
   themes, topics, and activities in, 163t
individualized grading plans, 158–159
instructional, 155–159
for leaving school, 162–164
life-planning curriculum, 163, 163t
person-centered, 59–60
positive behavioral support plans, 159–162
student support plans, 156–157
unit plans, 157–158
Policies and practices based on least dangerous assumption and high expectations, 26–30
Positive approaches to behavioral support, 216–217
   competencies associated with, 211
   examples, 216–217
Positive behavior, sample responses to, 235
Positive behavioral support plans, 159–162, 161–162
   sample, 233–238
   sample hypotheses for, 232
Positive behavioral supports, 216–217
Postintervention plans, 217
Practices based on least dangerous assumption and high expectations, 26–30
Preinternship and internship experiences, 204
Preservice education, 197–207
Principled negotiation, 120–123, 122
Problem solving
   involving students in, 130–132
   participatory, 111–119
Professional development, 191–193
   sample recommendations for, 237–239
Promising practices, 25–65
Public Law 88-352, see Civil Rights Act of 1964
Public Law 90-284, see Civil Rights Act of 1968

Public Law 101-336, *see* Americans with Disabilities Act of 1990
Public Law 101-476, *see* Individuals with Disabilities Education Act of 1990
Public Law 102-321, *see* Alcohol, Drug Abuse, and Mental Health Administration (ADAMHA) Reorganization Act
Public Law 105-17, *see* Individuals with Disabilities Education Act Amendments of 1997
Public Law 107-110, *see* No Child Left Behind Act of 2001
Public Law 108-446, *see* Individuals with Disabilities Education Act Improvement Act of 2004 (IDEA 2004)

Quality of instruction and supports, evaluating, 159
Questions
    for classroom assessment, 145–157
    focus, 221–222
    for student-focused assessment, 141
    for student-related assessment of school environment, 147
    for team member interviews, 146t

Reflective practice, 192
Reflective practice protocols
    elements of, 193
    leading, 193
Refocusing, 83
    characteristics of, 83t
    concerns about, case study, 91t
Reformer (personality type), 84
Related services, coordinating, 170–172
Related-services providers, 171
    role of, 188
    specialized roles in collaborative teams, 108–109, 109t

Relationships
    social, 104t, 211
    student, 125–137
Resource brokers, 167–182
Restructuring
    inclusive, 52–54
    to support inclusive education, 183–195
Roles
    changing, 183–188
    clarification of, 108–109
    distributed leadership, 111
    specialized, 108–109, 109t
Roncker v. Walter, 36

Sacramento City Unified School District v. Rachel H., 178
Schedules
    of elementary school special education teachers and inclusion facilitators, 186, 187t
    planning time, 188–190
School(s)
    assessment of, 139–165
    family and school partnerships, 39–41
    full membership and participation in, 37–39
    home and school partnerships, 133–134
    inclusive, 55–56
    leaving, 162–164
    liaison between school, home, and community, 13–15
    noninclusive, traditionally structured high school, 54–55
Schoolwide leadership, 11–13
Self-determination, 56–58
Self-efficacy, 70
Services
    bank of, 171–172
    community-based, 174t
    individualized, 174t
    outcome-based, 174t
    related, 170–172
    strengths-based, 174t
Setting events, 229–230
Shared framework of understanding, 116–117
Skills, 7–8

Skills—*continued*
  of effective communication,
      119–120
  of effective inclusion facilitators/
      change agents, 70–77
  fundamental facilitation, 113
  to reach sustainable agreements,
      115–116
  sample skills to teach, 235
SoC (Stages of Concern)
      Questionnaire, 89
Social inclusion
  facilitation of, 133–134
  fostering, 125–137
  How to Know It When You See
      It, 52
Social justice, 78*t*, 81, 98–99
Social relationships, 104*t*
  competencies associated with,
      211
  importance of, 128
  involving students in problem
      solving to remove barriers
      to, 130–132
  and status, 126
Special education reform, 52–56
Special education teachers
  case study, 87, 89, 93–94
  elementary school schedule, 186,
      187*t*
  inclusion story, 185
  roles of, 1–23, 184–186
    new, 2–16
    specialized, 108–109, 109*t*
Speech-language pathologists, case
      study, 87, 97
Standardized agendas, 110–111
Standards, 150
  critical function of, 150
  links with IEP skills, 151, 151*f*
  personalized learning, 217–218
Standards-based IEPs
  characteristics of, 153*t*
  development of, 148–155
  example goals, objectives, and
      supports of, 153–155, 154*f*
  model for writing, 151–152
Student assessment, 104*t*, 141–145
  competencies associated with,
      209–210
  evaluation of learning, 158–159
  sample functional behavior
      assessment, 225–227

Student assessment reports, 145
Student-focused assessment, 141
Student support plans, 156–157
Student-related assessment of
      school environment, 147
Students
  age 18–21, 190–191
  case study, 86
  with disabilities
    and education of classmates,
        34
    focused planning for, 163–164
    self-determination of, 58
    teaching of, 35
    values and beliefs about, 160
  facilitating relationships among,
      125–137
  graduation planning for all stu-
      dents, 162–163
  negative effects of separation
      from peers on, 36–37
  providing means of communica-
      tion for, 128–129
  with significant disabilities
    benefits of inclusive class-
        rooms for, 31–32
    negative effects of separation
        from peers for, 36–37
    supports for, 213–218
    teacher of, case study, 87
    treatment as competent, 136
Support(s)
  behavioral
    opportunities for teaching, 75*t*
    positive, 216–217
    positive approaches to, 211,
        216–217
    positive plans, 161–162,
        233–234
  classroom strategies, 75*t*
  communication, 214–215
  creative use of, 171–172
  design of, 104*t*, 210
  emotional, 213
  evaluating, 46, 159
  facilitators of, 10–11
  for families, 134
  How to Know It When You See
      It, 46–47
  implementing, 45
  indicators of, 46
  natural, 130, 174*t*
  nontraditional, 167–182

physical, 213
planning, 45
sensory, 213
standards-based IEP, examples,
    153–155, 154f
strategies that help without hov-
    ering, 75t
student support plans, 156–157
for students with significant dis-
    abilities, 213–218
traditional IEP, 149f
in ways that encourage interde-
    pendence and independ-
    ence, 130
Support plans
    behavioral
        high-quality, 161
        positive, 159–162, 233–234
    chapter or unit, 158
    positive behavioral support plans,
        159–162
Sustainability
    celebrating success for, 16–21
    creating, 15–16
Sustainable agreements
    how to reach, 115–119
    skills to reach, 115–116
Systems change, 211–212
Systems of care, comprehensive,
    172–176

TASH, 8, 198, 201, 202
Task functions, effective, 120t
Teacher certification, 199–200
Teachers
    advocate, 3
    as change agents, 68–69
    classroom, 10–11
    general education
        role of, 187–188
        specialized roles in collabora-
            tive teams, 108–109, 109t
    inclusion support, 3
    life skills, 5
        case study, 87–88, 89–90, 97
    special education
        case study, 87, 89, 93–94
        elementary school schedule,
            186, 187t
        role of, 184–186
        role revelations and revolu-
            tions, 1–23

specialized roles in collabora-
    tive teams, 108–109, 109t
Teaching
    about inclusive education, 74, 75t
    of functional skills, 32–33
Team leaders, collaborative,
    103–124
    inclusion facilitators as, 106–123
    role competencies, 103,
        104t–105t
Team meetings, 110–111
    agendas for
        standardized, 110–111
        template, 219–220
    difficult dynamics, 115
    purposes of, 110
Team members
    assessment of, 106–108
    identity assessment results, case
        study, 89–90, 91t–92t
    interviews with, 145, 146t
    levels of agreement among, 118,
        118t
Teams
    assessment of, 139–165
    collaboration to implement best
        practices, 148
    collaborative, 10–11, 41–43,
        105–106
        characteristics of, 42–43
        How to Know It When You See
            It, 42–43
    leaders of, 103–124
    disruptive dynamics, 119
    family, 174t
    recommendations for, sample,
        237–239
    wrap-around, 174–175
Technology
    accessible, 190
    provision of, 214
Terminology, 32
    derogatory, 136
    IEPs, 151
    person-first language, 30
    standards, 150
    suggested phrases for changes
        agents or facilitators, 73
Time management, 188–190
Transformation
    case study, 85–99
    definition of, 65
    of hearts and minds, 98–99

Transformation—*continued*
  inclusion facilitators as change
    agents for, 65–101
  of individuals, 66–68
Triggers, 228
  sample, 228–229

University of New Hampshire
    (UNH)
  conversion of rubric scores to
    grades, 203*t*
  Inclusion Facilitator Option pro-
    gram, 198, 199, 200–205
    competencies associated with,
      209–212
  Institute on Disability (IOD), 6,
    200
    Beyond Access Model
      Demonstration Project, 47
    Equity & Excellence confer-
      ence, 57
    mentoring from faculty and
      staff, 204–205

New Hampshire Leadership
    Series, 204

Value(s)
  assessing, case study, 88–89
  bottom-line, 77–81
  of diversity, 75*t*
  of inclusive placement, 35–36
  primary, 78, 78*t*
  of students with disabilities, 160
Value-added contributions, 35

Wrap-around approach, 13–14
Wrap-around comprehensive sys-
    tems of care, 172–176
  essential philosophical elements
    of, 174*t*
  process, 172–173, 174*t*
Writing standards-based IEPs,
    151–152